The Foundations of Human Society

DONALD McINTOSH

The Foundations of Human Society

The University of Chicago Press

CHICAGO & LONDON

301
M18f
90840
Nov. 1974

Standard Book Number: 226:55935-1
Library of Congress Catalog Card Number: 79-84771
The University of Chicago Press, Chicago 60637
The University of Chicago Press, Ltd., London

Acknowledgments

I AM GRATEFUL *for the advice and encouragement of Professors* NORMAN BAILEY, JULIAN FRANKLIN, *and* M. M. GOLDSMITH *in connection with an early draft of this book. Messrs.* MARK DONNELLY *and* T. J. PEMPEL *assisted in the preparation of footnotes, figures, tables, the Bibliography, and the Index.*

Contents

List of Figures

I /

INTRODUCTION

T HIS IS THE FIRST part of a projected three-volume systematic political theory. It inquires what it is to be a human,
a human group, an organized or governed human group, and
the political system of an organized human group. The answers
are worked out in terms of a general theory of human action,
constructed in stages: first individual action, then interaction
among individuals, followed by social interaction, and finally
the beginnings of a theory of group action and interaction. A
typology of the ways in which individuals and groups influence
each other's actions is developed, and the patterns of influence
which characterize and hold together human groups, organizations, and political systems are examined.

   As preparation for the presentation of the theory which
follows, this chapter will describe the general method of approach as well as some of the reasons why this approach has
been adopted. Included will be a discussion of the sense in which
the inquiry is and is not intended to be scientific, and a description of the main categories of analysis chosen, along with an indication of the sources from which they have been drawn and
the reasons for their adoption.

A. *The Status of This Work as Scientific Inquiry*

Scientific method is a specialization and formalization of the process of coming to understand reality which is indispensable to the attainment of goals in this world (as distinguished from other-worldly pursuits).[1] This is not to say that knowledge cannot be pursued simply for its own sake, but rather that when goals are sought knowledge is useful.

The nature of the process of knowing is still far from fully understood, but we are not totally ignorant on the subject. It involves thought—that is, the formation of concepts in the mind—which at least in principle is capable of being formed into propositions which are meaningful in the sense that they may be true or false. These propositions are then directly or indirectly tested by observation. Such a process is carried out constantly by almost everyone, although mostly in an incomplete or distorted way. What distinguishes scientific inquiry is not only that it involves elaborate refinements of this procedure but also that the inquiry is public in the sense that the concepts must be communicable and the process of testing repeatable by anyone willing and able to take the trouble.

A fully developed system of scientific explanation has four distinct components or aspects, although in practice the lines between these components may be ambiguous or shifting, even in the most advanced cases. In the first place, it contains a set of intelligible concepts. These concepts are often worked out into a model, for example, the familiar Bohr model of the atom. Models have an ambiguous character; they are more than metaphor and less than the "literal truth," whatever that phrase may mean.[2] On the one hand, by thinking about the model it is

1. The following discussion owes a good deal to Braithwaite (1953) and Nagel (1961). See also Carnap (1966) and Popper (1934). For the application of scientific method to the social sciences, see Kaplan (1964) and Meehan (1965, 1968).

2. The problem, exactly what a model is, leads to very deep philosophical waters. Following Whitehead and Plato, I am inclined to believe that the rela-

often possible to arrive at new propositions which, upon testing, turn out to be true. On the other hand, certain elements in a model may not correspond to anything observable or may be untrue when applied to the reality the model is supposed to describe. For example, in the Bohr model the picture of an electron as a very small particle spinning around the central nucleus in a particular orbit, much as the planets spin around the sun, contradicts certain facts known about atoms. Such discrepancies need not destroy the validity or usefulness of a model.

While not every theory is worked out in terms of a model, I would hold that a set of intelligible concepts is essential to scientific explanation. A theory is a set of intelligible concepts which, if true, correspond to (may be lined up with) the reality which is the subject matter of the theory. This correspondence theory of truth, first clearly developed by Aristotle,[3] springs from the view that knowledge consists of true propositions in the mind (where a proposition is a set of concepts of which truth or falsity may be asserted). This means that untrue propositions may nevertheless be intelligible. The aim of this work is to develop such a set of intelligible propositions. On the question of the truth of these propositions the aim is more modest.

Second, the concepts of a theory are arranged in a formal structure, which will emerge if meaningless symbols are substituted for all of the concepts. In other words, formalization involves the draining of conceptual meaning from a system of

---

tion of theory to empirical reality is essentially the relation of concept to thing conceptualized, and that a certain tension or lack of correspondence will always exist between the two realms. From this point of view, the function of a model is to *exemplify* the concept and *correspond to* certain observables. As an intermediary between concept and empirical reality, models perform much the same function as the myth in Plato. Compare this formulation with Braithwaite (1953), chap. 4.

3. Aristotle, *Metaphysics,* 1027b. 18 ff. For a modern formulation of the correspondence theory see Russell (1912).

thought. For example, in formal logic the proposition $((a \supset b) \cdot a) \supset b$ is valid (logically true) even if no meaning whatsoever is assigned to the various symbols, while the assertion $a \cdot Na$, whether meaningful or not, is logically untrue. The point is that formal logic posits a set of rules which states which orderings and reorderings of symbols are permissible and which are not. It is true that these rules, which state in a "meta language" what may and may not be done in the "object language" of logical symbols, must be made up of propositions which are formed of intelligible concepts, or if the meta language is formalized, there must be a conceptually meaningful meta meta language. The point is, however, that a purely formal set of propositions has no meaning in the language in which these propositions are stated.

The formal structure of a theory has two main functions. First, it establishes logical relations among the propositions which are entirely independent of the conceptual meaning that the propositions have within the language of the theory. The formal structure, it is hoped, hooks the theory together into a coherent whole. Second, the formal relations among the concepts serve as a set of implicit definitions of these concepts. That is, there is a sense in which the concepts of a theory are defined by their purely formal relations to the other concepts. Thus if one considers Newtonian mechanics only in its formal aspect, the statement "Force equals mass times acceleration" amounts to a definition of force. The statement, in its formal aspect, has no empirical standing; it is true by definition.[4]

There is thus a sense in which all theories, in common with formal logic, are a set of definitions and tautologies which have no empirical reference. The propositions advanced in this book are no exception to this general rule. Much of it is purely definitional or tautological in character. The formal structure of

4. Nagel's treatment of the empirical bearing of Newtonian mechanics throws a bright light on the general question of the empirical standing of theoretical systems. Nagel (1961), chap. 7, pp. 153–202.

the theory presented here, however, is by no means rigorously worked out. Often the logical relations among the concepts have been only sketched in or indicated in an informal, impressionistic way. This rather free way of developing the formal structure creates the danger that, despite the author's earnest efforts, non sequiturs or contradictions exist in the formal structure. Although the author believes that a rigorous development of the theory is possible, the current stage of advancement in social science does not seem to warrant such a formidable project. It is likely to the point of inevitability that if the theory presented here proves fruitful, further work will reveal that important modification or even a completely new theory is needed, in which case complete formalization will prove to have been a waste of time. Full formalization is most appropriate to theories which show signs of becoming well validated, and what is presented here is far from that.

Third, a scientific theory must contain a set of empirical generalizations. In common with most present-day philosophers of science, the author sees a radical distinction between a theoretical proposition and an empirical generalization and believes that the latter are most profitably understood in operational or instrumental terms. While a theoretical statement asserts relations among concepts, an empirical generalization states relations among the observable properties or results of activity.

For example, take the statement, "This table is four feet long." Presumably one could program a computer to measure the table and record its length. The process would not involve the use of concepts by the computer at all. The *interpretation* of the results of the computer's activity, however, must involve the use of concepts—that is, after observing the activity of the computer one may say, "This table is four feet long," and that statement is a set of concepts. While the operation of measuring and the concepts by which the operation is interpreted are distinct, the meaning of the concepts is defined by and exhibited by the operation. Thus the empirical statement, "This table is four feet long," means no more than "When the ruler was laid on the surface, the symbol zero corresponded to one edge, and the symbol 48 to the other edge." The statement does not give meaning to the operation; rather the operation gives meaning to the statement.[5]

In contrast to an empirical statement, a theoretical statement does not derive its meaning from any operational reference it may have. I am reminded of a physics class I once attended in which a student asked the instructor what an electron was. He replied by placing a long equation on the blackboard. When asked what the equation meant, he answered that it was a symbolic representation of the way his laboratory instruments behaved under certain circumstances.[6]

Impressed as I was by this explanation, I now regard it as one-sided. The theoretical concept of an electron in the atomic theory of the time, as at the present time, cannot be identified with a set of observations; rather it is *associated* with such observations. To derive empirical generalizations from a theory it is first necessary to posit a set of translation rules, by which certain elements of the theory are associated with observable variables. Once these translation rules are established, empirical generalizations may be deduced from the theory and then tested by controlled observation. These translation rules are also normally accompanied by a set of boundary conditions, which limit the range of empirical generalizations which one is permitted to derive from the theory. Thus when translation rules were established for the wave theory of light, it was found that, in addition to many true generalizations which could be logically derived from the theory, there were a number of untrue

5. There are other ways of measuring length than by laying a ruler alongside an object. Thus the empirical meaning of the statement, "This table is four feet long," is defined by a broad, perhaps indeterminate, class of operations which are understood to be operationally equivalent. Nagel (1961), pp. 117–29, 250–51.

6. Such a radical operationalism is perhaps most closely associated with Bridgeman (1927).

statements which were also derivable. The boundary conditions of the theory rule these untrue deductions out of order, and the theory is used to explain only a restricted range of phenomena associated with light. In addition, not every concept or proposition in a theory need be associated with an empirical context. On the contrary, the bulk of statements in most theories cannot be so translated.[7]

The foregoing discussion of the distinction between a theoretical statement and an empirical generalization is only a taste of a subject on which much has been written, and the reader is referred to the citations for fuller discussions and entrée to the literature.

In summary, a fully developed scientific theory contains four distinct things: a set of theoretical concepts and propositions, a formal structure, a set of empirical generalizations, and a set of translation rules and boundary conditions which connect the empirical generalizations to the theory.

The present work contains very few empirical generalizations. As such it is not a fully developed scientific theory. Rather it is a work of pure or speculative theory of the type exhibited by the bulk of traditional political theory, or "political philosophy," as it is sometimes pejoratively called. Nevertheless, the question of supplying empirical content to this work has received considerable attention, as the following discussion will indicate.

B. *The Use of Psychoanalytic Theory*

In its main features the theory presented in this book represents the use of Freudian theory to explain the fundamental relations which form human society and hold it together. The approach is hence basically psychological. A psychological approach has been chosen because it seems clear that, on the most elementary level, all or virtually all social behavior consists of

7. Nagel (1961), chaps. 5, 6.

acts by individuals which spring from their mental disposition and are in the broadest sense voluntary. It is true that social behavior is regularly strongly influenced by the behavior and attitudes of others, and by other external factors as well. Even so, to take an extreme example, suppose that a person is threatened by a revolver and ordered to hand over his money. Despite the coercive threat, if he hands over his money the act is voluntary, first in the sense that the action is directed by certain mental processes, and second because other choices were available (for example, an attempt to resist the robber), however harmful the exercise of such alternatives might have been.

It is also true that behavior is regularly motivated by unconscious forces. Here again, however, although the term "voluntary" might need some qualification, it would still seem to be applicable.

I thus follow general usage in treating all social behavior as voluntary and motivated and, indeed, use this as one of its defining characteristics. It follows that there is a level on which all social and political events can potentially be understood as complexes of individual behavior motivated by the psychic states of the individuals involved. (The question of the relation of psychological to sociological and political levels of explanation will be discussed later in this chapter.) Freudian psychology has been chosen, first because the author believes it to be the most adequate of the theories with which he is acquainted, and second because it appears to lend itself well to the analysis of social and political events. The latter point, however, must be qualified, for a set of rather severe difficulties is involved.

In the first place, Freudian psychology focuses almost entirely on understanding the individual psyche in a context largely divorced from the social and political milieu in which the individual finds himself. To attempt to ascertain the relevance of this theory to social and political questions is not easy and runs the risk of producing either bad psychology or bad social and political analysis. It is true that Freud addressed himself to social and political questions, notably in *Group Psychology and the Analysis of the Ego, Civilization and Its Discontents*, and *The Future of an Illusion*. But Freud's treatment of these questions is very sketchy and tentative. Despite the extraordinarily illuminating nature of many of his remarks, his views are not worked out in concrete detail, and they stand in sharp contrast to his deep and detailed examination of the human psyche. In fact, the main thrust of these works is to use social and political material to throw light on the human psyche, rather than vice versa. A good deal has been written on social and political questions from a psychoanalytic point of view since Freud's time, but with a handful of exceptions the author does not find these works to have contributed much.[8]

In the second place, psychoanalysis developed around the clinical problem of treating psychic disorders, and the main lines of Freud's work constitute an analysis of psychic pathology. Perhaps as a consequence much of the application of psychoanalysis to social and political questions has tended to treat "society as patient," as many of the titles—for example, *Escape from Freedom, The Authoritarian Personality, Psychopathology and Politics*, to cite three of the best-known works in the field—indicate.[9] The reasons for my misgivings about the use of psychoanalysis to demonstrate the existence of "pathological" social and political forces will be found in my doctoral dissertation, cited above. Here, suffice it to say that the present project is a different undertaking. The attempt will be to discover what psychological forces operate to form and maintain society, and, with the exception of an occasional remark, we are not interested in whether these forces are pathological or

8. Some of this literature is examined in my unpublished doctoral dissertation (1959).

9. Fromm (1942); Adorno et al. (1950); Lasswell (1930).

not. We are interested in "normal" processes in the sense of "usual," or "characteristic," and the presumption is that a good deal of this is normal in the sense of nonpathological.

Fortunately, late in his life Freud turned to an examination of normal mental states (this time the term "normal" refers to the psychic processes which enable the individual to deal adaptively with his environment), focusing on the ego as the part of the psyche concerned with environmental relations. These beginnings have been extensively developed by such psycho-analytic writers as Anna Freud, Heinz Hartmann, David Rapa-port, and Erik Erikson. This literature has proved most useful to me.

In the third place, there is the question of the scientific standing of Freudian theory. There are two problems here, one general to all accounts which treat of "subjective" mental states (what the adjective "subjective" adds to the meaning of the phrase is not clear), and the other specific to psychoanalytic theory. First, what is the empirical reference of statements about mental processes? Thoughts are not directly observable —indeed the behavior of some infinitesimal subatomic particles is far closer to being directly observable than mental states. But the example is instructive, for atomic particles are not ob-servable either. Their existence is inferred by theoretical reason-ing or from the behavior of laboratory apparatus, and often the chain of inference is quite long.

Accordingly, when a proposition such as "He became an-gry" occurs in a scientific account, it must be understood as a theoretical construct, which presumably may be inferred from a set of observables, for example, "His blood pressure went up"; "Adrenalin was pumped into his veins"; "He punched the man in the nose"; etc. In line with the previous discussion of the distinction between theoretical and empirical statements, it is important to note that such empirical observables do not con-stitute anger; they are its index—the data from which it can be inferred. This point was overlooked by early behavioristic psychology and is still not clearly grasped by some behaviorist social scientists, whose emphasis on careful empirical verification is commendable but whose insistence that only the observable is real or meaningful is not.

There is thus in principle no special problem in using ideas about mental states in a scientific theory. All that is required is that translation rules be adopted such that the concept of a mental state is associated with observable variables, in such a way that one can deduce propositions about such observables from propositions about mental states, and propositions about mental states from such observables.[10] In practice, however, this is not easy. Of course on a common sense level this is what everyone is constantly doing in his relations with others. We infer the feelings and thoughts of a person from his overt behavior. Indeed this is often possible even when deception is attempted. But such judgments are based on complex and subtle factors, many of which are not fully conscious and, moreover, are not always reliable. They do not make up an adequate basis for a scientific formulation, however useful and valid they may be in everyday human relations.

The second question of verifiability concerns Freudian theory itself. The vast bulk of the evidence for this theory consists of case studies, usually reports by psychoanalysts about the patients they have treated. Freud himself often presented his findings as conclusions he drew from such material. This body of evidence is by now very large; moreover, psychoanalytic writers regularly draw on their case experience in their writings even if these cases are not always explicitly reported. In addition, from the point of view of the psychoanalyst, a critical part of the therapeutic process consists of the progressive formulation and testing of hypotheses about the psychic dynamics of the patient—a process that clearly qualifies as controlled observation.[11]

10. Nagel (1961), pp. 473–85.
11. Fenichel (1945), pp. 23–32.

It is true that in order for one to verify Freudian theory it is in principle necessary to become a psychoanalyst, but it is perhaps equally true that in order to verify atomic theory for oneself it is necessary first to become a nuclear physicist. The term "public" in "public verifiability" refers to the fellow specialists of the scientist, not the man on the street.

It is also true that the translation rules whereby a psychoanalyst can draw conclusions about the psychic dynamics of a patient from his statements and behavior are not as rigorously worked out as they are in the science of physics. Physics, however, is far and away the most advanced of the sciences in this respect, and psychoanalysis would come off better if compared to other sciences. If the translation rules are not rigorously worked out, nevertheless there exist numerous works which describe in considerable detail how the psychoanalyst is to draw conclusions from what he observes. In sum, while there are undoubtedly difficulties connected with the question of the empirical base of psychoanalytic theory, these difficulties do not appear sufficiently severe to cause serious question about psychoanalysis as a scientific discipline.[12]

It is otherwise, however, when one comes to apply psychoanalytic theory to broad social and political questions. While the empirical base of psychoanalysis seems sufficient to support it as a theory of the individual psyche and as a technique of treatment, I am convinced that this base in itself is inadequate to support propositions about social and political phenomena. The best of the psychoanalytically oriented works in this genre —including, in my view, the above-mentioned works by Freud, some of the writings of Erik Erikson, and Dodds's work *The Greeks and the Irrational*[13]—must be regarded as purely specu-

12. For an extensive discussion of the issues, see Hook (1959), especially the articles by Nagel (con) and Kubie (pro).

13. Freud (1921, 1927, 1930); Erikson (1950), esp. chaps. 4, 8, 9, and 10; Dodds (1951).

lative, and between the speculation and the solidly established theory lies 90 percent of the march of science.

The problem of the empirical reference of a psychoanalytic account of a social and political phenomenon is thus formidable indeed. In order to deal with this problem the author has introduced into his theoretical framework a body of concepts and propositions drawn from the modern theories of utility, games, and decisions (hereafter referred to as "decision theory").

C. *The Use of Decision Theory*

At first glance, the two disciplines appear to be poles apart, certain to separate out into unrelated layers, like oil and water, shortly after the mixing activity has ceased. Yet three important factors seem to me to warrant such a radical procedure.

In the first place, decision theory has been worked out with great formal rigor. The use of this theory here thus serves, it is hoped, to supply a firm formal structure to the material presented below, even though, as has been stated, full rigor has not been attempted, nor felt to be warranted.

Second, in common with psychoanalysis, decision theory is strongly voluntaristic in orientation. This is especially true of the branch known as the theory of games. Since other writers have made the point convincingly, I will not here argue the superiority of voluntaristic over stimulus-response theories,[14] except to state that between stimulus and response lie not only perceptual selection and attitudinal predisposition but, most fundamentally, thought. As a consequence, stimulus-response theories are most successful in areas where people think the least—for example, voting behavior—and least successful where people think the most—for example, policy formation in

14. The topic is brilliantly and exhaustively treated in Parsons (1937). See also Weber (1903–17).

formal organizations. Since the analysis of formal organizations will play a central role in later volumes, a voluntaristic
theory seems appropriate.

Third, and most importantly, decision theory seems to lend
itself well to the formation of translation rules and boundary
conditions capable of providing a clear empirical reference. If
certain psychoanalytic ideas can be expressed (if only partly) in
the language of decision theory, the way is then opened for the
formation of an empirical base for a psychoanalytic account of
social processes which is entirely independent of, and for the
purpose far more adequate than, the existing base in clinical
experience.

For example, considerable use will be made of the idea of
a utility scale, in the sense developed in the second edition of
Von Neumann and Morgenstern's *The Theory of Games and
Economic Behavior.* A utility scale is entirely a theoretical
idea, which normally cannot be exhibited as an observable pattern of choice by a particular individual. Nevertheless, research
which has been done encourages the hope that with suitable
translation rules and boundary conditions the theoretical idea
of a utility scale can be associated with observable patterns of
behavior. Furthermore, the psychoanalytic idea of the drive
orientation of an individual seems to be translatable into, or
at least possible of association with, the idea of a utility scale.
If so, the foundation has been laid for empirical testing of these
theoretical ideas.

It is not claimed that every theoretical idea can be translated into empirically meaningful terms. To take an important
example, I have been led to develop the idea of a "real general
will" of a group, for much the same reasons that Rousseau,
Durkheim, Mannheim, and Talcot Parsons have been led to
use the idea. In the language of decision theory this concept
emerges as a component or factor of the utility scales of the
individual group members which is the same for each. Al-

though I believe that the idea of a utility scale is capable of being translated into empirical terms, I am not certain and in fact am inclined to doubt that this can be done for the idea of a component of a utility scale. If so, the evidence for the existence of a real general will must perforce be indirect, resting on the logical relations of this idea, within the theory, with other ideas which themselves are capable of being empirically tested. Such a situation is very common in scientific explanation.

Although a number of suggestions have been made in this direction, this work does not develop a set of translation rules and boundary conditions for the derivation of testable empirical generalizations. My present view is that such a project would be most profitably undertaken in connection with actual research programs, since the possibilities and limitations of observation have much to do with the designing of appropriate translation rules.

In sum, the substantive concepts developed here rely heavily on psychoanalytic theory. Important parts of this theory are integrated with and expressed in terms of materials drawn from decision theory. This procedure provides a coherent (though not fully worked out) formal structure to the theory and enables its expression in a form which, it is hoped, will be capable of empirical testing. Translation rules and boundary conditions for the derivation of empirical generalizations from the theory are, however, not provided. The work is hence more than pure speculation but less than a complete scientific theory.

D. *The Use of the Theory of Rational Action*

In view of the fact that Freudian theory is generally held to lay a heavy stress on the irrational components of human thought and behavior—and rightly so—it may seem strange that a theory of rational action is one of the two fulcrums on which this work turns (the other being the psychoanalytic theory of identification). There are several interconnected reasons for adopting this procedure, the first of which lies in the history of Western political theory and Western culture in general.

It was mentioned earlier that all human action is voluntary, with those activities which are not voluntary, such as the beating of the heart or reflex responses, being by definition excluded from the idea of action. Voluntary action is purposive—that is, directed by the conception of a goal in the mind of the actor—with the referent of the conception the object of the action. A central idea in the Western tradition, with its main origins in Greek culture and philosophy, is that the principal instrument with which man can achieve his purposes is his intelligence—and the use of intelligence to achieve purposes is nothing but rational action.

This view can be contrasted with two others, the magical and fatalistic. The first seeks to achieve purposes by magical means. In the process of maturation every individual goes through a phase in which he adopts this attitude, and it is a brave man who can assert that he has abandoned it entirely. In the same way, most primitive cultures rely heavily on magical practices, while the most advanced cultures can by no means be said to be free of them altogether. The weakness in the use of magic to achieve purposes is, of course, that it does not work—it is unintelligent.

The fatalistic view holds that it is not within human power to control one's destiny. In its pure form this attitude is psychologically very difficult to maintain, and it usually slips over into either a magical or a religious approach. It has the virtue, however, of tending to correct the *hubris* sometimes associated with a purely rationalistic view.

Three types of approach which seek to use intelligence to achieve purpose may be distinguished, according to whether the purposes are otherworldly, innerworldly, or outerworldly.

If one separates religion and magic sharply, which appears conceptually justified, however much the two may mingle in practice, and if one rules out (perhaps wrongly) a view such as appears to be adopted by Tillich—that religion is a symbolic but potentially not unrealistic way of dealing with worldly problems and that no religious dogma is to be taken as literally true[15]—then the phrase "otherworldly religion" is a redundancy. Religion *is* otherworldliness. It may appear paradoxical to speak of a "rational" religion, at least if one agrees with Freud that religion is irrational at its core, but as Weber has shown there is an important sense in which certain religious attitudes and practices can be described as rational. These matters, however, will not be discussed in the present work.

The essence of the innerworldly approach is perhaps best exemplified by Stoicism. In common with the fatalistic view, Stoicism holds that it is impossible to achieve outerworldly purposes with any reliability. The events of man's social and physical environment are subject to forces which he can perhaps understand, but not control. Hence the main purposes in life should be the cultivation and maintenance of certain inner mental states and certain ways of behaving which are right in themselves, regardless of their external effects. Such purposes are achievable by the systematic application of intelligence. Stoicism does not proscribe outerworldly activity, but it tends to be indifferent to its results.[16]

In contrast, modern Western culture strongly emphasizes the outward aspect of purposive behavior. Although the trend can be seen developing considerably earlier, the classic expression is Hume's "Reason is, and ought only to be, the slave of the passions,"[17] a formulation altogether antithetical to the Stoic. The purposes which motivate behavior are given: to be

15. Tillich (1951).

16. Hicks (1910). It is perhaps significant that an extensive bibliography on the history of philosophy covering the Stoic period published in 1965, was able to list only three works in English on Stoicism published since 1923, one on Seneca, one on Stoic logic, and one on Stoic physics. See Bréhier (1965).

17. Hume (1739), bk. 2, sec. 5.

found by simple introspection. The thrust of intelligence is strongly outward, toward the determination of means for purposes which are claimed to be neither rational nor irrational, but simply given. It is the age of technology, or more broadly of technique. As such, the most barbarous and irrational purposes can be pursued by the most sophisticated and rational means, as with Nazi Germany, not to mention examples closer to home. Typical is Hillary's conquest of Mount Everest, achieved by sophisticated technological means "because it is there." The intelligence expended in the determination of the means on the one hand, and of the purpose on the other hand, is quite disproportionate. Similar, but on a much larger scale, is the current drive toward the conquest of space.

The approach to the nature of rational action adopted in this work is a return to the classic Greek view, as exemplified by Plato and Aristotle, which sees the inward and the outward manifestations of rational action as indissolubly interconnected. For Plato, the rational order of the polis mirrors the rational order of the psyche, and neither can exist without the other. While Aristotle's formulation is more complex and realistic, less black and white, at bottom he shares the Platonic view, and I agree with him. It is true, as Aristotle was aware, that there are forces within both the psyche and the external environment which are not entirely amenable to intelligent direction. Nor can the creative potential of human action be entirely reduced to a question of intelligence. Nevertheless, if exercised in a way which balances the internal and the external factors, intelligence is the only human capacity which is not double-edged but, instead, is wholly constructive.

Post-Freudian psychoanalytic theory, particularly the works of Heinz Hartmann, has approached the question of rational action from the point of view of the theory of adaption (or adaptation, as it is sometimes called). Contrary to the charge sometimes leveled at the aim of psychoanalysis, adaption in general involves more than the adjusting of the aims and the activities of the individual to the imperatives prescribed by the environment. It also regularly involves action within and upon the environment to change it in such a way that it is more suitable to the satisfaction of the needs of the individual. Failing this, acceptance of a more or less permanent tension between the individual and his environment may be the most adaptive (although not in principle the ideal) course. Nevertheless, it remains true that the psychoanalytic theory of adaption concentrates on the internal phase.

In its pure, or mathematical, form, the modern theory of decisions is essentially a theory of rational action. It is devoted to answering the question, "Under certain abstract conditions what constitutes rational action?" Thus Von Neumann and Morgenstern, in the work which is the foundation of this theory, say that their aim is "to find the mathematically complete principles which define 'rational behavior' for the participants in a social economy, and to derive from them the general characteristics of that behavior."[18] The Von Neumann and Morgenstern work, along with the theory of decisions as it has developed since, is strongly oriented toward the outward facet of rational action, and indeed is the most advanced and rigorous version of the modern theory of rational action, most of which has been developed within the utilitarian tradition. Nevertheless, an examination of this theory has led me to the conclusion that it logically presupposes a certain kind of internal psychic organization which in fact fits in well with the psychoanalytic theory of adaption. Once this point had been perceived (and it took some time) it was a relatively easy matter to construct a general theory of rational action which integrates the internal and the external aspects—that is, the formulations found in psychoanalytic theory and the theory of decisions. I feel that it is this part of the work which is most likely to stand the test of time. This is not to say that a complete theory of rational action is

18. Von Neumann and Morgenstern (1944), p. 31.

here presented—far from it—but rather that I am convinced that I have hit upon the correct categories of analysis, in a way which integrates the internal and external aspects which have been more or less separated since the rise of Stoicism.

In the modern tradition, the question of rational action has generally been presented in terms of the relation of means to ends and, as has been pointed out, tends to be applied exclusively to problems of choosing means. This formulation, however, is subject to a number of difficulties which have led me to reject the means-ends distinction as an analytic idea. A large literature exists on the subject,[19] and a full treatment cannot be here attempted; so a few brief points will have to suffice.

In the first place, Freudian theory distinguishes between the aim and the object of a drive, so that the concept of an end, or goal, of action turns out to be complex rather than simple. While the *aim* of a drive is genetically given, the *object* is worked out by the individual and may be more or less appropriate to the aim. The determination of a drive object turns out to be, to a certain extent although by no means exclusively, a matter of intelligent choice. Hence the choice of goals as well as means can be a matter of rational action.[20]

Furthermore, quite apart from the fact that means and ends tend to shift and interchange with the passage of time, as pointed out by Dewey among others, at a given instant what is a means from one point of view may be an end from another, and vice versa. In addition, many activities provide their own satisfaction and hence qualify both as means and as ends.

Finally, it is almost always true that the events which ensue after a course of action is undertaken are only partly, often only to a minor degree, determined by this course of action. The end

19. I have found the following discussions illuminating: Weber (1919); Niebuhr (1932); Maritain (1951); Parsons (1937); Dostoevsky (1880) ("The Grand Inquisitor," pt. 2, bk. 5, chap. 5). I discussed the problem at some length, although now I feel not in an entirely satisfactory way, in my doctoral dissertation (1959).

20. This topic is treated in chapter 6.

is normally only partly a result of the means employed by a given individual or group. As a consequence, when Max Weber asserts that the results of the means employed regularly stand in a paradoxical relation to the intended consequence,[21] he is, I maintain, pointing out, not a tragic dilemma of human existence, but rather the inadequacy of the analytic idea of ends and means.

Accordingly, the fundamental distinction employed in analyzing rational acts is between strategy and state, a strategy being any course of action and a state the sum total of events (including the course of action itself) which occurs at the same time or subsequently to the execution of the course of action and is significant to the values of the actors, regardless of the causal relations involved. This distinction, which is drawn from the theory of decisions but is both broader and less precise, is not to be confused with the distinction between ends and means, which does not play an important role in this work. This reflects a more modest view of the role of intelligence as an instrument of human welfare than is characteristic of the intellectual tradition of the West. In contradistinction to the view of classic Greek philosophy, and of many subsequent thinkers, it is not asserted that if everyone were perfectly intelligent utopia would result. Important as rational action is, its limits must be understood.

The idea of power is often considered the fundamental concept of political science and has usually been defined in terms of the means-ends relation, mostly as some variant of the idea of "ability to achieve intended results." From this point of view it is power which enables means to achieve ends. Power thus springs from rational action. While the means-ends dichotomy has been abandoned, the traditional idea that power is an attribute of rational action has been retained and has been worked out in a systematic way. After much study, I have con-

21. Weber (1919), p. 117.

cluded that the idea of power is commonly employed in three distinct senses (which, however, are by no means always distinguished). Although my typology of power is derived in a formal way from the abstract theory of rational action, it has been constructed to conform to these three senses.

The abandonment of the means-ends dichotomy has, however, led to an innovation. Two of the senses of power (relative power and comparative power) are not causal, in that the actor's purposes and actions do not determine the result. The third sense (independent power) is causal but, I believe, rarely occurs in human interaction. The central idea is that a person "determines," in a causal sense, only his own actions. Ensuing events are normally the product of a multiplicity of factors, of which the individual's actions are but one component. Had he acted otherwise, however, the results would have been different. Hence, power is to be understood as the range of choice opened up by the alternatives available to the individual.

Since human action is purposive, and rational action is behavior which is appropriate to these purposes, there is a sense in which rational action is to be regarded as "normal," in that rational action fits in with or is congruent to purpose, while irrational action is not. This is the reason which led the Greeks to define man as a rational animal. Since the theoretical assumption here is that actors will behave rationally, and since theoretical terms are implicitly defined by their relation to the formal structure of a theory, this work follows the Greeks in this respect. Once the Greeks had adopted this definition, the vexing question arose, "If man is a rational animal, why is so much of his behavior irrational?" This question has plagued philosophy ever since, and it was perhaps handled successfully only by Spinoza—and at that only at a very high level of abstraction.[22] With the advent of Freudian theory, of course, the question is no longer puzzling.

22. Spinoza (1677).

The point is that the implicit definition of man as a rational animal is a theoretical assumption, not an empirical generalization. Although this distinction has already been explained, perhaps another example is in order. Galileo's law asserts that, for any time interval, the distance a falling object will travel downward equals one-half a gravitational constant times the square of the numerical value of time elapsed (if suitable units of measurement are chosen). As stated, this is not an empirical generalization, but a theoretical statement, since it posits a number of conditions which have no empirical meaning. The body is supposed to have a point mass, to be falling in a vacuum, etc., whereas in fact there is no such thing as a point mass or a perfect vacuum, etc. Suppose that we associate certain empirical states with these ideas—for example, define a point mass as the limit of a series of observations, a vacuum as no more than a very small pressure (that is, a near vacuum), etc. In that form the law would be empirically descriptive, but of very little that happens in this world. It would be necessary to pump the air out of a long vertical column, etc. A further alteration of the boundary conditions, by allowing for atmosphere and expanding the permissible margin of error, would result in an adequate description of a lead shot, but not a feather, dropped from the Tower of Pisa.

A more constructive way to derive empirical generalizations from Galileo's law, once suitable translation rules have been established, is to introduce "correcting factors." In describing falling bodies, one observes not only distance and time but the size, shape, mass, mass distribution of the falling body, atmospheric pressure, wind velocity, water vapor pressure, etc. One then introduces a large set of additional formulas to correct the results predicted by the law itself. The end product is the science of ballistics.

The fact that people regularly act irrationally no more invalidates the theoretical postulate of rational action than dropping a handful of feathers from the Tower of Pisa would invalidate Galileo's law. The idea is to build a theoretical structure on a relatively parsimonious set of premises and to use this framework to organize the enormous set of empirical variables that obviously must be employed for an accurate factual explanation of social behavior.

E. *The Use of the Concept of Identification*

At the beginning of his *Politics,* Aristotle defines man as "a social and political animal."[23] As with Plato, this formula does not stand in tension or contrast with the definition of man as a rational animal; rather man is a social being *because* he is rational. Man's rational nature implies a harmonious and cooperative social and political order.[24] This idea dominates the intellectual tradition of the West. There is hardly a major figure prior to the twentieth century who does not, in some way or to some extent, subscribe to this idea, although the point could be questioned with some force for Augustine and Machiavelli and, less justifiably, I feel, for Rousseau. More pertinently, I do not know of a single figure who asserts the essential rationality of human nature who does not go on to argue that it is the course of reason for men to enter into a cooperative society. Nevertheless, I do not accept this view, at least not in an unqualified way. Several points are involved here:

1. Plato and Aristotle, and many following them, have held that man's potentiality for rational action can develop only in a cooperative society. This view appears incontestable.

2. They also felt that a certain kind of social order will especially encourage the development of an individual's rational potential. This argument may have merit, but it is not treated in this work.

3. Beginning with Plato, it has also been argued that it is necessary only that people be rational for them to form a coop-

23. Aristotle, *The Politics,* bk. 1, chap. 2, par. 9.
24. Plato, *The Republic,* 372–445, esp. 427–45.

erative society.[25] This viewpoint is rejected, for reasons developed in chapter 12. I see nothing more rational about the comforts and safety of civilization than about the life of Rousseau's savage, subsisting on acorns and roots, or about the war of each against all in Hobbes's state of nature. This rejection is based on arguments which I believe to be weighty but not conclusive; that is, a fully conclusive refutation has not been attempted. Accordingly, all the conclusions which are supported by this view are also supported on other grounds.

4. Finally, some have argued that certain kinds of social organization are more rational than others: that among persons there is always one and only one fully rational cooperative arrangement. Not just any kind of cooperative arrangement, but a particular cooperative arrangement is the course of reason. This view is also rejected, for reasons found in chapter 4. While the arguments for this position are also not definitive, certain major conclusions follow from them and them alone, in contrast to the previous point. The soundness of these conclusions depends squarely on the correctness of the position adopted on this question.

I have been led to these views by various routes. In the first place, my examination of the many attempts to show that sociability is the course of reason has left me unconvinced. To develop this point would take a volume in itself, and nothing more will be said on the subject except to make one brief point. The writers who hold a social order to be rational generally mean "sociable" by "social." Cooperation, not conflict, is held to be the course of reason. Even Marx, the apostle of social conflict, felt that the time would one day come when men would live together in total harmony. Yet conflict seems as fully the essence of society as cooperation. Not only is conflict endemic, it is *essential* to social order.[26] The only question is, What form will the conflict take? Various writers have been worried by

25. Plato advances this argument but does not accept it. Ibid., 357–64.
26. Coser (1956) has made this point.

the aggressive forces they find in people, which so unfortunately tend to find their outlet in war, and they have sought to find the "moral equivalent of war." The answer is that society itself is the moral equivalent of war.

The second route that led to the author's view on the matter was his study of psychoanalytic theory. From a psychoanalytic point of view, what holds society together is identification, and identification seems to be neither rational nor irrational, but a nonrational process. Like birth and death, it is not a matter of choice—it just happens, and to everyone. It follows that man is indeed a social animal, but this is entirely different from the statement that he is a rational animal.

The third route was my study of the theory of decisions. The point emerges most strikingly from an examination of Von Neumann and Morgenstern's work, cited above, and in particular from their treatment of competitive non zero-sum games. Although worked out in very abstract terms, this type of game seems typical of the situation facing man in society, in that the interests of the actors partly coincide and partly conflict with each other. That everyone in a society can potentially benefit from agreed-on cooperative plans of action, but that their interests conflict on the question of what particular form the cooperation will take, seems to me to be basic, irreducible, and the proper starting point for the analysis of social action. The analysis of various abstract forms of this situation is thus of very great potential importance to political theory.

The conclusions that Von Neumann and Morgenstern came to in this matter are most interesting. In the abstract situations involving interaction between actors which they analyzed, they concluded that a specific rational solution will occur only for two-person zero-sum games (two persons whose interests conflict totally). For all other situations, their solutions were in terms of "imputation sets" (as against "unique imputations"). They interpreted this to imply that, in general, rationality dictates that men cooperate with each other (point 3 above), but that there is a wide range of possible specific solutions, among which there is no rational basis for choosing (point 4 above). For such a specific solution to occur, they contended, it is necessary to posit a perfectly arbitrary (nonrational) social standard. These conclusions have been supported by the independent work of Arrow.[27]

The evidence on this question is by no means all in. Since the publication of Von Neumann and Morgenstern's book, decision theorists have expended much effort on this question, and solutions have been found for a few of the situations which those authors felt to be insolvable. Many workers in the field hope and even expect that it will eventually be possible to work out a unique solution for every case. The whole endeavor is the latest of many attempts in the history of political thought to show that if men would only act rationally they would all agree on a particular kind of organized society. My examination of this theory has tended to reinforce my already-formed skepticism on this point, and I have used some of this material to support my views, despite the fact that it is far from conclusive.

An examination of the premises of the theory of decisions reveals that the process of identification is ruled out. It is assumed that the actors in a social situation do not identify with each other. If, however, certain kinds and degrees of identification among the actors are *postulated*, the way is opened to rational and cooperative solutions to previously intractable situations. Accordingly, a central theoretical argument of this work is that if men are rational *and* identify with each other in certain ways, they will form into stable patterns of cooperation and conflict called social groups. This is not necessarily to say that society is in fact produced by rationality and identification, but rather that it can be accounted for (i.e., explained) by these factors.

27. Arrow (1951).

What has been done is to translate the Freudian theory of identification into the language of decision theory. A good deal of the concrete content of this theory is lost in translation; what is gained, it is hoped, is the greater amenability of the theory thus formed to empirical investigation.

F. *The Use of an Interdisciplinary Approach*

It has been indicated so far that this volume draws heavily from three fields—traditional political philosophy, psychoanalytic theory, and the theory of decisions. In addition, certain elementary sociological ideas such as legitimacy, authority, norm, role, and social group will be introduced and defined. Later volumes will deal mainly with materials usually associated with sociology and political science. The approach is thus heavily interdisciplinary and raises the question, What kind of connection is being drawn among these disciplines? A question of this kind seems incapable of a clear answer until the exact empirical reference of the theory itself and the material from the various fields which it incorporates have been established. Therefore my discussion will be brief and tentative.

I am not attempting a full-scale general theory of human behavior, although I hope I am helping to prepare the ground for the development of such a theory. The connections which I am establishing among the disciplines are loose and conventional, rather than tight and organic. Perhaps the example of the use of the idea of identification already discussed will help clarify this point. The idea of identification as it is used in psychoanalysis is not identical with the idea of identification as it is here developed in the language of decision theory. Rather, certain elements in the former are translated into the language of decision theory, where they take the form of postulates. Hence propositions about identification derived from the decision theory may suggest (by way of translation) propositions in psychoanalytic theory, but strictly speaking they do not constitute evidence for them, since the connection is conventional, not logical. The two ideas of identification are not deducible from each other. Nagel has pointed out that for one theory to be reduced to another it is not only necessary that the propositions in the second be connectible with propositions in the first but also that they be deducible from them.[28] The first and not the second is here attempted as the means of relating the various disciplines employed. Accordingly, sociology and political science are not here reduced to psychology or the theory of decisions. In a general theory of human behavior the disciplines of psychology, sociology, and political science would all speak the same language. Here the attempt is to provide a method whereby some of the material in these disciplines may be translated into the language of the others. It is hoped that a useful exchange of ideas can result.

28. Nagel (1961), p. 355, n. 5.

2/

RATIONAL ACTION

RATIONAL ACTION has four phases: assessment, evaluation, choice, and execution. The process of working these four phases out in the language of decision theory will involve the development of material which is highly abstract, much of which will appear to have little if any bearing on concrete reality. The question of the relation of this purely theoretical framework to empirical reality will be discussed toward the close of the following chapter.[1]

In addition, for the sake of simplicity, a number of special conditions will be posited. One of these simplifying conditions is that the interaction of only two individuals will be analyzed. The assumption (probably unfounded) is that the conclusions drawn for two actors can be extended to an indefinitely larger number. These individuals, *A* and *B*, will be termed *actors* until such time as we are in a position to call them *persons*. The

1. This chapter and part *A* of chapter 3 draw heavily on the theory of decisions, but these materials are placed in an interpretative context which is my own. The reader is not getting a straightforward summary of decision theory, except in the purely technical or mathematical passages. The author's main debts are to Von Neumann and Morgenstern (1944); Luce and Raiffa (1957); Rapoport (1966). Luce and Raiffa's treatment is mainly followed.

theory of action will presume only one actor, A, while B will enter with the theory of interaction.

A. *Assessment*

It is assumed that a number of courses of action are open to the actor. These courses of action will be called *strategies* (or, later on, *programs*) and symbolized by $a_1, a_2, a_3, \ldots$, etc., and $b_1, b_2, b_3, \ldots$, etc. They may be indefinitely numerous, but it is assumed that they are all known to the actor in precise detail.

Each strategy is associated with a *state*, $s_1, s_2, s_3, \ldots$, etc., which consists of everything that happens or will happen simultaneously with or subsequently to the institution of the strategy which is significant to the values of the actors. Put simply, it is assumed that the actor knows precisely what courses of action are open to him and precisely what the *results* will be for him. The term "result" must not be understood in a causal sense. The result of going out in the rain is that we get wet, but this does not mean that going out in the rain caused us to get wet. It is just as true to say that the water falling from the sky caused us to get wet. No implication is intended about the degree to which the state that ensues the adoption of a strategy is produced by that strategy, although such a question will arise later in connection with our discussion of power. It is simply asserted that for every strategy a_n there is a state s_n such that if a_n occurs then s_n will occur. The set of these states, $\mathbf{S}_a$, is the *field of action* with respect to A.

It is furthermore assumed that a strategy is composed of a set of many possible discrete actions, which are chosen in advance on the basis of the contingencies faced. Thus most people have a "strategy" concerning the clothing they will wear on leaving home in the morning. If it is raining they plan to wear a raincoat, if it is cold an overcoat, etc. The idea of strategy presupposes complete beforehand planning for every possible contingency. Moreover, the temporal extension may be indefinitely long; a strategy may be conceived of as a plan of action involving many actions arranged in temporal succession. The idea is essentially the same as the idea of a program, as when we speak of programming a computer, or an organizational program of action.

These provisos produce an enormous proliferation of possible strategies for even the simplest cases. For example, take the game of tic-tac-toe. Actor *A* has nine possible first moves: there are nine possible first-move strategies. Actor *B* has eight possible replies, to each of which *A* has seven possible answers. The number of strategies available to *A* for his first two moves is thus nine times eight times seven, or 504. As the moves continue the number of possible strategies quickly becomes very large. There are in fact over three hundred thousand strategies available to the first player for a whole game of tic-tac-toe, although the number can be reduced considerably by various simplifying procedures.[2] This practical complexity of the idea of a strategy is counterbalanced by the great theoretical simplification that it enables.

The assumption that the results of a strategy are known in advance by the actor needs two qualifications. First, knowledge of a result is assumed normally to be probabilistic. Thus, a result is usually a set of states, each with a certain probability of occurrence. For example, if there is a 50 percent chance of rain, the result of the strategy of going for a day-long walk without a raincoat is a 50 percent chance of getting wet and a 50 percent chance of staying dry. It is in this sense that the result of a strategy is assumed to be known in advance. In other words, to make a rational decision whether or not to wear a raincoat, it is sufficient to know the chances of rain, without knowing for a fact whether or not it will. Second, as we shall see, there are special cases where the rational strategy can be determined when the various possible events which may ensue upon the adoption

2. This example is drawn from Rapoport (1966), pp. 41–43. The actual figures, however, are my own; Rapoport's seem to be in error.

of a strategy are known but their probabilities of occurrence are not. Thus each strategy is associated with a set of states, one for each possible complex of events pursuant to the strategy, and a *result*, which is the probability of occurrence of the various states. It is always assumed that these states are known, but not always assumed that the result is known.

Finally, it may be added that a state may include the strategy with which it is associated. A state has been defined as a possible total eventuality, including everything significant to the values of the actor which is simultaneous with or subsequent to the initiation of a strategy. But a strategy must normally be supposed to meet these conditions; for example, in calculating the result of a strategy the cost of executing the strategy must normally be taken into account. Hence a strategy is usually a component of its associated states, and hence of its result. This point tends to undermine the means-end dichotomy.

B. *Evaluation*

Since the set of strategies $(a_1, a_2, a_3, \ldots)$ is the full set of alternative strategies available to A (one of which presumably is the strategy of doing nothing at all), and the set of associated states comprises all the possible events pursuant to these strategies, the action field S_a includes everything that can possibly happen to A that is significant for his values. Let us now broaden the concept of an action field still further by including all possible probabilistic combinations of states.[3] Thus, if the actor's field has only two states, s_1 and s_2, we now combine these two states into a set of "lotteries" $L_1, L_2, L_3, \ldots$, etc., which includes all possible probabilistic combinations of the two states. For example, if s_1 is "rain," and s_2 "shine," there is an infinite set of probabilistic combinations (lotteries), starting with 100

3. This section and the first paragraph of the next are a straightforward summary of the modern theory of utility and follow Luce and Raiffa (1957), pp. 12–34, closely.

percent chance of rain and 0 percent chance of shine, and ending with 0 percent chance of rain and 100 percent chance of shine. It can be seen that a lottery is a "possible result." The idea of the action field has thus been expanded to include the infinite set of possible results of all the possible strategies available to the actor.

The theory of rational action posits the following assumptions about A's evaluation of the action field, understood as this infinite set of lotteries or possible results.

1. For any two lotteries, A will prefer one to the other or he will be indifferent between them.

2. Preferences are transitive: for example, if A prefers L_1 to L_2 ($L_1 > L_2$), and L_2 to L_3 ($L_2 > L_3$) then he will prefer L_1 to L_3 ($L_1 > L_3$).

3. Through the use of probability calculus, compound lotteries are decomposable into equivalent simple lotteries among the states of the field. For example, where p stands for "the probability of," the lottery $ps_1 = 0.5; p(s_2 = 0.6, s_3 = 0.4) = 0.5$ can be restated as $ps_1 = 0.5; ps_2 = 0.3; ps_4 = 0.2; ps_5 = 0$.

4. If A is indifferent to two lotteries, then they are interchangeable as alternatives in any compound lottery.

5. If two lotteries involve the same two alternatives, the one in which the more preferred alternative has the higher probability is itself preferred: for example, for the lotteries $L_1 = (ps_1 = n; ps_2 = 1 - n)$ and $L_2 = (ps_1 = m; ps_2 = 1 - m)$, if $s_1 > s_2$ and n is more probable than m, then $L_1 > L_2$.

6. If $L_1 > L_2$ and $L_2 > L_3$, there exists a lottery involving L_1 and L_3 which is indifferent to L_2. For example, if A prefers s_1 to s_2 and s_2 to s_3, there exists a lottery of the form $ps_1 = n$, $ps_3 = 1 - n$ (either s_1 or s_3 with a certain probability), which is indifferent to s_2.

These postulates amount to a definition of *consistent preference* and have been worked out rigorously by the modern theory of utility. In effect, they assert that a rational individual will be able to determine his preferences between any two states of the field of action, and between any two probabilistic combinations of states, and that the preferences will be consistent one with the other. For example, it is inconsistent (involves an intransitivity) for A to prefer s_1 to s_2, s_2 to s_3, and s_3 to s_1. The second postulate asserts that this will not occur, and that preferences will be transitive: that is, if $s_1 > s_2$ and $s_2 > \cdot s_3$, then $s_1 > s_3$.

The postulates outlined so far in this section form the grounds of the modern theory of utility. On the basis of a more rigorous version of these postulates, it has proved possible to demonstrate three major conclusions: first, that preferences can be arranged in rank order; second, that these preferences can be quantified; and third, that on the postulates stated an individual will always act to maximize his expected utility. These conclusions will now be examined.

The first conclusion, that preferences can be uniquely ranked, follows quickly from the postulates. If for any two states, or for probabilistic combinations of states, A can tell which is preferable, and if preferences are transitive, then clearly all states and probabilistic combinations can be ranked in a unique order of preference, starting with the most preferable and ending with the least preferable: $L_1 > L_2 > L_3 > L_4 > \ldots > L_n$.

The mathematical demonstration of the second conclusion, that preferences can not only be uniquely ranked but also quantified, is somewhat complex and will not be explained here. But the underlying idea of the proof can readily be seen from an examination of postulate number 6—that, if $L_1 > L_2 > L_3$, there is a lottery, $pL_1 = n$; $pL_3 = 1 - n$, which is indifferent to $pL_2 = 1$. Granted that L_2 is preferred to L_3 and less preferred than L_1, the question is, How does the degree of preference of L_1 to L_2 compare to the degree of preference of L_2 to L_3? Assuming that there is such a thing as a degree of preference (not just an order of preference), such a degree of preference can be visualized as a point on a line. If L_1 and L_3 are points on this line, at what comparative distance between L_1 and L_3 does L_2 lie? Figure 1 illustrates this problem.

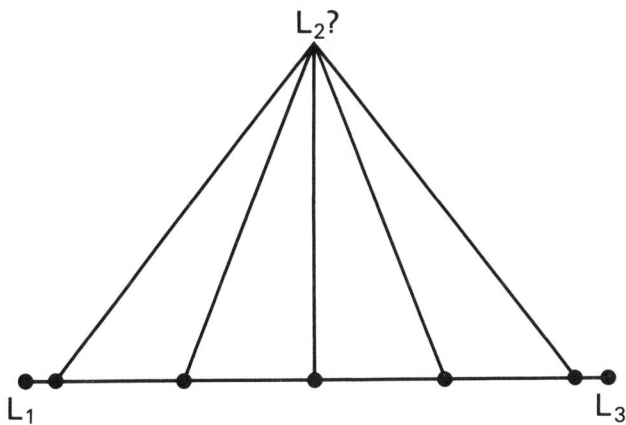

Fig. 1. The problem of degree of preference

Using postulate number 6, *A* determines what probabilistic combination of L_1 and L_3 is indifferent to (equal in degree of preference to) L_2. Suppose this combination is $pL_1 = 0.6$, $pL_3 = 0.4$. This combination can be pictured as lying 0.6 of the way from L_3 to L_1, or 0.4 of the way from L_1 to L_3. Since its degree of preference is the same as L_2, then L_2 is also 0.6 of the way between L_3 and L_1. In other words, the ratio of the interval between L_1 and L_2 to the interval between L_2 and L_3, $(L_1 - L_2)/(L_2 - L_3)$, equals $\frac{4}{6}$. If any arbitrary values are assigned L_1 and L_3, for example 10 and 20, respectively, we can then determine the numerical value for L_2, in this case 14. This illustrates the principle on which a utility scale can be constructed and a numerical value assigned to the degree of preference of every lottery in the field. These numerical values are called *utility numbers*, or simply *utilities*.

A utility scale may be visualized as a line upon which the utilities of the lotteries occupy points. The absolute length of the line is unknown; it may be one inch or one mile. Any numerical values may be chosen to represent the positions of the points on the line, as long as these values express the relative lengths of the segments (distances or intervals) between the points. In terms of the example just given, any numbers may be chosen as long as the ratio of the intervals $(L_1 - L_2)/(L_1 - L_3)$ comes to 0.6.

This kind of scale is called an interval scale. An example of the use of an interval scale is a thermometer measuring temperature. An interval scale is less powerful mathematically than the more commonly used ratio scale, along which, for example, distance, mass, and time are usually measured. On an interval scale, one can meaningfully add intervals between points, but not the values of the points themselves. Thus, where u stands for "the utility of," if $uL_1 = 30$, $uL_2 = 15$, $uL_3 = 10$, we can conclude that the degree of preference of L_2 over L_3 is one-fourth the degree of preference of L_1 over L_3 $[(uL_2 - uL_3)/(uL_1 - uL_3) = \frac{1}{4}]$, but not that L_1 is twice as preferable as L_2 and three times as preferable as L_3. On the other hand, both types of operation can be performed on a ratio scale.

An interval scale is sufficient, however, to give meaning to the idea of preference as a matter of quantifiable degree and, hence, to enable a mathematical expression for the process of formulating goals. On the premises of rational preference outlined above, it can be demonstrated that every state of an action field, and every probabilistic combination of states, can be assigned a utility number, which measures the degree of preference of this state or combination of states, as compared with all other states or combinations of states.

This conclusion can be expressed in the following way: After the individual has assessed the contents of the action field, he evaluates all the possible results of his strategies by assigning to each a utility number which expresses his comparative degree of preference for each possible result.

C. *Choice*

A preference is defined as an intention to act if choice is possible. If an individual is first asked to state his preference between s_1 and s_2 and indicates that he prefers s_1, and then is given a choice between s_1 and s_2, he will choose s_1, provided that his preferences were correctly stated, and that they have not changed. On this assumption, and from the conclusions developed in the previous section on grasp of reality and evaluation of reality, it can be shown in a rigorous way that an individual will always act to maximize his expected utility. This conclusion, sometimes called Bernouli's Theorem, constitutes a definition of rational action. Rational action is the choice of that strategy which will maximize an individual's expected utility.[4]

It must be emphasized that this theorem, that an actor will always act rationally, tells us nothing whatsoever about the real world. The whole theory is purely mathematical and simply demonstrates the logical connections among a certain set of propositions. Let us attempt to state Bernouli's theorem as factually true. For example: "If it is (in fact) true that there is an individual A who is able to grasp reality, who has coherent and consistent preferences, who acts according to his preferences, then it is also (in fact) true that A will act rationally—that is, will act to maximize his expected utility."

This statement of "fact," however, contains much less than appears at first glance. It is of the same order as the following statement: "If there is in fact an individual A, and if A in fact is a biped, then A in fact has two legs." The conclusion contains no information that is not already logically contained in the

4. The idea of "expected" utility involves probabilistic considerations. For example, if I risk $2.00 in a gamble for a $2.00 gain, and if the odds are two-to-one in my favor, then in the long run for every three tries I will on average win $2.00 twice and lose $2.00 once, for a net gain of $2.00 in three tries, or $.66⅔ for each try. Here, $.66⅔ is the "expected" gain of a single try. Luce and Raiffa (1957), pp. 19–20.

premises. In the Introduction it was pointed out that this is regularly the case with theoretical statements if their empirical reference is defined solely in terms of the theoretical meaning of the terms.

Thus the whole theory of utility amounts simply to a precise definition of the concept of rational action. But in addition, and perhaps more importantly, it serves implicitly to define the psychological prerequisites for rational action. Let us examine briefly what must be the case if an individual is to act rationally.[5] First he must be able to grasp reality (assessment). This leads to the question: How and under what circumstances is the mind able to grasp reality?

Second, action is assumed to be purposive: the choice of action is governed by a conception of its results, and some possible results are preferred to others.

Third, continuity of purpose is assumed. If an actor's utility scale were to shift from minute to minute there would be no way of telling in advance what the utility of a course of action was going to be and hence no reasonable basis for choice. Of course purposes do change from time to time, and when this happens the program of action can be expected to change, but at least a relative stability of purpose is essential to rational choice.

Fourth, coherence of purpose is assumed. Suppose that I want to go to the theater and also want to go to the concert. I should, of course, consult my preferences and go to the one I want most or, if they are equally preferable, flip a coin. But suppose the two desires are somehow incommensurable, as in a genuine psychic conflict. Suppose my feelings are ambivalent— I want to go to the theater and not to go. In such cases, where it is impossible to assign a clear order of preference, rational choice is impossible. Psychic conflict normally implies lack of full psychic integration: failure to form a fully coherent self.

---

5. The following points represent my own conclusions.

Part of me wants one thing; part of me wants another.[6]

In sum, rational action implies a *self*, which is purposive, stable, coherent, consistent, and able to grasp reality. Only to the extent that such a self is formed will action be rational. Only to the extent that such a self is formed will an actor be a *person*. This, of course, is what Aristotle had in mind when he defined man as a rational animal. An animal is a man only to the extent that he is rational. From now on, the term "person," will be used to mean a rational actor.

Thus, far from being empirically empty, modern utility theory implicitly states the psychological requirements for rational action. Using psychoanalytic concepts, the nature of these requirements will be more fully explored later.

D. *The Solution of the Field*

The treatment of rational choice is not yet complete. Given the fact that A has determined the contents of the action field and the utility of each state and possible combination of states, the question remains, How is A to calculate which strategy will maximize his expected utility? that is, How is he to determine which state or combination of states will ensue on the adoption of his various possible strategies? This problem may be classified under two headings, probabilistic choice and strategic choice.[7]

Probabilistic choice occurs where a single result can be associated with each strategy. This result is normally a probabilistic combination of states, that is, a lottery. As we have seen, a utility number can be assigned each such result. Thus each strategy has a result with a utility number, and this number can be associated with the strategy.

6. Classical and modern utilitarianism have consistently been unable to develop a coherent psychological theory of the self on the basis of their premises. We here adopt a different approach, by arguing that utilitarian premises logically presuppose a psychological theory of the self.

7. The remainder of this section draws on Rapoport (1966), pp. 28–38.

The problem of probabilistic choice has been called the Robinson Crusoe problem, because it is typical of action in a nonhuman environment.[8] From the point of view of the theory of decisions, the problem of choice (as distinct from assessment and evaluation) presents no difficulty in this case. A rational actor will simply choose that strategy whose result has the highest utility. The only theoretical problem is precisely what meaning shall be assigned the term "probability," a question that will not be examined here.

In contrast to probabilistic choice, the problem of strategic choice presents a hornets' nest of difficulties, only some of which can be said to have been solved. Strategic choice typically occurs in the interactions of thinking beings. It is thus par excellence the problem of choice in a social context, and will be considered in the following chapter on interaction.

E. Execution

From the point of view of a mathematical theory of action, choice and execution are not separable. The choice of a strategy involves a decision on how to act under any circumstance that may arise; hence execution is simply the already predecided process of putting choice into effect.

The two ideas only begin to assume separate status when we have moved a good way toward describing actual processes of action. In particular, when we come to organizational action, the persons who choose the organizational program (strategy) are often different from those who put it into effect (execute the program). Under such circumstances, choice and execution become quite different things. Meanwhile, however, the theory of execution will not receive any substantial separate analysis; it is mostly subsumed under "choice."

8. Von Neumann and Morgenstern (1944), pp. 9–13.

3/

RATIONAL CHOICE

IN INTERACTION

A. *Strategic Choice*

WE MOVE NOW from action to interaction by introducing our second actor, *B*.

Like *A*, actor *B* is assumed to have a set of strategies, b_1, b_2, b_3, ... A *strategy pair*, or *interaction*, consists of the combination of one strategy by *A* with one strategy by *B*. In strategic choice a single result (a state or a lottery of states) is associated with each strategy pair, not with each strategy, as in probabilistic choice. The point is that in interaction, as against action, the result of a given strategy by *A* will vary according to the strategy chosen by *B*, and vice versa. A single result requires two choices, one by *A* and one by *B*. The sum of the results of these interaction pairs is an *interaction field* ($\mathbf{S}_{ab}$), which is represented symbolically in figure 2. (The symbol *s* now stands for a state or a lottery of states.)

The knowledge required for rational choice needs some restatement for the case of interaction fields. Assuming that reality has been grasped and evaluated, the actor must know, as previously stated, which strategies are open to him and what the utilities of the resulting states are to him, but in addition he must know what strategies are available to *B*, and what the

	b_1	b_2	$\cdots$	b_j	$\cdots$	b_n
a_1	$s_{1.1}$	$s_{1.2}$	$\cdots$	$s_{1.j}$	$\cdots$	$s_{1.n}$
a_2	$s_{2.1}$	$s_{2.2}$	$\cdots$	$s_{2,j}$	$\cdots$	$s_{2,n}$
$\vdots$	$\vdots$	$\vdots$	$\cdots$	$\vdots$	$\cdots$	$\vdots$
a_1	$s_{i.1}$	$s_{i.2}$	$\cdots$	$s_{i,j}$	$\cdots$	$s_{i,n}$
$\vdots$	$\vdots$	$\vdots$	$\cdots$	$\vdots$	$\cdots$	$\vdots$
a_m	$s_{m.1}$	$s_{m.2}$	$\cdots$	$s_{m,j}$	$\cdots$	$s_{m,n}$

Fig. 2. The interaction field

utilities of the various states of the field are to B. This situation can be represented graphically by substituting in the representation of the interaction field the utilities of the states for the states themselves. Thus for the result s_{ij} we substitute the *outcome* of the result, which is the two utilities of the result, first for A and second for B($u_a s_{ij}$ and $u_b s_{ij}$, or O_{ij}). In other words, the outcome of a state is the set of utilities associated with that state. This substitution generates the *outcome matrix* of an interaction field.[1]

	b_1	b_2	$\cdots$	b_j	$\cdots$	b_n
a_1	$O_{1.1}$	$O_{1.2}$	$\cdots$	$O_{1.j}$	$\cdots$	$O_{1,n}$
a_2	$O_{2.1}$	$O_{2.2}$	$\cdots$	$O_{2.j}$	$\cdots$	$O_{2.n}$
$\vdots$	$\vdots$	$\vdots$	$\cdots$	$\vdots$	$\cdots$	$\vdots$
a_i	$O_{i.1}$	$O_{i.2}$	$\cdots$	$O_{i,j}$	$\cdots$	$O_{i,n}$
$\vdots$	$\vdots$	$\vdots$	$\cdots$	$\vdots$	$\cdots$	$\vdots$
a_m	$O_{m.1}$	$O_{m.2}$	$\cdots$	$O_{m,j}$	$\cdots$	$O_{m,n}$

Fig. 3. The outcome matrix

1. The sharp distinction between interaction field and output matrix, which plays a fundamental role in the theory presented here, is an interpretation of the basic analytic ideas developed by Von Neumann and Morgenstern, since I feel that this distinction is implicit in their approach. See Von Neumann and Morgenstern (1944), chap. 1. The form of the output matrix is taken from Luce and Raiffa (1957), p. 58.

The question of strategic choice is, assuming that the actors know the contents of the output matrix, Can they calculate their rational strategies, and if so, how? What characterizes the problem of strategic choice is that it appears in general impossible for either actor to know what the other's choice is going to be, either on a determinate or a probabilistic basis, and as a consequence it appears impossible to ascertain a rational strategy. For suppose that A is trying to find out which strategy will maximize his expected utility. Since the outcome of each of his strategies will depend on what B will do or is likely to do (otherwise the problem is not strategic) it appears that he has no basis for choosing a strategy unless B's strategy is known at least probabilistically. But it appears that B cannot choose his strategy rationally unless he knows something about A's likely choice. Hence, on the assumption that each actor is rational, or at least on the assumption that each actor must provide for the contingency that the other may act rationally, there seems to be a complete logical impasse similar to the dilemma created by the law which stated that when two trains meet at a crossing neither can proceed until the other has passed. It seems that neither can choose until he knows how the other will choose.

Certain special cases do admit of a simple solution. For example, see figure 4. In this matrix, the numbers in each

	b_1	b_2	b_3	b_4
a_1	5,6	8,7	6,2	4,3
a_2	7,4	9,6	12,3	8,5
a_3	2,7	4,9	8,8	5,4
a_4	6,4	7,8	10,5	6,3

Fig. 4. Dominant strategies

square are the utilities of A and B, in that order, for the result of the interaction pair which defines the square. Here, a_2 is A's *dominant* strategy because it is his best choice *whatever B does*.

In the same way B's dominant strategy is b_2; so the solution to the field is $s_{2,2}$, with the outcome $O_{2,2}$, ($ua = 9$, $ub = 6$), which represents what will happen if A and B are rational. Also, if B has a dominant strategy and A does not, then on the assumption that B is rational A can be sure that B will adopt his dominant strategy, and A will choose his own strategy with this in mind.[2]

Where neither side has a dominant strategy the problem at first glance is insolvable. Nevertheless, solutions have been developed for some situations. The most impressive is Von Neumann and Morgenstern's general solution for the "two-person zero-sum game." A zero-sum game is defined by an output matrix such that, for any two outcomes, if A prefers the first B will prefer the second and vice versa. In other words the situation is one of total conflict between A and B. By appropriate linear transformations such a matrix can be expressed in a form in which the sum of the utilities for the two actors will equal zero for every outcome, whence the term "zero-sum." Von Neumann's solution is both elegant and ingenious and represents a major advance in the theory of rational action. It will not, however, be treated here, first because it has been described many times both in technical and popular works,[3] and second because the present volume is concerned with social interaction, where by definition the interests of the conflicting parties are not in total conflict.

It is obvious that for a situation of total harmony, where the outcome which has the highest utility in the matrix for A is also the outcome which has the highest utility for B, there is a solution at this point. In between the zero-sum and the perfect harmony situations lie those matrices where the interests of the persons involved partly coincide and partly conflict. It is this situation in which a theory of social action is particularly inter-

2. Rapoport (1966), pp. 54–56. The introduction of additional assumptions can create situations where the dominant strategy is not the rational one. Nigel (1966).

3. For example, Rapoport (1966), pp. 57–93.

ested. At present the general solution for these situations is far from having been accomplished, although solutions have been found for some special cases. Indeed, as has already been mentioned, many decision theorists, including Von Neumann and Morgenstern, believe that no general solution can be achieved. For the sake of the argument, however, at present it will be assumed that every outcome matrix has a solution in the sense that for each actor there is a calculable strategy which will yield an outcome equal to or higher than the outcome for any other strategy, and that persons will choose such strategies, yielding a solution to every matrix which represents what will happen if the actors are rational. Later this assumption will be withdrawn and some aspects of the question of solutions for these matrices examined.

B. *Empirical Reference*

With the above proviso, this completes our critique of pure reason. The remainder of the chapter will be devoted to a discussion of whether and how this theory of rational action can be given empirical reference.

In general outline the procedure might be as follows:

1. Establish a set of empirical variables which are associated with certain key terms of the theory, leading to the development of empirical generalizations about rational behavior. This would result in a set of propositions about what constitutes rational behavior in actual situations.

2. Measure actual behavior against these standards.

3. Develop and test subsidiary hypotheses to explain irrational behavior.

4. Incorporate these subsidiary hypotheses into an enlarged theory which would thus constitute a general theory of behavior.

Some of these questions will be treated later on in this work, but a few remarks on the subject seem appropriate at this point.

With regard to grasp of reality, the theory developed here

says nothing about the process of assessment which actually occurs, but simply posits that it has occurred. Even this goes beyond the existing theory of decisions and represents my own enlargement of it, for game theory proper asserts a purely logical relationship between only two ideas—preference and choice.

Choice may be interpreted as a decision to act, rather than the act itself. Alternatively, both preference and choice could be interpreted in terms of action, along the lines laid down by behaviorist psychology, without regarding mental states as independent variables. Here the former interpretation is preferred because, as is pointed out in the Introduction, it is felt that a theory of rational behavior must treat thought and action as separate things. The relation between thought and action thus becomes problematic. This dictates the enlargement of utility theory proposed here.

As here defined, rational action presupposes (1) that the assessment of reality is correct—that the concept is congruent to that which is conceptualized; (2) that when s_1 is preferred to s_2, and achieved, it will turn out in fact to have been preferable; (3) that the results which are conceptualized as following the adoption of a strategy will actually occur if the strategy is adopted. These provisions are obviously too strong for direct empirical application, and so an empirically based definition of "reasonable" (as distinct from "rational") action must be worked out, and this associated with the theoretical idea of rational action by way of translation rules and boundary conditions. This definition of reasonable action would take into account the limitations of available information, time, effort, mental capacity, etc.[4]

If action is observed to be reasonable, it will then be explained by the theory, which in effect states that people will

---

4. This idea has been developed by a number of people. For example, see March and Simon (1958), pp. 136–71, for a treatment of the cognitive limits of rationality, including their idea of "satisficing."

behave rationally unless some factor prevents this, analogously to the Newtonian formula: that a body will continue in motion in a straight line at a constant velocity unless an outside force acts on it. The construction and use of an index of reasonable behavior would reveal that much actual behavior is irrational. This is no threat to the theory of rational action, even though some writers have felt it to be. For example, in discussing intransitivities in preference formation (as pointed out above, utility theory posits transitivity of preference formation), Luce and Raiffa say:

> No matter how intransitivities arise, we must recognize that they exist, and we can take only little comfort in the thought that they are an anathema to most of what constitutes theory in the behaviorial sciences today. We may say that we are only concerned with behavior which is transitive, adding hopefully that we believe this need not always be a vacuous study. Or we may contend that the transitive description is often a "close" approximation to reality. Or we may limit our interest to "normative" or "idealized" behavior in the hope that such studies will have a metatheoretic impact on more realistic studies.[5]

I feel that this passage misconstrues the epistemological status of decision theory. Decision theory defines the concept of rational behavior. Even when this concept is translated into empirically meaningful terms, nothing in the theory asserts or implies that actual behavior will be rational. Luce and Raiffa's position makes sense only on the assumption that they regard a theory as nothing but a set of logically integrated empirical generalizations. An examination of decision theory itself, however, reveals that it is a theory in the sense developed in the Introduction. Unfortunately, some game theorists, sharing Luce and Raiffa's apparent view of the matter, have attempted to apply game theory directly to the solution of actual

5. Luce and Raiffa (1957), p. 25.

policy problems without devoting sufficient attention to the problem of translation rules and boundary conditions.[6]

While the fact of irrational behavior does not invalidate the theory developed so far, it points up its incompleteness. In order to explain why behavior is sometimes rational and sometimes not it would be necessary to develop an account of the process whereby reality is assessed, preferences are formed, and choices are made, as well as of the circumstances under which these processes will or will not meet the canons of rational action. At present the theory simply posits that these processes have been accomplished.

To use decision theory in an explanatory way, the theory must contain an account of the formation and operation of personality. In other words, an examination of the formal structure and empirical bearing of decision theory, even in the enlarged form developed here, reveals that it cannot be used to explain actual behavior unless a psychological theory is associated with it or integrated into it.[7] A step in this direction has already been taken by pointing out that the theory in its present form implies certain psychological traits on the part of a rational actor which can be summarized by saying that the actor must be a person. This theme will be developed later.

While decision theory itself contains no account of the process whereby reality is assessed or preferences formed, it does develop ideas about how, once preferences have been formed, they are worked into coherent and quantified utility scales, and about how strategies are chosen. The question

6. The question of the epistemological status of decision theory has divided decision theorists rather sharply into two camps, as exemplified by Anatol Rapoport on the one hand and Thomas Schelling on the other. No one denies that present models are not adequate. The basic issue is whether the main line of progress of decision theory lies in refining existing models or in enlarging the underlying theoretical postulates. I share Rapoport's views on the matter. See Rapoport (1960) and Schelling (1960).

7. See Rapoport (1966), pp. 202–14.

arises, What if any actual empirical events are these processes to be placed in correspondence with? It should first be noted that it is not absolutely necessary that such a correspondence be established. For example, suppose that in one way or another we find out what the actual preferences of an individual are in a specific instance, then calculate on the basis of the theory what his rational decision is, and finally observe what decision he actually makes. Supposing this decision to be entirely rational, still there is no necessity to assume that the actual process by which the individual arrived at the decision bore any resemblance whatsoever to the process whereby the theorist figured out this decision from his information about the preferences of the actor. The subject need not work his preference into a quantified utility scale, assign numerical values to each box in the outcome matrix, and then perform a sophisticated mathematical calculation to arrive at his strategy, even if these ideas are translated into a clear empirical meaning. The actual process could be of an entirely different kind. As has been pointed out, not every proposition or chain of propositions in a theory need be translated into empirical terms; in fact the use of entirely artificial constructions is common in scientific explanation.

In point of fact it appears that the actual situation is mixed. Certain formal organizations, for example, seem to use processes corresponding to those developed by decision theory in situations where individuals might not. For example, the type of analysis carried out by the United States Department of Defense in connection with choosing one weapons system over another appears to be consonant with the process developed by decision theory (and this is no accident, since decision theory has influenced the ways in which such decisions are made), while an individual choosing between two job offers might decide by a radically different method. On the other hand, if such an individual were interested only in maximizing his net income, his choice of a job might be based on a gain-versus-cost analysis similar in principle, if simpler in practice, to a Department of Defense decision. Decisions springing from a complex and subtle intermingling of various kinds of preferences, each of which is in principle recalcitrant to quantification, as is common in human choice, seem more likely to be based on different kinds of processes.

Recent decades have seen an enormous development of "mechanical" methods of reaching decisions, as exemplified by the use of the modern computer, a process which has been accompanied by an interaction between this technological development and the growth of modern decision and cybernetic theory. These developments seem, however, to mirror only a part of the typical process by which individuals reach decisions. In particular, there is no analogue or correspondence to the operation of preconscious and, through the preconscious, unconscious mental processes which seem to play a central role not only in the making of decisions but in perception itself. The game of chess provides an example of this point. Given the complexity of the game, the limitations of the human mental apparatus, and the limits imposed by tournament conditions, it is often impossible for even the strongest player to calculate all the possible consequences of a given move. In this situation, strong chess players regularly lean heavily on preconscious (intuitive) thought processes in making their decisions. The chess master will first subject the position to as extensive a conscious analysis as time permits, and if this does not clearly indicate what the best move is, as it often will not, he will make the move that "feels" best. The process is called "letting the fingers decide," and in the hands of an international grand master it can produce truly startling results. There are many games on record played under a time limit of ten seconds a move which have a profound conception executed with flawless precision.

Preconscious thought normally plays a central role in individual decision making. It is through preconscious thought that the resources of the unconscious mind can be brought to bear in seeking solutions to problems and in creative activity.[8] The use of the unconscious in making decisions has, however, a double edge, for unconscious thought does not operate according to the canons of rationality. As a result, the play of chess players, especially the strongest, always has a distinct personal style which reflects the personality of the player and often his emotions of the moment.

It is possible to take advantage of this by "playing the opponent, not the board." On the basis of one's knowledge of the opponent, estimates are formed of what moves he is likely to make in a given situation and plans are laid accordingly. Often a move is chosen which is objectively (by strategic analysis) not the best move but which is calculated to create difficulties for this particular opponent in this particular situation.

Probably the most eminent proponents of "playing the board" were Aaron Nimzovitch and Akiba Rubinstein. Both produced many games of flawless perfection, but, perhaps significantly, neither became world champion. In contrast, the games of Emanuel Lasker, world champion for twenty years, abound in "bad" moves designed to discomfit his opponents. Alekhine and Tal, both of whom also became world champions, also made heavy use of such psychological strategy. The same conclusion also holds for poker, in which, as all good players know, success depends mainly on psychological factors and only secondarily on mathematical considerations.

In the realm of military strategy the issue between a strategic and a probabilistic approach to choice is put in terms of laying plans on the basis of the capabilities or, alternatively, the intentions of possible enemies. From the above discussion it is clear that the latter is the preferable procedure if sufficiently reliable estimates of intentions are possible. As Mao Tse-tung

8. On the role of the preconscious in decision making see Kris (1950).

put it, "Know the enemy and know yourself, and you can fight a hundred battles with no danger of defeat."[9] Therefore, strategic decision making might not be the rational course as often as at first glance appears. The premise of rationality on the part of other actors ignores the fact that preconscious thought is regularly used when people make decisions in situations where the properties of the interaction field present great difficulties of analysis, and that, as a consequence, in these cases deviations from full rationality must be expected as a matter of course. This reservation in no way vitiates the theoretical significance of the modern theory of games and decisions but must be kept in mind when attempts are made to base empirical statements upon the theoretical analysis. It does, however, raise the question why in recent decades so much actual decision making has come to approach the canons of decision theory.

Part of the answer to this may lie in the growth of large formal organizations as the central units of decision making in modern society. It has already been suggested that the goals of formal organizations may in many cases be amenable to a simplification and quantification impossible in the case of one person. In addition, the technical necessities of decision making in an organization may require ruling out certain intuitive methods of evaluation and decision available to individuals. Thus in situations where an individual, through the use of preconscious mental resources, may be able to establish a probabilistic or even a determinate analysis of a situation, an organization, because of technical necessities of decision making, may be required to rely on strategic analysis alone. For example, it is hard to imagine a modern defense establishment making military judgments on the intuitive basis employed by a Caesar or a Napoleon, even though the judgments made in this manner might be superior.

An example is the melancholy and Cassandra-like career

9. Mao Tse-tung (1965), vol. 1, p. 190. Chairman Mao is here quoting Sun Wu-tsu.

of George Kennan since 1948. Mr. Kennan's views, which in my judgment have been uniformly correct, have just as uniformly been ignored, and rightly so, since they were based solely on Mr. Kennan's personal reflections and experience and as such did not constitute an adequate basis for organizational decisions.[10]

These considerations suggest a split between personal and organizational requirements for rational decision making and imply that decision theory may be a more adequate basis for the latter than for the former. This in turn raises the question of how the persons who are members of a large formal organization are to come to terms with an organizational system whose requirements and standards are at odds with their own; that is, it raises the question of alienation. A treatment of this problem must, however, await a later volume.

10. Kennan (1967).

4/

SIMPLE POSITIVE

IDENTIFICATION

A. *The Problem of Solutions for Matrices of Partial Conflict (Nonstrictly Competitive Games)*

IN THE PREVIOUS chapter it was assumed that for any interaction field there is always a rational strategy for every
actor and that this strategy is always calculable in principle.
This assumption will now be examined.[1]

As has been pointed out, Von Neumann and Morgenstern
felt that this assumption is not true.[2] By this must be understood, not a statement about actual behavior, but a claim that
certain propositions cannot be derived from certain premises.
The problem is purely theoretical but nevertheless of great
importance because of the central role of the concept of reason
or rationality in the intellectual tradition of the West, and because the Von Neumann and Morgenstern formulation is a
refinement and extension of that concept. There is of course a
large literature on this subject,[3] but here the nature of the

1. The discussion in this section is based mainly on Rapoport (1966), pp. 94–
144, and Luce and Raiffa (1957), pp. 88–154, 327–70.

2. Von Neumann and Morgenstern (1944), pp. 31–43, 608, n. 1; Luce and
Raiffa (1957), pp. 152, 218–19.

3. Shubik's annotated Bibliography provides a good entrée into this literature.
Shubik, (1964), pp. 363–76.

problem will be illustrated by an examination of only one instance.

$$
\begin{array}{c|cc}
 & b_1 & b_2 \\
\hline
a_1 & 2,1 & -2,-1 \\
a_2 & -1,-1 & 1,2 \\
\end{array}
$$

Fig. 5. The rowboat problem: Outcome matrix

Consider figure 5. Here the interests of A and B both coincide and conflict. Their interests coincide in that both prefer a_1b_1 and a_2b_2 to a_1b_2 and a_2b_1. They agree that each of the former outcomes is preferable to either of the latter. On the other hand, their interests conflict over which of the two former outcomes is preferable: A prefers a_1b_1 to a_2b_2 while B prefers a_2b_2 to a_1b_1.

Figure 5 seems to present the bare bones of the central problem of voluntary social cooperation: men are all better off if they join into cooperative relations with each other; but such cooperation can take various forms, and each of these various possible cooperative arrangements will affect the interests of the cooperating parties in a different way. It is to their interests to cooperate, but which form of cooperation should be chosen?

In the literature of decision theory, the situation presented in figure 5 is usually entitled "The Battle of the Sexes," but here another interpretation will be given. Suppose that two persons cast into the sea by a shipwreck come upon a boat and climb in. The boat requires two persons to operate it, one to row and one to bail. Assume that there are two sets of oars and oarlocks and two bailing buckets. If both row, the boat will sink and they will have to swim for shore, while if both bail, it will stay afloat but get nowhere. It is to their interests to act cooperatively— one should row and one bail—but suppose each party prefers bailing to rowing? What is the solution?

It might seem that the reasonable solution is a fifty-fifty split

—each rows and bails half the time—and in fact that is perhaps what would happen with two actual persons in such circumstances, but there appears to be no way to show that such a solution is more rational than any other on the premises of decision theory.

A closely related situation is the "Bargaining Problem," which can be stated as follows: Person *B* has a bushel of wheat which *A* wishes to buy. The utilities of *A* and *B* are as follows: Person *A* prefers the bushel of wheat to $10.00, but not to $10.01—that is, $10.00 is the most he is willing to pay. On the other hand, *B* prefers $5.00 to the bushel of wheat, but not $4.99—that is, $5.00 is the least he will accept for the wheat. Clearly a sale at somewhere between $5.00 and $10.00 is advantageous to both—but what price represents a rational solution? Again, a price of $7.50 seems to be a fair bargain, but it is not clear why. Furthermore, it is not clear that $7.50 amounts to "splitting the difference," for we do not know how the utility scales of *A* and *B* are to be compared. Possibly the $7.50 price might represent a greater gain for one party than for the other. The main difference between this and the previous problem is that it has a clear "no sale" point, which will occur if agreement proves impossible. The actors may not be "in the same boat," as in the previous example. This difference may or may not be significant.

Returning to the problem presented in figure 5, there are two ways to treat it, depending on whether or not communication between *A* and *B* toward a possible negotiated settlement is "allowed." We will treat the negotiated game because it seems reasonable that *A* and *B* would enter into discussion about how their conflict might be solved. It will not be assumed, however, that either party will stick to his side of the bargain if it is not to his interest to do so. No moral scruples are assumed, nor is there posited any party capable of enforcing an agreement made.

Assuming only pure strategies, the four possible solutions may be pictured as in figure 6.

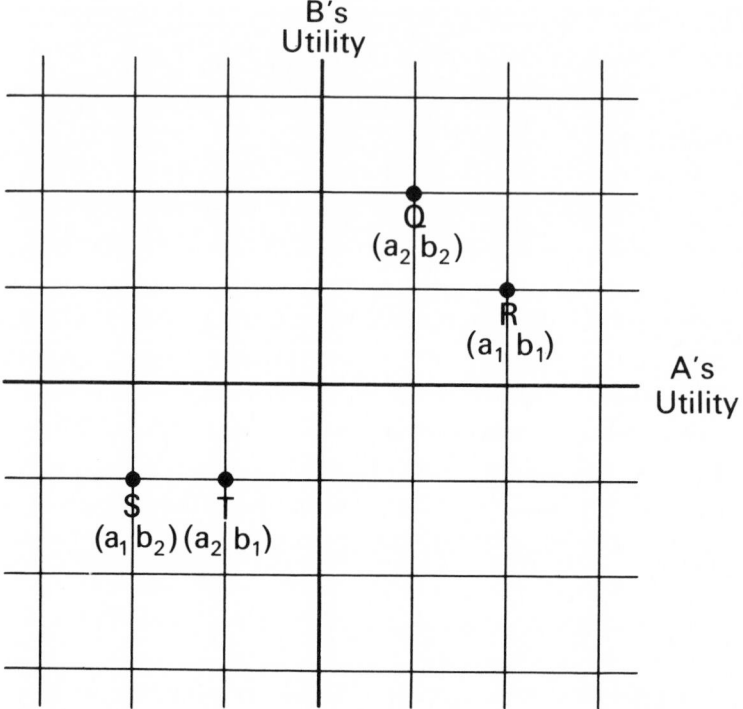

Fig. 6. The rowboat problem: Outcomes with pure strategies

Using mixed strategies—that is, random choice at a given probability between a_1 and a_2 and b_1 and b_2—we get a field of possible outcomes which forms a quadrangle, with the four "pure" strategies the outcomes at the corners, as in figure 7.

In the example, this field may be considered to be generated by different combinations of rowing and bailing by A and B, where the possibilities that both may bail or both may row for various lengths of time are taken into account, as well as the possibility that one may bail while the other rows for various lengths of time. This matrix has been much studied, and certain conclusions have emerged.

First, it is clear that if there is a cooperative solution, it will

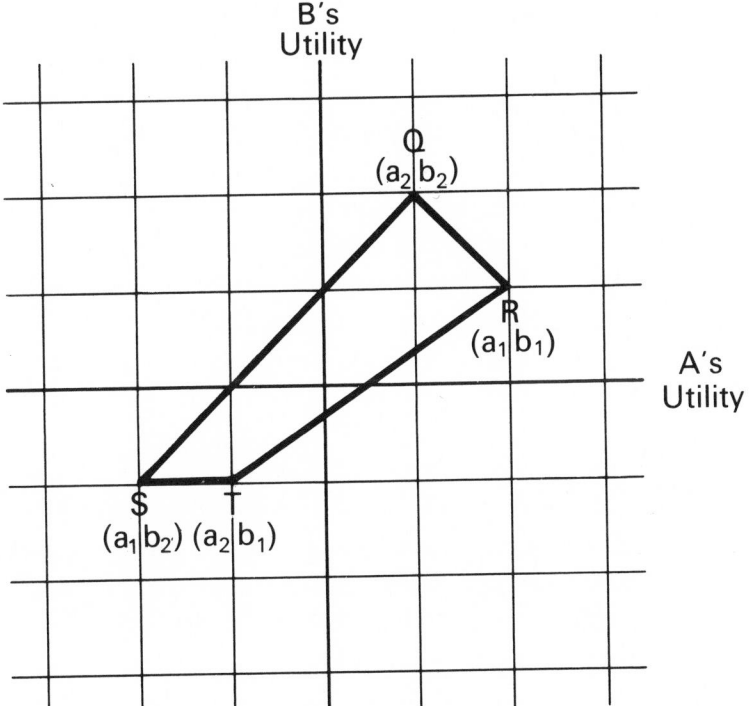

Fig. 7. The rowboat problem: Outcomes with mixed strategies

lie on the line on the edge of the quadrangle between the points *Q* and *R*. For assume that there is a solution within the quadrangle. For any such point, there will be at least one point (above and to the right of the so-called solution) which has a higher utility for both *A* and *B*. If *A* and *B* are cooperating, they will agree to shift to such a point, since it will increase the expected utility for both *A* and *B*. This condition is not true, however, for solutions along the line *QR*. As long as *A* and *B* are at any point within the quadrangle, their interests coincide in moving toward *QR*. Once they reach this line, the conflict of interests built into the situation emerges, since any motion along the line will benefit one at the expense of the other. The line

QR is called the "negotiation set" of the matrix. This illustrates the essence of Von Neumann and Morgenstern's solution of the *n*-person game. The solution is a set of strategy pairs, in this case and, in general (but not for every case), an infinite set. The course of reason is for the parties to choose one member of the set. According to Von Neumann and Morgenstern any one will do, for all are equally rational.

In terms of the example, if *A* and *B* are cooperating, they will agree that at all times one should be rowing and the other bailing, that is, at no time would both be rowing or both bailing. The negotiation set is those ways in which the time can be divided between the two alternatives: *A* rows while *B* bails, or *B* rows while *A* bails.

The above analysis suggests a possible approach to a unique solution (i.e., a single strategy pair). If a starting point for negotiation could be established, along with a rational bargaining procedure, the two negotiators, starting at this point, would proceed through successive stages toward the line *QR* until the boundary is reached, as in figure 8.

A number of attempts to use such a procedure have been made, but there are two difficulties: First, it is not clear where the starting point should be, and second, out of the several possible bargaining procedures there is none which is clearly more rational than the others.

One idea for a starting point is to use the minimax point: the solution which would occur if each used his minimax strategy. Unfortunately the minimax strategy for games of partial conflict has different properties than for zero-sum games. For zero-sum situations, the strategy which guarantees that *A*'s result will not be below a certain minimum also guarantees that *B*'s result will not be above a certain maximum, since their utilities will always sum zero. Here, however, the strategy which will guarantee the best result, regardless of the opponent's strategy, does not guarantee the worst result for the opponent, re-

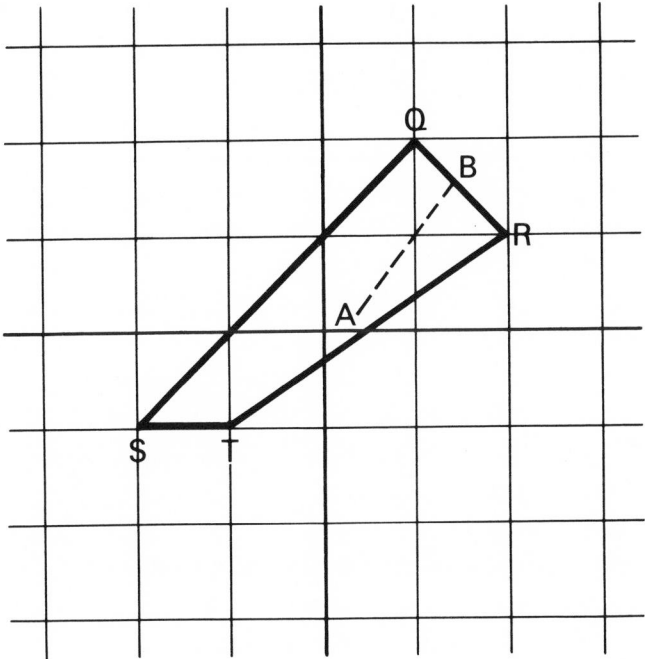

Fig. 8. The rowboat problem: Negotiation toward a solution

gardless of his strategy. The zero-sum minimax strategy breaks down into two strategies, a defensive strategy which will place a floor under one's possible losses and an aggressive strategy which will place a ceiling over the opponent's possible gains. This has the effect of undermining the rationality of the whole minimax procedure, either for finding a starting point or for defining the bargaining process. There exist a number of different attempts, each of which seems reasonable, but it appears impossible to say which is the more rational.

Another attempted solution, due to Nash, argues first, that if there is a solution it must satisfy certain conditions, and second, that there is only one point (on the negotiation set) which satisfies these conditions.[4] To complete Nash's proof, however, it would also be necessary to show that there is in fact a rational solution, but this is precisely the point in question.

It is the apparent nonsolvability of the bargaining problem that creates the difficulties for zero-sum games with more than two players. With three or more players, opportunities for coalitions occur, in which some of the players "gang up" on others. The exact terms of such coalitions, however, involve a bargaining problem similar to the one just treated. If the bargaining problem could be solved, the way would be open for the solution of *n*-person zero-sum games.

A central reason for the intractability of this and similar matrices in yielding solutions lies in the possibility of the "double cross." For many negotiated solutions, the results will hold only if both parties keep faith and do not renege on the agreement. It is a general property of many of these matrices that if *B* keeps faithfully to his side of the bargain then *A* will have the option of reneging and choosing a strategy which will give him a better result than the agreed-on solution (and *B* a worse result). Hence, if the opportunity to double-cross occurs, it is rational that it be taken.

To eliminate the double-cross possibility, it is necessary that the solution be at an equilibrium point. At equilibrium, if one actor changes his strategy while the others do not, he cannot improve his outcome and he may worsen it. Hence all actors will continue to pursue the same strategy, once the equilibrium has been reached.

The problem discussed so far in this chapter and the difficulties in achieving a solution are strongly reminiscent of traditional social contract theories and the objections which have been raised to them. For example, both Plato and Rousseau used the double-cross argument in rejecting social contract

4. Nash (1950).

theories.[5] All are supposed to benefit equally from joining into the contract and creating a cooperative society. But the crafty and unscrupulous will renege on the contract and take advantage of their more gullible neighbors; in fact, the rules of the social contract will aid rather than hinder their nefarious purposes. The ostensible equality of the laws will cloak the real exploitation by the more capable rascals. The contract, though apparently just, actually furthers the interests of the strong at the expense of the weak. In the language of decision theory, while the "solution" of the social contract may benefit all parties, it is not at an equilibrium point.

In essence, the arguments of Plato and Rousseau assert that if people are motivated by the values and interests necessarily presupposed by social contract theories, they will double-cross whenever they get a chance to do so advantageously, and a rational social order will be impossible. Their next step is to inquire what sort of values and interests must motivate the members of a society to make a rational social order possible, and what conditions might produce such values and interests. This is essentially the course of the argument in this volume.

One matrix, often called "The Prisoner's Dilemma," bears a strong resemblance to Hobbes's idea of the state of nature. The matrix was thought to involve an insolvable paradox, but recently a solution has been found, which, however, does not appear to resemble Hobbes's method of escape from the dilemma. To treat this question would require too long a digression, however.[6]

It is undoubtedly premature to assert that Von Neumann and Morgenstern's pessimism on the possibility of unique cooperative solutions of matrices of partial conflict was justified. The recent solution of "The Prisoner's Dilemma" is a sufficient

5. Plato, *The Republic*, 364–65; Rousseau (1754), pp. 78–79.

6. Nigel (1966); Rapoport and Chammah (1965).

reminder, if one is needed, that what today appears insolvable may tomorrow be solved. The difficulties involved, however, are illustrated by the very simple and suggestive matrix (fig. 5) treated above and at least seriously raise the possibility that the premises of decision theory are too narrow a base on which to construct a theory of social interaction.

The discussion so far in this chapter suggests the following definitions and conclusions: The underlying problem of co-operative social interaction seems to be well exhibited by inter-action matrices of partial conflict. These lie between zero-sum matrices (where, for any two states, A prefers one if B prefers the other) and matrices of total harmony (where, for any two states, the preference of A is the same as the preference of B). That is, a matrix of partial conflict will have some pairs where the preferences of the two actors are opposed, and others where their preferences are the same. It is assumed that A and B can communicate with each other with a view to reaching an agreement about what strategy each is to choose.

A cooperative solution will be said to occur when A and B both have a rational strategy, with a result that lies within the negotiation set. A negotiation set is the subset of the states for which, (1) both A and B prefer every state within the subset to every state not within the subset, and (2) within the subset, for every possible pairing of states, if one prefers the first, the other will prefer the second.

A central obstacle to an agreement between A and B is that neither will have any reason to suppose that the other will keep the agreement if it is not clearly to his interest to do so. Mutual confidence that the other will honor the agreement is justified only if the matrix has a solution which lies at an equilibrium point within the negotiation set.

Even though the view has not been demonstrated, and may be false, I agree with Von Neumann and Morgenstern that it cannot be shown that there is a unique cooperative solution to any but some special cases of matrices of partial conflict, that is, that there is in general no "solution" in the sense of a pair of rational strategies which maximize the expected utilities of the actors. Hence, no specific cooperative interaction can be shown to be the course of reason in the most general and typical situations of partial conflict.

B. *The Comparison of Utilities*

On the basis of the theory of utility, there appears to be no way to compare the utilities of one actor with those of another. In fact, this impossibility seems to be built into the method of deriving utility scales. What is posited by the theory is that an actor can rank any set of alternatives in order of preference in a consistent way. The theory of utility is simply a development of the mathematical implications of this premise. A utility scale is an expression of a ranking of preferences worked out in such a way that it is possible to speak in a meaningful and quantified way of the degree of preference among three or more alternatives; for example, *a* is twice as preferable to *b* as *b* is to *c*. (That is, things are not preferred in themselves, but in relation to each other.) The idea of "quantity of utility" is not derivable from this scheme.

It is as if two persons had thermometers of unknown and possibly different calibrations. A statement such as "My temperature is two degrees higher than it was an hour ago" has no intrinsic meaning other than that the temperature is higher, for the calibrations on the thermometers are unknown. One can only make statements of the kind, "My temperature rose twice as much between nine and ten as it did between ten and eleven." This conclusion will hold regardless of the way the thermometer is calibrated.

Suppose, further, that we wish to compare the temperature of *A* to *B*. Obviously the answer is to take the temperature of both with the same thermometer. But this is precisely what cannot be done with utility scales. By definition, as it were, *A*'s thermometer can be used to measure A's temperature only, and B's to measure B's temperature only. It is hence impossible to compare A's temperature with B's.[7]

In sum, utilities can be compared in two senses but not in two other senses. First, they can be compared in the sense that "A prefers x to y, while B prefers y to x." Second, they can be compared in the sense that "A prefers x to y twice as much as he prefers x to z, while B prefers x to y three times as much as he prefers x to z." Third, however, we cannot tell whether the utility of x to A is greater, the same, or less than the utility of x to B, nor, fourth, can we tell how the degree of A's preference of x to y compares to the degree of B's preference of y to x. It is the latter two senses that are referred to by the phrase "the incomparability of utilities."

It was earlier pointed out that the contents of an interaction field included everything which was of significance to the utilities of the actors, and nothing whatsoever was ruled out as of possible significance to a given actor. As a result of the considerations just introduced, it is now necessary to conclude that, on the premises developed so far, there are two kinds of things which cannot be of significance to the utilities of a given actor —namely, the intensity or degree of the preferences of the other actors, and the degree to which another actor prefers one alternative to another. These cannot be significant for an actor's own preferences because he cannot know what they are as compared with his own, and hence they cannot enter into his preference formations. Interactions where the actors are indifferent to these aspects of the utilities of others will be defined as "impersonal." Hence the theory of utility and the theory of decisions based on the theory of utility presume or posit impersonality of interaction.

It is important to understand what is intended by the above

---

7. This analogy ignores the existence of the Kelvin Scale.

argument. Utilitarianism has often been accused of being a philosophy of self-interest in the sense that it holds that in making their decisions people are always indifferent to the welfare of others. While this charge may be valid for some of the earlier formulations of utilitarianism, it is not true for the theory in question. There is no logical reason in the theory why a person should not prefer actions which benefit others to actions which benefit themselves, for a utility scale simply measures preferences, without stipulating what these preferences are. Nor does the theory rule out the possibility of "sympathy," in the sense of the term used, for example, by David Hume,[8] where the sight of pain to others is painful to ourselves, and of pleasure to others is pleasurable to ourselves. What is ruled out is that in forming our preferences we cannot weigh our own benefits or harm against the benefit or harm to another *as the other defines them.*[9]

Common sense indicates that in practice people do compare utilities. For example, suppose that the two people in the hypothetical boat described above were friends. It is likely that after it had been ascertained that both preferred bailing to rowing, each would then inquire how much the other preferred bailing to rowing. If the first strongly preferred bailing while the second mildly preferred bailing, friendship obviously would dictate that the former bail and the latter row. If they are equally adverse to rowing, it is reasonable to suppose that they would decide to divide their time equally between rowing and bailing. This procedure logically presupposes a comparison of utilities in a sense ruled out above.

A little reflection will reveal that this kind of method of resolving conflicts of interest is exceedingly common, and the more personal the relation the more common, the less personal

8. Hume (1739), bk. 2, pt. 1, sec. 2.

9. The point that in the above sentence no basis has been laid for the idea of benefits or harm as independent of preferences will be treated below.

the less common. In fact, widely accepted principles of equity hold that, where these are the only two alternatives, the lesser injury to one is preferable to the greater injury to another, and that the greater benefit to one is preferable to the lesser benefit to another. Hence it would seem necessary to introduce the idea of comparison of utility in some way in order to account for the way in which situations of partial conflict are in fact often settled.

But there seems to be a contradiction here, for it has been asserted that in forming their preferences people often compare their utilities to those of others, but the existence of utilities assumes that the preferences in question have already been formed. In other words, the idea of comparison of utilities as a step in decision making seems to suppose that the utility precedes the preference formation, whereas in the theory of utility a utility is simply a preference. To handle this problem, it is necessary to develop a theory for that which is simply posited by utility theory—the process of preference formation. Briefly, the contradiction is resolved by the assumption that in principle preferences are formed in stages—that is, in effect utilities are first formed without comparison of utilities, utilities are then compared, and, as a consequence, the original preferences are altered to form new utility scales.

The method adopted for comparing utilities will be simplicity itself—we will let our actors do it for us. That is, the act of comparing utilities will simply be posited, just as the act of forming preferences is posited. However, although in the logic of the theory these acts will simply be posited without explanation or defense, implicit support for this procedure will be drawn from psychoanalytic theory. That is, the "givens" of the theory will be associated with ideas that are the product of another theory. In this way, the word "preferences" will be associated with the term "object choice," the words "utility scale" with the words "drive orientation," while the process of comparing utilities will have the same name in both theories: "identification."

C. *Identification*

1. The importance of identification with others to the process of forming a clear self-concept has been pointed out by Piaget,[10] G. H. Mead,[11] and Freud, among others. Freud states, "Identification is known to psychoanalysis as the earliest expression of an emotional tie with another person."[12] In the psychoanalytic view, the very first object relations partake of identification: "At the very beginning, in the primitive oral phase of the individual's existence, object-cathexis and identification are hardly to be distinguished from each other."[13]

At this early stage the distinction between the self and the external world is not well formed; hence an object relation can just as well be described as a self-relation ("primary narcissism").

These primitive object-identification relations are crucial to the development of the idea of one's self as distinct from others. Rapaport says, "From certain vantage points, the ego is the precipitate of abandoned drive-objects, that is, of *identifications.*"[14]

Identification first occurs through introjection: the incorporation into one's self of something from the outside.[15] In its primitive and unconscious form, this process is psychologically quite literal, as can be seen from certain magical practices; for example, eating the flesh of a brave person can make one brave, and of a divine person can make one divine. Such ideas

---

10. Piaget (1947, 1953); See the selections from *The Psychology of Intelligence,* with extensive discussion, in Rapaport (1951), pp. 154–75.

11. Mead (1934).

12. Freud (1921), p. 105.

13. Freud (1923), p. 75.

14. Rapaport (1951), p. 725. Rapaport is here referring to Freud (1923), p. 29. (Italics Rapaport's.)

15. Rapaport (1951), pp. 724–25.

can play an important role even in religions which have advanced a considerable degree beyond the primitive level.

It must be stressed that the self is not a material thing, but a concept which a biological-psychological entity has about itself as a biological-psychological entity. Since the self is a concept, the notion that this concept includes as a component the concept that one has of another biological-psychological entity is in no way stranger than, and just as literal as, the Euclidian idea that congruent triangles are identical in all respects. Our concept of ourselves is what we choose it to be, and we are perfectly free to identify this concept with the concept we have of another person.

If another person has preferences, and we identify with him, then his preferences become our own. In other words the idea of identification includes the idea of adopting a utility scale of another person as our own. This phenomenon is readily observable in all cases of close identification. (This will be qualified presently.)

Despite a great deal of material in psychological theory on the nature of identification, the exact process whereby such comparisons are made does not seem to have been examined. This question, however, need not concern the present inquiry—it is enough to point out that people in fact do compare utilities. Such comparisons cannot be judged either right or wrong except in the sense that any act of preference can be judged right or wrong. Just as an individual is free to decide, for example, that his preference of steak to hamburger is twice his preference of hamburger to beans, so he is free to decide that the utility of steak to another person is twice its utility to himself. Notice that the idea of an absolute magnitude of utilities is not involved here—just as people compare the utility of one state with the utility of another for themselves, so they compare the utility of a given state for themselves with its utility for another. The relationship is purely relative in both cases. Nor would there be anything contradictory about A and B each deciding that the utility of state S is worth twice to the other what it is to himself, although in practice such a combination of judgments might lead to an Alphonse-Gaston kind of struggle.

In sum, if the utilities of other actors are significant for one's own utilities, it is logically necessary that utilities be compared (except in certain cases to be treated presently). From a psychological point of view, the process of identification would also seem to involve such a comparison of utilities.

2. Identification admits of degree. At one extreme, an identification may be so strong that it swallows up the whole ego; at the other, it may be so slight that it hardly affects behavior at all. It seems that there are two dimensions along which degree of identification can occur: first, the area of the ego involved; second, the intensity of the identification. As to the first, identification is frequently only partial. For example, a member of an occupational group can be expected to identify with other members of his group, but his concept of himself as a person who holds a particular occupation is normally only a part of his total self-concept, since this internalized role is normally only one of many. Hence only part of himself will identify with others who have the same occupation. This factor will not be analyzed further, but it is assumed to be included in the construction which will be developed shortly.

The intensity of the identification will vary with a number of factors. Some of these will be analyzed in a future volume, and here I will make only one or two remarks. The frequency of the interaction is obviously a factor, as is the nature of the interaction. Identifications outside the family are normally derivative formations, springing from earlier parental or sibling identifications. Here the closeness of the character of the person identified with to the original object of identification may be a factor, and also the degree of similarity of the role he plays to the original family role. Obviously the more intense the identification, the greater will be the influence of the other's utilities.

3. Projection frequently plays an important role in the for-

mation of identifications. The internalized father image in the superego is normally to a certain extent idealized; its characteristics are partly what one wishes the father to be, rather than what he actually is. This internalized father image may then be projected onto the father himself: he is perceived as similar to the internal picture. Subsequent identifications may involve the projection of this father image, or some aspect of it, onto other people whose actual preferences may in fact be different from those of the projected image.[16] (When one takes into account the unconscious components of the relationship, however, such projections are often less erroneous than they superficially might seem to be.) For the sake of simplicity, this problem will be handled by assuming that identification involves a correct perception of the utility scale of the other, in line with the assumptions of utility theory already developed. However, nothing is assumed about the "correctness" or "incorrectness" of the comparison of utilities. Like the formation of preferences, it is simply something the actor does; it is a part of the process of evaluation.

4. In identification, the significance of the utilities of the others may be negative, rather than positive. The relationship can express hate as well as love. While the psychological mechanisms involved in hatred have not been as thoroughly explored as with love, identification also seems to be involved.[17] What happens is that unwanted, often largely unconscious emotions, feelings, and characteristics of the person's own self are projected outward onto somebody else. Hostility toward the other thus partly takes the place of the more painful self-hostility which is the basis for the projection. While in a positive identification, or love, a gain in satisfaction to the other is automatically a gain in satisfaction to one's self, in negative identification, or hate, the situation is reversed. Intense mutual hatred may

16. "The belief in authority in general is always due to a projection of superego qualities." Fenichel (1945), p. 110.

17. Adorno (1950), pp. 240–41 et passim.

produce a zero-sum situation even where there is no overt conflict of interests. This is not to say, however, that the zero-sum utility relationship is necessarily one of hatred. People's interests often conflict quite apart from the feelings they have toward one another.

D. *The Formation of the Particular Will*

In the original formulation of the idea of interaction, it was posited that the relationship was impersonal; that is, that the actors were indifferent to the utilities of the other actors in the sense developed. This was reflected in the fact that the utilities of the other actors were not included as properties of the possible results. The introduction of the idea of personal relations has the effect of making the utilities of others a component of the interaction field which is significant for the actor's own utilities. Preferences are formed by evaluating the total contents of the field, including the utilities of others. Since identification plays such a crucial role in the formation of social groups, however, it is convenient for analytic purposes to separate these factors out and to imagine the utility scale of the individual as the combination of two sets of factors: first, the utilities of the interaction field apart from the influence of identification, and second, the influence of identification on these utilities. As will be seen, this separation is not entirely artificial and, to some extent, corresponds to actual divisions within the psyche.

1. *The private will and the particular will.* For any interaction field, the *private will* of an actor will be defined as his utility scale apart from the influence of the utilities of others: what his actual utility scale would be if the relations within the field were impersonal. For any interaction field, the *particular will* of an actor will be defined as his actual utility scale when all the factors of the possible interaction states, including the influence of the utilities of others, are taken into account. The term "par-

ticular will" is taken from Jean-Jacques Rousseau, for reasons which will become apparent later on.

The use of the terms "private will" and "particular will" imply a specific interaction field as referent. Thus an actor will have as many private and particular wills as there are interaction fields in which he participates. The division of the position of an actor vis-à-vis his environment into discrete interaction fields is of course artificial, because in practice the utilities of one field will normally interact with the utilities of another. The division therefore is justifiable only if it is analytically useful. Actually there is only one private will and one particular will, with the interaction field constituting the entire set of possible interactions with the environment.

It might be argued, as some sociologists have seemed to do, that there is no such thing as a private will as distinct from a particular will, since the preferences of an individual are entirely a social product made up of nothing but the various social identifications he has formed. Freud's assertion, previously cited,[18] that the ego is nothing but a precipitate of the individual's identifications, also seems to support such a view. This, however, is going too far.[19] The psychic system springs from the genetically determined instinctual drives, and no matter how strongly shaped and altered by the social environment, an individual's preferences must to some extent be influenced by and reflect this instinctual system. Identifications are, so to speak, the stones from which the individual forms his self-concept, but these stones are shaped and fitted together in ways which are unique to each person. Furthermore, although it is the ego which forms the preferences of the individual, these preferences must not be regarded as those of the ego only, but rather of the entire person, at least if the ego has been successful in its task.

18. See note 14 above.
19. For a more balanced statement see Brenner (1955), pp. 113–40.

The idea of the particular will also implies that what is involved is the person's preferences at a given moment, or over a relatively short period of time. The contents of the interaction field keep changing, and so do the preferences of the individual. Certain features of the particular will, over a longer period of time, will be found to be relatively consistent through the progressive alteration of the field and of the individual's preferences. This constant structure or content of preferences constitutes the *personality* of the individual. When these more stable factors change, the actor's personality is said to change.

The distinction between private and particular will may or may not correspond to a distinction in the mind of the individual. If superego identifications are involved, the distinction between particular and private will may correspond to the distinction between superego and ego. Or more generally, we may be aware of our desire to further our own interests as distinct from our sympathy and concern for the welfare of others.

2. *Total identification.* Identification clearly admits of degree. At one extreme the identification may be so slight that the private will and the particular will for all purposes are the same. At the other extreme, as a polar case which may at times be approached in practice, we have total identification. Consider the utilities shown in figure 9. There the identification is "total": A

	s_1	s_2	s_3	s_4	s_5
A's Private Will	8	6	4	2	0
B's Particular Will	1	2	3	4	5
A's Particular Will	1	2	3	4	5

Fig. 9. Total identification

and B are still discrete actors, but A has taken B's utility scale over as his own. The utility for all possible interactions will be the same for each. A's attitude toward B is "Thy will be done."

Hence, *B*'s utility scale will determine *A*'s actions. Whatever *B* commands, *A* will do, assuming that obedience to this command will maximize *B*'s expected utility as far as the relationship between them goes. In fact, such a command will never be necessary. All that is needed is for *B* to communicate his utilities to *A*.

While a pure type of this relationship cannot be expected in practice, it is occasionally approached in certain human relationships and, more frequently, is expressed as an ideal. For example, it is the heart of the Judaic and Christian conceptions of the proper relationship between man and God. ("Thy will be done.") Sin is nothing but a refusal to accept God's will as one's own. Charismatic leadership and hero worship share this quality, as does the conception of paternal authority as absolute and unbounded. The political view that law is simply the will of the sovereign also reflects this idea, although the authority involved is not necessarily personal. Another level is reached, however, when the sovereign is considered to be the whole body politic.

3. *Partial identification.* According to the theory being developed here, identification admits of degree. For the two polar cases, total identification and no identification, *A*'s particular will in the first instance will be the same as *B*'s particular will, and in the second instance the same as *A*'s private will. In between, his particular will is an amalgam of his private will and *B*'s particular will, with the weight accorded to each dependent on the degree of identification.

There are two steps or stages which are logically required for such an operation. First, *A* must compare his utilities to *B*'s: that is, he must form the idea of a comparative standard of utility, so that *A*'s private will and *B*'s particular will can be measured on the same scale. It must be emphasized that this comparison is entirely *A*'s doing—it is a judgment which he alone makes. An outside observer measuring utilities in terms, let us say, of chemical reactions or electrical discharges might arrive at a different standard of comparison. Second, *A* decides how much a given utility for *B* is worth to him, compared with the same "amount" of utility to his own private will. On that basis he forms his particular utilities as an amalgam of his private and *B*'s particular utilities.

Perhaps an example will make this outline of the logical requirements of identification clear. Let us assume an interaction field of four states, s_1, s_2, s_3, s_4.

a. Actor *A* determines his private utilities for the four states; for example, *A*'s private will:

s_1	s_2	s_3	s_4
1	2	4	7

It will be recalled from chapter 2 that the figures on this scale are arbitrary in the sense that any linear transformation of this scale (multiplying all numbers by the same number, and/or adding the same number to all numbers) will yield an equivalent scale. What is constant throughout all such transformations is the ratio of the numerical distances between the utilities. Thus, let the distance between s_1 and s_2 be x, between s_2 and s_3 be y, and between s_3 and s_4 be z. Then the ratios $x/y = 1/2$, $x/z = 1/3$, and (hence) $y/z = 2/3$ are constant throughout any linear transformation.

b. Since *A* knows *B*'s preferences, he can construct *B*'s utility scale just as well as *B* can. Any one of an infinite number of scales, each a linear transformation of the others, will do to express *B*'s scale. The ratios between the intervals, however, will be the same for all such transformations. Let the ratios for *B* be $x/y = 1/3$, $x/z = 1/4$, and (hence) $y/z = 3/4$. Any set of numbers which satisfies these ratios will express *B*'s utility scale. Note that these ratios are set by *B*'s preferences. Actor *A* merely observes them.

c. Now *A* compares utilities as follows: For at least two states, he decides what each state is worth to his own private will compared with what it is worth to B. Suppose, for example, that he decides s_1 is worth twice as much to B as to his private will, or 2, and s_3 is worth three times as much to B as it is to him, or 12. From this it is possible to calculate the rest of B's scale as follows:

1. For B, $\dfrac{x}{y} = \dfrac{1}{3} = \dfrac{u_b s_2 - 2}{12 - u_b s_2}$. Solving, $u_b s_2 = 4.5$.

2. For B, $\dfrac{x}{z} = \dfrac{1}{4} = \dfrac{2.5}{u_b s_4 - 12}$. Solving, $u_b s_4 = 22$.

3. Etc.

Thus B's particular will is:

s_1	s_2	s_3	s_4
2	4.5	12	22

This is B's particular will, *expressed in A's units.* It is as if A has measured B's utilities on his own "thermometer." It will be seen that the ratios which satisfy B's scale hold: $x/y = 1/3$, $x/z = 1/4$, and (hence) $y/z = 3/4$. These ratios are determined by B. But in addition the scale now has a form in which it is comparable with A's private will. This comparison has been made by A.

3. From these two scales A now forms his particular will. See, for example, figure 10. Here A's particular will was formed

	s_1	s_2	s_3	s_4
A's Private Will	1	2	4	7
B's Particular Will	2	4.5	12	22
A's Particular Will	1.5	3.25	8	14.5

Fig. 10. Identification of 0.5

by weighing his private and B's particular utilities equally: $ua_{par}s_n = 0.5ua_{pvt}s_n + 0.5ubs_n$. (The utility to A's particular will of state s_n is one-half the utility to A's private will of state s_n

plus one-half the utility to B's particular will of state s_n (measured in A's units).) This will be called 50 percent, or 0.5, identification. For a 0.7 identification the formula will be $ua_{par}s_n = 0.3ua_{pvt}s_n + 0.7ubs_n$.

The situation becomes much more complicated if it is assumed that A gives different weights to B's utilities for different ranges of B's scale. For example, I have observed the following situation in the game of poker: Some players have no compunction about winning money from other players within a given range of loss, but once the others' losses exceed a certain sum, they become uncomfortable, are reluctant to press their advantage when they hold strong cards, and are generally unhappy about any further losses by their opponents. It seems that the monetary utilities of the other players are of no consequence to such players as long as their losses do not exceed a certain sum, but for larger losses the others' utilities become a significant factor.

Figure 11 shows one instance of this type of problem. Here

	s_1	s_2	s_3	s_4	s_5
A's Private Will	1	2	3	4	5
B's Particular Will	1	3	6	12	20
A's Particular Will	2	4	7	10	12

Fig. 11. Nonlinear identification

there is no linear transformation to B's particular will producing a scale which, when added to A's private will, produces his particular will. Rather, B's utilities in the lower range of his scale are worth more to A than B's utilities in their higher range. What seems to be involved is the establishment of an *absolute* (ratio) scale (by A), along which the utilities of A and B are compared.

To attempt—on the basis of our current knowledge of how, in practice, people compare their utilities one with the other—

to work this idea out on a theoretical basis would be to go beyond speculation into fancy. This question must be deferred until there is some research on the matter. The theory developed here will not go beyond the idea that the particular will of an actor is formed by the interaction of his private will and the particular will of the other actors who are identified with, and whose utilities are hence compared (in a nondefined way) with the actor's and combined with them to form his own particular will. Fortunately, even this slim basis is enough to support the points we wish to make.

We see no reason why this theory of the process of identification could not be empirically tested. Of course, actual preferences regularly violate the principle of consistent choice, and so this factor would have to be controlled. Whatever the actual findings, it seems logically necessary for the process to have two aspects or stages: first, comparison of utilities; second, weighing of utilities. The way in which the two operations are performed might differ from that outlined here, however.

E. *Mutual Identification and Cooperation*

When individuals interact with each other regularly, especially if this interaction is cooperative, ties of mutual identification will spring up. One-way identification must be considered exceptional, and mutual identification the rule. For mutual identification each party to the interaction field goes through exactly the same process of forming a particular will as has just been outlined for a single actor.

There is no logical reason to suppose that when two people identify mutually each compares his utilities to the other's in the same way, or that they identify with each other to the same degree. On the first point, it will here be assumed that the comparisons are in fact the same. If A judges s_n to be twice as useful to himself as to B, then B will judge s_n to be half as useful to himself as to A. This assumption is adopted purely for the sake of simplicity; empirical research would likely show that the comparisons can differ and there is no reason why a more fully developed theory could not take account of this. On the second point, degree of identification, it would also seem to be true that people in interaction often identify with each other to different degrees for different interactions. This possibility will also be ignored, solely for the sake of simplicity.

The formation or ties of mutual identification may produce solutions, or cooperative solutions, for matrices where these were not previously present. For example, mutual identification may produce a cooperative solution from a zero-sum matrix. Assume that the private wills of A and B are those in figure 12 after comparisons have been made but before identification has occurred.

	s_1	s_2	s_3	s_4
A	0.1	0.2	0.3	0.4
B	40	30	20	10

Fig. 12. Conflicting private wills of A and B

Previously, this matrix could have been converted to zero-sum, first by multiplying all of A's utilities by 10 and dividing all of B's utilities by 10, and then by subtracting 2.5 from the utilities of both actors, producing the zero-sum matrix in figure 13. Such a transformation, however, would fail to

	s_1	s_2	s_3	s_4
A	−1.5	−0.5	0.5	1.5
B	1.5	0.5	−0.5	−1.5

Fig. 13. Transformation of figure 12 to zero-sum

reflect any comparisons of utility which may have occurred and obscure the fact that in the original matrix, a 0.1 identification of A with B would produce the matrix in figure 14.

	s_1	s_2	s_3	s_4
A	4.9	4.8	4.7	4.6
B	40	30	20	10

Fig. 14. Utilities after 0.1 identification of A with B,
from figure 12.

Here s_1 has the highest utility for both parties, who will then cooperate by choosing strategies to produce this result. On the other hand, in the original matrix, if A does not identify at all with B, very high identification of over 0.99 is required on B's part for a cooperative solution. A little reflection will show that a sum of identifications on the part of the two actors of 1 or more will produce a cooperative solution for any matrix whatsoever.

Hence the generalization follows that in any interaction between two actors, if each of the actors follows the golden rule literally, and loves his neighbor equally as well as himself (0.5 identification), all possible interactions between them will have a cooperative solution. If we assume that the political situation always involves conflict, the corollary follows that in politics not everyone obeys the golden rule.

A further generalization is possible: In a situation where the private wills of the actors are in total conflict—that is, where for any two states B will prefer s_n to s_m when A prefers s_m to s_n (which is now no longer automatically a zero-sum interaction) —if the stakes of one actor in the interaction (the magnitude of possible gain or loss) are considerably higher than the stakes of the other, a cooperative solution can be reached if the actor with the lower stakes identifies only slightly with the other. For roughly equal stakes (which approach zero-sum), at least one of the actors must identify heavily (around 0.5) with the other for a cooperative solution to be possible.

This conclusion holds for the "rowboat problem." If it makes a major difference to one party, and a minor difference to the other, whether he rows or bails, then a slight identification by the one to whom it makes a slight difference will produce a cooperative solution. If the difference is about the same for both, then a heavy identification by at least one party is necessary. In other words the more intensely two people identify (positively) with each other, the less frequently will their relationships involve struggle. I feel that no very substantial practical problems stand in the way of setting up translation rules so that the above propositions can be tested empirically.

This is perhaps an opportune moment to defend myself against the charge of using an elaborate theoretical apparatus to demonstrate the obvious. The principal conclusion of Whitehead and Russell's *Principia Mathematica* is that one plus one equals two, a fact that was already fairly widely known before this work was published. We are not aware, however, that this has been used for the basis of the charge that the work is a trivial one. The point is that they derive the idea of number, and addition of number, on the basis of formal logic alone, thus demonstrating that mathematics is in effect a branch of logic. In the same way, to derive elementary, common-sense propositions about the way people behave on the basis of an axiomatic development of certain postulates is to show the applicability of the theory in explaining human relations.

F. *Conclusion*

The process of identification adds a new dimension to the analysis of human relations in terms of interaction matrices. In this chapter the greater emphasis has been laid on positive identification, which tends to mitigate otherwise "irreconcilable" conflicts of interest between actors. It must not automatically be assumed, however, that human identifications are predominantly positive. The relationship of hate (negative identification) is perhaps nearly as common, or even more common, than that of love (positive identification). More accurately, human relations are often complex combinations of both factors.

By itself, positive identification is capable of producing co-operative behavior in some situations but not in others (assuming rationality of decisions). When the component of negative identification is taken into account, cooperative relations seem to be rarer.

In general, the greater the degree of positive identification, the more interaction matrices will yield a cooperative solution. It is possible that the process of identification, as developed in this chapter, is a sufficient basis on which to explain the stability of small, intimate, face-to-face groups, such as the family. In larger groups, where the interactions are less frequent, emotional relations less intense, and hence identifications not as strong, simple identification seems inadequate to produce stable cooperation. In addition, the operation of simple identification seems to produce all-or-nothing situations—either cooperation and stability or conflict and instability. In contrast, actual group relations regularly exhibit a mixture of cooperation and conflict.

What is needed is a stronger bond. Such a bond, one in which the negative identifications as well as the positive ones will serve to bind men into cooperative relations, and where cooperation and conflict can exist side by side, will be described later, after a typology of influence has been developed.

5/

POWER

A. *Introduction*

THE IDEA OF POWER, as it has developed in the intellectual tradition of the West, has two main components. The first is the idea of purposive control, and the second is the idea of technique, whereby the control is exercised. Central to both components is the idea of rational thought and action. It has been traditional to distinguish among power over nature (level of technology), power over other people (political or social power), and power over one's own purposes and actions (self-control). While the field of application of each of these three types differs, the idea is the same.

The idea of internal mastery and external control through rational thought and action is perhaps the most important theme in the political and social thought of Plato and Aristotle. For them, the relationship between the two provides the answer to the problem of human conflict. If the internal lives of the members of society are properly ordered, their external lives will be harmonious, not in conflict. Failing this, says Plato, the State will be not one but many; conflict will be irresolvable, and the political system will disintegrate.[1]

1. Plato, *Republic*, 422–23.

The more policy-oriented Aristotle was more ready to deal with the fact that men cannot be expected to behave according to a wholly rational conception of justice. The division of labor in society produces different interests and values and, as a consequence, a struggle for power among classes.[2] As long as these views are not thoroughly perverted, however, an equilibrium, or balance of power—and through this a relative degree of justice—may be attainable.[3] Or (in a passage strongly but deceptively similar to the content of Machiavelli's *Prince*) an enlightened tyrant can, through the manipulation of the instrumentalities of power, establish a regime which exhibits some degree of justice.[4]

Despite the striking modernity of books 4–6 of Aristotle's *Politics*, however, his central point, like Plato's, is the intrinsic connection between rational thought and action as an internal process whereby men govern their own actions, and an external process, whereby they govern the actions of others. It is precisely this connection which is lacking in the modern conception of power. True, it has not altogether vanished in Machiavelli's treatment of the subject. He makes it quite clear that the Prince's use of power is thrust on him by the moral degeneration of those whom he rules.[5] In a state with a virtuous citizenry, the political process takes a different form, and the operation of political

2. While this idea is not fully developed by Aristotle, it seems to me implicit in his analysis. For example, book 4 of the *Politics* links the social structure with the distribution of both power and opinion (and all three with the constitutional system).

3. For example, *Politics*, bk. 4, chap. 11. The idea of a harmonious balance, or middle between extremes, is of course basic to Aristotle. The idea, however, is not always formulated in a dynamic way.

4. Aristotle, *Politics*, bk. 5, chap. 11, pars. 17–33.

5. "Therefore a prudent ruler ought not to keep faith, when by doing so it would be against his interest, and when the reasons which made him bind himself no longer exist. If men were all good, this precept would not be a good one; but as they are bad, and would not observe their faith with you, so you are not bound to keep faith with them." Machiavelli (1532a), chap. 18.

power becomes less central.[6] But the decisive step has already been taken by Machiavelli: virtue is no longer equated with rational self-control.

In the modern era, the idea of purposive control turns strongly outward, toward the environment and, as a consequence, becomes preoccupied with the techniques of power—both power over nature and power over other men. The political situation presupposes that certain conflicts between men or organizations cannot be resolved by rational discourse and voluntary mutual accommodation, and hence that the relationship will become coercive. The quest for power becomes the quest for the means of exercising coercive influence, and for expertise in the use of coercion.

The term "coercion," however, is too narrow. Power operates not only through the threat of deprivation but also by means of the promise of reward. Hence, the word "sanction" will be employed as encompassing the wide range of threats (negative sanctions) and promises (positive sanctions) involved in the uses of power.

The treatment of power adopted here will be within the framework of the Western tradition. The weight of attention will be on the modern idea of power as a form of interaction between individuals. But it will be found, as the classic tradition maintained, that this form of power cannot be understood without delving into the inner psychological aspects.

The principal difficulty in using the concept of power is that in complex interactions involving many individuals it is commonly difficult to untangle the thread of the influence of one particular individual or group of individuals from that of others. This is especially true of decisions made by large organizations. Since the focus of this work is purely theoretical, such problems of empirical applicability will not receive more than passing attention. The idea of a field of interaction will

6. Machiavelli (1532*b*). For example, bk. 1, chap. 55.

enable a treatment of the theoretical—as distinct from the practical—problem of distinguishing the degree of power exercised by an actor in such a complex interaction.

The modern idea of power implies a purely external connection between the purposes or wills of the interacting individuals. As Kant puts it, the actors treat each other purely as objects, not as persons (ends in themselves).[7] Power relationships are impersonal. The same theoretical tendency has already been noted in the modern theory of utility, which, as has been pointed out, presumes impersonality of interaction, in the sense defined.

In fact, however, such impersonal power relations must be regarded as altogether exceptional, for truly impersonal interaction is rare. This will be readily understood if one contemplates the relationship of man to nature, even inanimate nature. In primitive cultures, it is commonplace for nature to become personified, invested with human attributes, and treated accordingly. In more sophisticated cultures, these attitudes become overlaid with more rational levels of understanding. On the level of factual assertion it is understood that man and nature are distinct. Yet in our emotions (now perhaps partly unconsciously) and, to a certain extent, in our actions we continue to personify nature: to treat it as if it were human—perhaps with some justification, for, as Spinoza has argued, while the distinction between man and nature is great, it is not ultimate.[8]

But if it is emotionally difficult to treat inanimate nature as if it were not human, how much more difficult to treat other human beings as objects, not as persons. With any regular interaction between human beings, we can expect emotional ties to spring up, whether these be of love or of hate. (It makes no sense to hate a thing.) This points up a weakness of much of current theory about international relations, which proceeds from the assump-

7. Kant (1785), pp. 22–60.

8. Spinoza (1677); Hampshire (1951), pp. 46–54.

tion that the foreign policy of states is not set by human beings. Nor was Marx exempt from this kind of misapprehension. Under capitalist production, he felt, the relationships between people become relationships between things, a view that was probably much too lenient on the capitalists.

Even apparently impersonal relations may be deceptive ("I cannot admit my emotions toward you even to myself, and in an attempt to deny these emotions I will treat you as a thing."). What at first appears as an impersonal relation may in the end turn out to be a special kind of personal relation.

The introduction of the process of identification into the theory of social interaction here being developed enables a formulation of the concept of power potentially capable of a more valid descriptive account of actual power relations. The power relation can be defined as one of "pure" power if it is completely impersonal (a polar case) in the sense that the actors do not identify with each other at all. At the other extreme, as has been argued, if mutual positive identification is "complete" (i.e., sums one or more), no conflict will occur, and power will not be exercised over others (only *with* others). The normal case, partial identification, is between these two extremes. It is thus possible to speak of the degree to which a power interaction is personal or impersonal. Theories which assume impersonality as an attribute of interaction in the social process, for example, Weber's theory of bureaucracy,[9] are using an artificial assumption, which is not necessarily a fault, for all theories must use artificial assumptions. In a later volume it will be argued that in practice the degree of impersonalization in bureaucracies is normally far smaller than has often been supposed, and that this fact is crucial to the understanding of how they work.

9. "[Bureaucracy] develops the more perfectly the more [it] is 'dehumanized,' the more completely it succeeds in eliminating from official business, love, hatred, and all purely personal, irrational, and emotional elements which escape calculation. This is the specific nature of bureaucracy." Weber (1925), p. 216. Note that, as he often does, Weber here takes a view which Marx applies to capitalism and casts it on to a larger screen.

If impersonality of interaction is posited in the theory, the descriptive fact that relations are personal must be handled by the introduction of boundary conditions which account for the discrepancy between the theoretical predictions and the observed behavior and are logically unrelated to the theory itself. On the other hand, the tactic employed here is to account for such relations within the theory itself.

From another point of view, purely impersonal power relations are not polar, but a midpoint on a continuum, at one end of which is complete $(+1)$ positive identification (perfect love) and, on the other, complete (-1) negative identification (perfect hate), while the zero point is one of indifference (impersonality). For a given interaction field with a given set of private utilities, the degree of conflict between the actors will be a function of the degree and kind of identification.

B. *Power as a Causal Idea*

In the earlier chapter on rational action, no causal relation was assumed between a strategy employed and the result, or outcome, of the interaction field. The term "result" means result of the field, not result of a strategy employed, or even the result of the whole set of possible strategies for each actor. For example, in a battle between two armies the terrain is usually an important feature of the interaction field, whose properties cannot be influenced by the various strategies of the actors. The result of a battle is often strongly influenced by certain features of the terrain and hence cannot be considered solely the product of the strategies employed. This point has additional force when applied to the strategy of an actor, for not only the terrain but also the possible strategies of the other actors are not of his making, nor can he normally use his influence over the other actors' choices of strategy to the extent of achieving total control. The theory of rational action thus posits only a functional (in the mathematical sense) relation between strategy and outcome, in that for every strategy there will be a result, without implying that this result was caused or even necessarily influenced by this strategy.

The idea of power is generally taken to imply a stronger connection between strategy and result than this. When we say that someone has power over something, the implication is that the strategy in some sense produces the result. To the extent that the result of a strategy is accidental or fortuitous—that is, due to factors beyond the control of the actor—it seems intuitively evident that the result did not represent an act of power. The idea of power as control over events seems to imply a *causal* relation between strategy and result.[10] On the other hand, this idea seems to fly in the face of the equally evident fact that a given actor rarely, if ever, has control over all the factors which determine a result.

For example, assume that the star of a baseball team is said to be responsible for his team's winning the pennant. On examination, this can be seen not to be a causal idea. In the first place, supposing that he had not played at all, his replacement might have played equally well. It may also have been true that the contribution of other members of the team was also indispensable. Furthermore, for example, if the star of an opposing team had not broken a leg and been out half the season, the team would perhaps not have won the pennant. To put it in an old-fashioned way, the star's contribution may not have been a necessary condition, and clearly it was not a sufficient condition, for winning the pennant.

It would hence seem necessary to inquire to what degree the player's contribution was responsible for the victory, but this

10. The use of "causation" as a technical term in explanation has occurred less and less in recent decades, possibly because of the decline of its use in theoretical physics and the development of field theories, starting with Maxwell in the nineteenth century. In a field, everything causes everything else; hence the term loses explanatory force. In effect, the discussion of causation introduced here is an indirect way of examining the question to what extent our theory is a field theory.

may be like asking which leg of a three-legged stool is the most responsible for holding it up. Indispensability does not necessarily admit of degree.

It was considerations such as these which eventually led me to abandon the attempt to define power in causal terms. It may be that some kind of causal relation is involved, but the concept is here defined without using the idea. An attempt has nevertheless been made to formulate a definition which is consistent with the connotations of the term "power" as it is ordinarily used. Since the matter is of considerable theoretical importance, a short digression on the idea of causation and its relation to the scheme of analysis employed here seems worthwhile.

Following Hume, it is believed by many that the idea of cause cannot be demonstrated to contain anything objective, or to have a clear meaning, beyond the idea of constant conjunction and temporal succession.[11] In other words, it is held that the statement "x causes y" can mean no more than "For every observation which has been made, x has been followed by y." Recent developments in logic and the philosophy of science, however, seem to indicate that the idea of causation can be used to assert more than this, in a way that does not necessarily overthrow the Humian critique but at least deflects its force. The definition of causation presented here rests on this recent analysis, although some of the ideas here used were developed by Silberstein as early as 1933.[12]

A causal relation between x and y may be defined as follows:
1. *If—*

  i. there is a process, s_1, s_2, s_3, etc., such that each successive state follows the former in time;

  ii. each state can be defined as the sum of the particu-

---

11. Hume (1739), bk. 1, pt. 3.

12. The following discussion leans on Silberstein (1933) and Braithwaite (1953), pp. 293–341. See also Nagel (1961), pp. 73–78, 517, and Lenzen (1954). The problem of causation is closely tied up with the status of nomic universals. See Nagel (1961), pp. 68–70, and Braithwaite (1953), pp. 314–17.

lar values assumed by a set of variables, with **x** and **y** among these variables;

    iii. whenever x_a is the value of **x** in any state, y_a is the value of **y** in the temporally following state;

    then: x_a causes y_a.

    2. If x_a in s_1 causes y_a in s_2, and y_a in s_2 causes z_a in s_3, we can say that x_a causes z_a; that is, in a chain of causation each element in the chain causes every subsequent element in the chain.

    3. If for every x there is a y, and for every y there is an x, such that every x causes a y, then the variable **x** causes the variable **y**.

    4. *The above statements must all be understood to be "nomic" (as against "accidental") universals.*[13] It is this distinction which gets around the Humian critique. An accidental universal is simply a summary of observations made, while a nomic universal asserts a "necessary" connection. For example, the universal "All swans are white" is an accidental universal if it means "All swans so far observed have been white"; on the other hand, if it is a nomic universal it asserts, "For every x, past, present, or future, whether observed or not (or if in fact there is no x, past, present, or future, but if there *were* such an x), if x is a swan, then x is white." We cannot here go into the logical status of nomic universals and the question of the grounds on which they can be asserted, except to say that to be nomic, a universal must be deductible from generalizations, the evidence for which is independent of observations of the conjunctions of x and y and is hence part of an explanation (as against a description). Theoretical generalizations are nomic, while empirical generalizations are accidental.

    While the above formulation of the concept of causation is the author's own, he believes it to be consonant with recent

---

13. For a discussion of the nature, logical status, and implications for scientific explanation of nomic universals, see Nagel (1961), pp. 56–73.

treatments.[14] It may, however, be too narrow, in the sense that it may rule out certain relations which can be said to be causal.

The above definition of cause may be broadened into a definition of a field. Suppose that for a process, s_1, s_2, s_3, etc., the sum total of the values of the variables in s_n (any state) can be said to cause the sum total of the values of the variables in s_{n+1} (the following state). That is, suppose the variables $x_n + y_n + z_n$, etc., in s_n cause the variables $x_{n+1} + y_{n+1} + z_{n+1}$, etc., in s_{n+1}, or, in other words, s_n causes s_{n+1}. In that case, the process **S** may then be said to be *deterministic* or *self-governed*. The formula which defines the formal relations among the variables for every state may be said to be the *formal cause* of the process, in the sense of the term used by Aristotle.[15] (It also seems possible to distinguish an efficient and a material cause.) If the formal statement is interpreted, and the values of the variables for one of the states are known, then by using the formula one can calculate the values of the variables for every other state. (The purely formal statement and its interpretation seem to stand in the relation of *nous* to *logos*.) Such a process can be termed a *field*. In a field in general every variable is a function of every other variable and the causal process must be described as relations among the sum total of the values of these variables for a succession of states.

It follows that the variables of **S** are not functions of any variables outside the process. This may be interpreted in two ways. First, **S** may be an *isolated system*: that is, it operates in an environment which has no significant impact on its behavior. This idea is much used in the physical sciences. Of course in using the idea of an isolated system, it is always necessary to posit boundary conditions within which the system will be isolated, for no process is completely isolated unless, perhaps, one takes the universe as a whole.[16] Second, **S** may be

14. See the citations in note 12 above.

15. Aristotle, *Metaphysics,* bks. Alpha and Delta.

16. Meehan (1968), pp. 53–56; Nagel (1961), p. 461.

understood to be an aspect of an equilibrium system. It is assumed that there is a larger process whose operation enables
the process **S** to maintain its integrity despite the fact that it is
immersed in an environment with which it interacts. In that
case, the process **S** is a *function* of the equilibrium system.[17]
The application of this idea also requires boundary conditions,
for example, the range of environmental variation within which
S will be performed.

The interaction field posited in this work may be understood to constitute two states, or parts of two states, of a determinate or causal process, in the sense just developed. The first
state is the field before the interaction has occurred, and consists of the actors and the "entire circumstances in which they
find themselves" (a phrase which will not be carefully defined).
On examining these circumstances, the actors calculate possible
courses of action and the results which will occur if the various
possible combinations of strategies are chosen. They then evaluate these possible results and choose the strategy which will
maximize their expected utilities. The execution of the strategies
will produce a result. This result is the second state of the field.
It may also be understood as the first state of the next field, that
is, to contain a new entire set of circumstances, with the same
or other actors, who are again faced with choices. The interaction field thus consists of any two successive states of a determinate process. To continue this analysis would very possibly
lead to a general field theory of human behavior. In this work,
however, a more modest approach is taken.

Let us look at the situation of *A*. He assesses, evaluates,
chooses, and executes. For him to be able to cause anything,
one of these activities, or a combination of them, must be a
cause of something in the field. His assessments influence only

17. See Braithwaite (1953), pp. 322–42; Nagel (1961), pp. 401–28. In
adaptive equilibrium systems, to use Aristotle's terminology, the formal and
final causes are closely related; in fact if the adaptive behavior is purposive,
the two causes are the same.

his own behavior; so, ruling them out, we get the following kinds of influence as possibly causal:

1. His evaluations influence the evaluations of others, through identification, and hence possibly their choices and executions, and through this the result of the field, and the outcomes to the actors.

2. His choices influence the results of possible choices by others, and hence their choices and executions. For this to occur, he must choose first. Notice that if A's *possible* choices influence the behavior of others, this influence is not exercised by A since his possible choices are not at all his own doing, at least for the field under consideration. If his *likely* choice, however, influences the choices and executions of others, this constitutes influence by A. (We will not treat the interesting question how this is to be squared with the idea of temporal succession usually considered to be inherent in causality.)

3. His execution influences the resulting state of the field, and hence the utility of the result to the other actors and to himself.

This seems to summarize all possible ways for A to influence the field. The situation may be stated symbolically as follows:

The variables which may be causal are:

Va: an evaluation by A

Ca: a choice of strategy by A (or likely choice)

Ea: the execution of a choice by A

The variables which may be influenced by the above causal variables are:

Vb: an evaluation by B

Cb: a choice by B

Eb: an execution by B

R: the result of the field (which is an indefinitely large set of variables)

Oa: the outcome for A

Ob: the outcome for B

The aim of A is to maximize his utility. This is done by attaining the result for which his utility is the highest possible. Hence, it is ability to influence the result of the field which is crucial. Ability to influence B's evaluation, choice, execution, or outcome is significant only as these in turn influence the result (or, if it is these themselves which are desired, they are nevertheless components of the result). From the three headings above, and focusing on A's possible influence on R, we get the following three possible chains of influence:

1. $Va \rightarrow Vb \rightarrow Cb \rightarrow Eb \rightarrow R$ (personal influence)
2. $Ca \rightarrow R \rightarrow Cb \rightarrow Eb \rightarrow R$ (power)
3. $Ea \rightarrow R$ (power)

Let us examine under what circumstances such influence can be said to be causal. To take the first case, an evaluation can be said to cause the evaluation of another if it is true that (as a nomic universal) if Va_n then Vb_n. But this is true only for one case: if B identifies totally with A. In that instance, B's utility scale is uniquely determined by A's, and the influence is causal. Otherwise, while A's utilities may influence B's, other factors (i.e., B's private will or his identifications with others) will also exercise an influence, and it will not be true that if A performs a given evaluation Va_n, then B will always perform the evaluation Vb_n. Rather, for any evaluation by A, there will be a whole set of possible evaluations by B, and which member of this set will occur will depend on the values which are assigned to the other influencing variables. Hence the influence is causal only for the limiting case of total identification.

The same point can be made for each of the other two cases listed above. The influence will be causal only in limiting cases. Thus normally the choice of strategy by one actor is only one of the factors which influence the strategy of the responder. For example, in a war, suppose that one side launches an attack of a certain kind in a certain sector. The other side has various options. Its choice among these will be influenced not only by the nature of the attack but normally also by many other factors, such as terrain, weather, disposition and size of its own forces, etc. These are all variables of the field, and the attack will *cause* the response only if the response is the same for any value of any of these variables. The relationship between the execution of a strategy and the state of the field which results has the same characteristics.

To repeat a point made earlier, it is a defining characteristic of a field that in general every variable influences every other variable. Therefore, the only causal relation is between a state of the field and its following state. The sum of the variables of one state causes the sum of the variables of the next. Even this is true only under the very stiff requirement that the field constitute either an isolated system or the function of an equilibrium system.

Hence, it will not do to speak of power as the "ability to produce intended effects." In general, action does not produce (i.e., cause) results, but only influences them. What is meant by influence will be explained shortly. I have insisted on this point, and at some length, because I feel that a false and pernicious dream of omnipotence has run like a leitmotiv through much of modern Western culture, both in its ideational and technological aspects. I am instead asserting a more modest view of the potentialities of rational action.

C. *The Aim and the Object of a Strategy*

It has been pointed out that the exercise of power is, by definition, purposive. It is now necessary to specify more carefully what is meant by purpose, for the concept has two components. Freud distinguished between the aim and the object of a drive.[18] The aim of all drives is the same—need satisfaction—and drives may be distinguished according to the type of need: sexual, aggressive, etc. The aim of a drive is achieved through a satisfying

18. Freud (1915), pp. 122–23.

relation with an object (or drive object). The object of a drive is that element of the environment (or field) which will satisfy the drive when a need-satisfying relation to it is achieved. In other words, need satisfaction (the aim) is achieved through object relations (the object). The relation between aim and object is not one of end to means—the object relation *is* need satisfying (unless the psyche is subject to functional disturbances).

The distinction between the aim and the object of a drive resembles and can be associated with the distinction developed here between the outcome and the result of an interaction, except that in Freudian theory need satisfaction is assumed to have a physiological aspect, or basis, in terms of "reduction of tensions,"[19] which implies that it can be measured along a ratio scale (although as yet this point is purely theoretical), while the concept of utility contains no such implication and is understood to be measured on an interval scale. Otherwise, the two concepts are closely similar. Just as the aim of a drive is achieved if and when its object is attained, so the maximum expected utility is obtained if and when its associated state occurs. The *object* of a strategy—that which is conceptualized as the state of affairs toward whose occurrence strategy is to be directed—is that attainable state of the field which bears with it the highest expected utility. Similarly, psychoanalytic theory assumes that the individual seeks to maximize drive satisfaction.[20]

Hence the object of choice is to achieve a certain state of the field, and its aim is to maximize the actor's utility. The term "power" can thus refer to either a relation between strategy and state or a relation between strategy and outcome. The term "power" is often used to refer to the degree of satisfaction obtained, without regard to the amount of control over events required for the attainment of this aim, but strictly speaking such an accomplishment does not constitute power, and the term

19. Freud (1905), pp. 208–19.
20. Freud (1920), pp. 7–11, 26–43.

"autonomy" will be used to express the idea of ability to satisfy *aims* through purposive action. The term "power" will be reserved to designate a relation between strategy and result (object).

D. Power[21]

1. *The approach.* A state of the field is understood to contain an indefinitely large set of elements. In the general case this complex is not determined uniquely by the strategy of any one actor. Rather, it is determined by the sum of the strategies of the actors, plus an indefinitely large number of factors which are partly or wholly independent of the strategies adopted by the actors. The example of the terrain of a battlefield has already been used to illustrate this point. The weather is another factor independent of the strategies of the actors which many influence the result of a battle. It is important to an understanding of the concepts of interaction field and interaction state to realize that the weather is an invariant of the field. Each state of the field consists of a battle which will occur if each side chooses a particular strategy. The weather may vary within a given possible battle, but if so, it will vary in exactly the same way for every other possible battle. It is hence a constant of the field—an element which is the same for any state because it is not influenced by any possible strategies of the armies. Such constants may affect the result of different interactions in various ways; for example, for one pair of strategies the weather may have a strong

21. It is difficult to determine the specific works I am indebted to for the following definition of power. Most importantly, perhaps, this definition has been derived by reflection on the implications of the method of analysis created by Von Neumann and Morgenstern, in the light of the philosophical position which I have worked out for myself over the years. For some of the literature, see Bierstedt (1950); Dahl (1957); Dahl (1963), pp. 39–54; Emmet (1954); French (1956); Goldhammer and Shils (1939); Harsanyi (1962); Lasswell and Kaplan (1950); March (1955); Moore (1958); Riker (1962); Shapley and Shubik (1954); Simon (1953).

influence on the result, and for another strategy pair it may have little influence.

We are here concerned with those aspects of the field which can be influenced by the strategies of the actors—in particular, how the strategy of a given actor can influence the field, whether this influence can be expressed as a matter of degree, and finally whether the degree of power of one actor can be compared to the degree of power of another.

Those things which an actor can do unaided by his own efforts and regardless of what others might do are clearly aspects of his own power. In interaction fields, however, it is normal for the variables of the field to be products of a joint effort, whether of cooperation, conflict, or—the normal case— a mixture of the two. For example, suppose that A and B individually are unable to move a large stone but can move it by their joint efforts. Jointly, they have the power to move the stone. But for this case what are we to say about their power individually?

In general, when any element in the state of a field is genuinely a joint product, rather than a sum of individual products, it seems difficult to separate the part of the product caused by the efforts of the one from the part caused by the efforts of the other—at least I have been unable to do this, even after persistent effort; and the reasons why this seems to be so have been explained. Therefore another approach will be taken.[22]

In practice, the way in which "power" is used usually seems to imply a comparison of the results of more than one strategy. It is assumed that a very powerful individual's actions will produce very different results depending on the strategies he chooses. On the other hand, if a person is completely powerless, the results will be the same regardless of the strategy he chooses.

22. Modern factor analysis is an attempt to give causal weight to the members of a set of variables (factors) in the situation where each factor is a function of all the others. We are inclined to doubt that this technique would be useful in analyzing voluntaristic models. See Fruchter (1954).

A powerful nation-state may act with restraint on a question and hence have little influence on the actual course of events, but presumably if it had wished to do so it could have influenced the results greatly. Power thus has two senses—the capacity to influence events, and the actual influence exercised.

The problem is to find a particular strategy or strategies (and their associated results) which can serve as points of reference. When power is exercised, it makes a difference in the result. The question is, Different from what? It will not do to say, "The results of the strategy have this and this difference from the result if the actor had done nothing," for it is not clear what "doing nothing" means. For example, suppose that a powerful senator had the option of supporting, opposing, or remaining neutral towards the passage of a particular bill. It might seem that remaining neutral is doing nothing, but in fact this may be a definite strategy and strongly influence the fate of the bill.

Another approach is to assume that each strategy has a cost (negative utility), requiring the expenditure of resources. Power over a particular element of the field would then be the efficiency (production of the element per unit cost) times the resources, both measured in utility numbers. Such an approach has been taken by some writers, but it seems to me to involve a confusion between outcome and result.[23] In any event, the approach adopted here is different. Here, the difference the various strategies make will be measured against the situation produced by the assumption that the other actors will act rationally, regardless of the strategy employed by the wielder of power. In terms of the example given above, the power of a senator over a bill can be discovered by examining the different fates of the bill had the senator acted differently, assuming in each case that the other actors had continued to act rationally.

2. *Relative power.* Let y be any element of the interaction field which has a value (y_a, y_b, y_c, etc.), for each state, and which can

23. For example, Harsanyi (1962).

be expressed in quantitative terms. (The latter proviso enables quantified expression but is not indispensable to the general theory.) It is understood that in general the value of **y** is not a function of the strategies available to A, but rather a function of the interaction pairs and, possibly, of other variables or constants of the field. Let y_a be the lowest value of **y** for any state of the field, and y_z the highest value of **y** in the field. Then y_z minus y_a will be the *range* of values of **y**, or the "range of **y**."

Now, one by one, assume that A adopts each of the strategies at his disposal, a_1, a_2, a_3, etc., and that for each case B adopts his rational strategy, whatever it may be in that instance. For any strategy (a_n) by A, there will be a resulting value (y_n) of **y**. Let this class of values of **y** be **y'**. Now on the assumption that B's strategy is rational, A will always be able to choose which member of the subclass **y'** of the class **y** will occur. In other words, it is within A's power to determine which value of the class **y'** will occur. Notice that y_n is not a function of a_n with respect to the interaction field as a whole, but only for the much smaller set of states consisting of the interaction pairs determined by every strategy of A coupled with B's rational strategy for each case.

Let y_e be the lowest value of **y'**, and y_t the highest. Then y_t minus y_e is the *range* of A's power relative to **y**. The range of A's power relative to **y** divided by the range of **y**, $(y_t - y_e)/(y_z - y_a)$, is the *extent* of A's power relative to **y**. This number can vary from one (full power) to zero (no power). For the latter case, the value of **y** will be the same whatever A does. At the risk of repetition, it must be emphasized that A does not in general have the power to determine what the values of **y** are in the particular states. He does, however, have a degree of power in determining which interaction pair will occur (assuming B's rationality), and hence which value of **y** will occur.

Power relative to **y** can also be described in terms of *spread*. If the values of **y'** are spread out equidistantly from y_e to y_t, the spread will be said to be *even*. Alternatively the values could be mostly bunched together around one or more points in an *uneven* spread.

Suppose that the extent of A's power relative to **y** is large (for example, about one-half), and that the range of **y'** extends well down toward y_a. Then A can be said to have substantial power to deter or minimize **y**, while if the range extends well toward y_z, he can be said to have the power to enhance or maximize **y**.

Relative power can also be described with respect to *breadth*, that is, the number of variables **x**, **y**, **z**, etc., of the field of a specified set for which the range of power exceeds a specified number.

The range of power of different actors relative to a given variable can obviously be compared. Notice, however, that the range of power of A is not necessarily at the expense of the range of power of B, for each range is measured on the basis of a different assumption (the rationality of the other).[24]

Relative power gives us a measure of A's power with respect to **y**, but not of A's power with respect to **y** as against B's. A measurement of relative power, or a comparison of relative power, does not get at an important factor; we have no idea what the range of A's choice with respect to **y** owes to B's assistance or opposition. This problem can be handled by changing the assumption about B's strategies. Assume that B will always adopt the strategy which will minimize **y**, and now examine the value of **y** for every strategy by A. This will give us a range of choice on A's part which will be called A's power *over B* relative to **y**. Notice that A's relative power over **y** will be the same as his power over B relative to **y** under two conditions: first, if B has no influence over **y** in either case; or second, if in fact it is always B's rational strategy to minimize **y**. In the same way, by assuming that B will always act to maximize **y**, we can measure A's power *with B* relative to **y**. Actor A's power with

---

24. Compare this categorization of types of relative power with Dahl (1957).

B relative to **y** will be the same as *A*'s power relative to **y** if *B*'s rational strategy is to maximize **y**. Although we do not intend to use the term, perhaps this variant of relative power might be called concrete power.

3. *Independent power*. We have now defined three different senses of power relative to a variable of the field,[25] depending on the assumption made about the strategy employed by the other actor (or, by extension, the other actors). This creates three different ranges of **y** over which *A* has relative power. It is clear that *A*'s power relative to **y** depends on what strategy *B* will employ. It is assumed by our theory that *B* will always act rationally; therefore the range of *A*'s relative power will vary according to whether *B*'s rational strategy is to maximize **y**, minimize **y**, or some other strategy. In practice, since **y** is only one element in the field, and other elements are presumably also relevant to *B*'s utilities—and hence his strategy—*B* will not normally adopt a straightforward maximizing or minimizing strategy, but instead take a more complex position toward the value of **y**. What is central to note, however, is that *A*'s relative power is dependent on *B*'s choices unless *B* has *no* power relative to **y**. If *B*'s evaluation were to change, and hence his strategic objectives, *A*'s relative power would change (although his concrete relative power would not, since that is posited on specific strategies by *B*.) There may, however, be a range of values of **y** which *A* can choose regardless of what *B* does. This will be termed *independent* power relative to **y** with respect to *B*. To simplify, let us take the two extreme strategic positions by *B*, a minimizing and a maximizing strategy with respect to **y**. Actor *A* will have a different range of power relative to **y** with respect to *B* in each case. If there is no overlap between the two ranges, *A* has no independent power relative to **y** with respect to *B*. If there is an overlap, this overlap will define the range of *A*'s inde-

25. Or, alternatively, two senses: relative and concrete power, with concrete power subdivided into two types.

pendent power relative to **y** with respect to *B*. Presumably (although we have not considered all possibilities) *A* has the power to choose any value of **y** within this range, whatever *B* does.

Independent power is an exclusive property. If there is only one value of **y** relative to which *A* has independent power over *B*, then there is no value of **y** relative to which *B* has independent power over *A*. This, however, is not quite accurate. If *A* has independent power relative to **y** over *B* for one value of **y** only, it may be possible for *B* to have independent power over *A* relative to the same value of **y**. This can occur in certain zero-sum configurations, for example, in the game of matching pennies. If *A* randomizes his choice of heads or tails, he will have an expected monetary gain of zero regardless of the strategy *B* chooses. But *B* has the same independent power over *A*'s monetary result: by randomizing his own choice, he can insure that *A*'s expected gain is zero, whatever *A* does. The situation is less clear for poker, where the minimax strategy guarantees that the player will break even against any normal strategy of the opponent. If one's opponent, however, diligently plays "giveaway" —adopts his worst strategy—*A*'s minimax strategy will more than break even. To break even against giveaway poker, one must adopt a giveaway strategy, but this is presumably no guarantee that the opponent will continue his altruistic ways. Hence it is not clear whether either side has any independent power relative to the outcome of a poker game.

This question may not be of any great theoretical significance, but it warrants a slight modification of our generalization about the exclusiveness of independent power.

4. *Discussion.* The ideas of power just developed can be extended to more than one variable, and with respect to more than one actor. Power with respect to every actor in the field can be called "power with respect to the field," or simply "power" without qualification. In actual practice, "power," or "influence," are often used in the above senses, although generally not in a

precise way. For example, when one says that "*X* is a powerful senator," several ideas which are here distinguished one from the other appear to be mingled together. In the first place, the statement implies that the adoption of various different strategies by the senator with regard to legislation would make a considerable difference in the actual legislation passed or not passed (range of power relative to content of laws passed). In the second place, it is implied that his power is greater than most other senators' (comparative relative power). In the third place, it is implied that his influence will be substantial even if opposed by an (unspecified) number of other senators (power over other senators relative to legislation), and that this influence is large compared to that of many other senators (comparative relative power over other senators). On the other hand, surely his relative power over *all* his colleagues (acting in concert against him) will not be great. (He has little or no power over the senate relative to legislation.) Also, he obviously has no independent power over legislation; that is, he cannot uniquely determine any aspect of the content of legislation if opposed by all of his colleagues.

Independent power over the field is a causal idea. It asserts that if *A* adopts a given policy, or strategic position, then a given value of *y* will necessarily occur. It is difficult, however, to think of examples of independent power over any variable of a field of interaction, for presumably the other actors could gang up on *A* and forcibly prevent him from doing almost anything. It is necessary to conceive of a very small group, with one person of very great physical strength or dexterity, or to exercise one's fancy in terms of some instrument of extraordinary power solely in the hands of a single person, for example, Plato's Ring of Gyges, which gave its wearer a cloak of invisibility.[26] For all practical purposes, the category of independent power over the field is vacant relative to any significant variable. Nevertheless,

26. Plato, *Republic*, 360, or in Aristotle's terms, perhaps if we can imagine a person "of merit so outstanding as to surpass that of all the rest [taken collectively]." Aristotle, *Politics*, bk. 3, chap. 17, par. 5.

it is possible to conceive of independent power over a subset of individuals in the field, since it may be the rational strategy of some other members of the field to assist the wielder of such independent power. (Note that the definition does not rule out this possibility.)

The central point here is that statements that attribute power to an individual normally imply certain assumptions about what strategies the various other actors will adopt. The power of even a Hitler or a Stalin would be negligible without compliant actions by a very large set of individuals. This illustrates our assertion that in general individual power is not a causal idea.

Power is often defined as the ability to control the actions of other people. Presumably however, one wishes to control the actions of others because these actions will produce a desired result. This idea is implicitly covered by the theory already developed. For example, let A be a factory owner, B a worker, and y the weekly output of the worker. To the extent that A has power over y he controls the actions of B.

Note that the treatment of power has been developed without using the idea of comparison of utilities; in exercising power over variables of the field and over each other A and B may or may not identify with each other.

Since the definition of power advanced here is new, perhaps it will be helpful to give a detailed example. Suppose we wish to measure and compare the military power—say, air power—of two neighboring States, A and B.[27] First we must have some measurement of air power. It would be helpful if we could measure air power in terms of, say, a "standard unit of military effectiveness," but we may have to be content with the number of airplanes, or the number of wings. We must not fall into the trap of asking, "How much power does a medium-range bomber have?" because aircraft in themselves do not have power, since they do not act purposively. Only people or groups can have

27. I have capitalized State as political organization throughout to distinguish it from state as property of an interaction field.

purposes; hence only they can have power. This point is worth a short digression.

If we ask, "How much power does a medium bomber have?" we can only mean, "How much power does an actor get when he acquires a medium bomber?" As stated, this question has no answer, for his power will depend entirely on the interaction field in which he finds himself. It is necessary to specify either a particular interaction field, or something like an "average expectable interaction field."[28] In addition to specifying the interaction field, we must specify what the aircraft may possibly be used for—to blow up bridges, strafe ground troops, bring about political concessions, etc.—by asking what variables of the field may be influenced by possession or use of the aircraft.

Having specified the actor, the field, and the relevant variables, we then measure the actor's relative power over the field with respect to these variables, first ignoring all strategies which involve use of the medium bomber. We now add all the deleted strategies and the counterstrategies of other actors with respect to the medium bomber, and then we again measure the actor's power relative to the variables. The difference between the actor's power relative to the variables without the bomber and his power with the bomber measures the increment of power produced by the medium bomber for this actor, this field, and these variables. Unless all these factors are at least implied, a statement that the military power of a medium bomber is such and such has no clear meaning. If these conditions were fulfilled, then, in our example, we could speak of the power of *A* to produce military power, where military power refers to units of power relative to military objectives. This, however, is not necessary to our example, and instead we will speak of power to produce military aircraft, without regard to the military effectiveness of the aircraft themselves.

To return to our example, let **y** be the number of wings in

28. To paraphrase Hartmann's "average expectable environment." Hartmann (1939), p. 23 et passim.

the air force of country A. Where **x** is an integer, let us assume that if A is capable of producing x wings, he is also capable of producing $x - 1$ wings. To measure the range of A's power to produce wings, it is thus only necessary to inquire, What is the maximum number of wings A is capable of producing? This is not to say that it would be to A's interest to produce an absolute maximum; on the contrary, one would expect this to have a very low utility because of all the other presumably important objectives that would have to be sacrificed in the consuming drive to produce aircraft. We are simply inquiring how many wings A could produce if it really had to, without regard to the utility of such a course of action.

To get a meaningful answer to this question, it is necessary to adopt some assumption about what the neighboring countries will be doing meanwhile, since their activities will presumably have an impact on how many aircraft A can produce. If B likes the idea of A having a large air force, it might help A in various ways—lending money, sharing technical knowledge or technicians, etc.—while if B doesn't like the idea it might hinder A in various ways—refusing to sell strategic materials, distributing propaganda, engaging in sabotage, etc. We will therefore adopt the general assumption of this analysis, that B will adopt its rational strategy, whatever that may be. Under this assumption, the maximum value of **y** will represent what will actually happen if A goes all out to produce aircraft. Suppose that we now find that the power of A to produce aircraft ranges from 0 to 115 wings. This statement seems in accord with, but more precise than, a sense in which the term "power" is in practice often used. We can also compare the power of A to produce aircraft with the power of B to produce aircraft; for example, "Country B is capable of producing twice (or three times) as many planes as A."

Turning to our second sense of the term, we can also measure A's power to produce aircraft under the assumption that B, for any strategy employed by A, will adopt the strategy which will result in the minimum expected value of **y** or, alternatively, the maximum expected value of **y**. Suppose we find that A's power to produce aircraft *over B* is 0–95, and that its power *with B* is 20–125 wings. From this, we can see that A has quite a bit of independent power relative to aircraft produced with respect to B, for it can produce anywhere from 20 to 95 wings regardless of any strategy by B. The term "autonomy" is often used for this sense of power, but it is here reserved for another idea, which corresponds to another sense in which the word "power" is sometimes used.

We could go on to develop further variations and combinations of the three types of power here distinguished, but perhaps enough has been said to illustrate the meaning of the central concept as it is here employed, and its relation to the common-sense usages of the term "power."

E. *Autonomy*

Even though the utility of a state for an actor is uniquely determined by his evaluation of that state, power over states of the field and ability to satisfy preference are two different things. This is so for three reasons. First, unforeseen occurrences may make the result different than anticipated. As pointed out before, however, this problem is most appropriately handled by translation rules which connect the theoretical idea of rationality into the empirical idea of reasonableness. Second, owing to psychological problems, the actor may find that even if the result is as anticipated, its utility is not. This question will be dealt with in the following chapter. Third, and this is our main point, degree of power cannot be equated with degree of preference satisfaction. This point can be illustrated by two extremes. First, the legendary Faust, as interpreted by Goethe, has through his pact with Satan the power (to use the language employed here) to produce any state whatsoever; yet he cannot find satisfaction. At the other extreme is the Stoic philosopher who, ideally, can achieve his heart's desire without any control over events at all, and no matter what course they may take. In other words, if we substitute for an element of the field, y_n, the utility of that element, $u_a y_n$, and examine the extent to which A's choices determine $u_a y_n$, we may get an entirely different set of results from that of the analysis of A's power over $\mathbf{y}$. This we will now proceed to do.

Let $u_a \mathbf{y}$ be the set of utilities to A for the set of variables $\mathbf{y}$. For simplicity's sake, assume that $\mathbf{y}$ is the only variable with utility for A. Let $u_a y_{40}$ be the utility of $\mathbf{y}$ with the highest value to A, and $u_a y_0$ the utility with the lowest value. Let y_n be the result of the field, and $u_a y_n$ its utility for A. Obviously the closer $u_a y_n$ is to $u_a y_{40}$, the nearer will A's utility approach the highest possible for the field. This can be stated quantitatively: The *autonomy* of A with respect to the variable $\mathbf{y}$ is expressed by the fraction $(u_a y_n - u_a y_0)/(u_a y_{40} - u_a y_0)$. Autonomy can thus be measured along a scale from zero to one.

Autonomy can be related to relative power as follows: $u_a y_n$ will be the highest utility of any value of $\mathbf{y}$ which is within the range of A's power relative to $\mathbf{y}$ (i.e., the member of the set $\mathbf{y}'$ with the highest utility for A). In other words, A will always achieve the highest utility within the range of his power.

The idea of autonomy can be extended to the field as a whole, where A's autonomy with respect to the field is $(u_a s_n - u_a s_0)/(u_a s_{40} - u_a s_0)$.

High autonomy can be coupled with low relative power, while low autonomy can accompany high relative power. On the former point, suppose that A is powerless relative to $\mathbf{y}$: that is, the values of $\mathbf{y}$ are the same whatever A does. This must also mean that A has no power over B with respect to $\mathbf{y}$. However, as long as A's and B's interests do not conflict with respect to $\mathbf{y}$, the utility of the result for A can be anything at all. In other words, a powerless man may through fortunate circumstances obtain high autonomy. One of these fortunate circumstances, however, must be that his interests do not conflict with those of anyone who has high power relative to the variables which are significant for his own utilities.

On the other hand, assume that A has high and independent power with respect to **y**, but that all of the many values of **y** among which he may choose are of low utility to him, while the few he is powerless to achieve are of high utility. In that case his autonomy will be low. Only total independent power—ability to achieve any of the values of **y** in the field—will guarantee him high autonomy.

One special case out of the many possible is worth noting, because it appears to occur with relative frequency. Suppose that a variable **y** has the following properties:

1. The spread of A's power relative to **y** is relatively even.

2. The higher the value of **y**, the higher the utility of **y** for A. (The relation need not be linear.)

3. If A has the power to choose a value of **y**, he also has the power to choose any smaller value of **y**.

The variables of wealth and military power seem, by and large, to have these three properties. In general, the more a person or nation-state has of either, the better off he (or it) is. They admit of discrete and relatively even spread of variation; and, if one has the power to attain a given amount of either, one generally has the power to obtain a smaller amount.

In these circumstances, the higher the relative power, the higher the utility of the result. Greater power brings greater satisfaction. With respect to such variables, the quest for power and the quest for satisfaction are the same thing. This is not true for all variables, however. Note that wealth and military power are often thought to be means rather than ends. The present theory does not use this distinction; it merely asks to what degree a given amount of wealth or military power is preferred to other alternatives.

The Greek and Stoic philosophers were fully aware that, in the general case, power and satisfaction are not to be equated; indeed there is much discussion of this question in their writings.[29] Modern political theory has tended to forget this point—to follow Hobbes in defining power as the "present means to some apparent future good"[30] and to draw the implication, the greater the means the greater the satisfaction. If the analysis here presented is allowed, such a conclusion will be unwarranted. The general question of the relationship between power and autonomy will be clarified if the psychological aspect is considered. To this task we now turn.

29. The question is already discussed in Herodotus.
30. Hobbes (1651), p. 78.

6/

THE PSYCHOLOGY OF

RATIONAL ACTION

S O FAR WE HAVE been concentrating on the external aspect
of power: the ability to exercise purposive control over the
environment. Since power is exercised through rational thought
and action, the concept of rationality was first examined as a
foundation for the theory of power which followed. In chapter
2 it was pointed out that the mathematical theory of rational action presupposes an actor with a coherent self—that is, that
there are certain psychological requirements for rational action.
This theme, which was temporarily set aside at that point, will
now be taken up and will lead to an examination of the internal
psychological dimensions of rationality and power. As was
pointed out in the first chapter, the shapers of the classic tradition, especially Plato and Aristotle, saw the internal and the external aspects as interdependent, and this insight will be followed here. The internal aspect will be examined in its relation
to the external, and not as an entirely separate realm.

A. *The Development of Purposeful Action*

Rational action requires a person with a coherent set of purposes.[1] People are not born with coherent purposes, but with

1. The following discussion is based on Freud (1915, 1923, 1926, 1938);
Hartmann (1947, 1948, 1950, 1958); Hartmann, Kris, and Lowenstein
(1942); Rapaport (1951). See also Brenner (1955), chaps. 1–5.

needs (instinctual strivings), whose satisfaction requires the establishment of certain relationships with the external world. Even in infancy, and to a much more marked degree as maturation proceeds, need satisfaction requires appropriate behavior. In contrast with other animals, however, for humans almost none of such appropriate behavior patterns are genetically determined. These patterns must be worked out by the individual himself. This imparts an enormous range of flexibility in the ways in which an individual can satisfy his needs. The price of this greater potentiality is the possibility that the actual modes of behavior worked out may be imperfectly adaptive.

The principal means by which the individual works out his mode of bringing his instinctual needs to terms with his environment is his psychic system. Adaption requires the successful performance by the psychic system of the following functions:

1. *Development of a drive apparatus.* Instinctual strivings in themselves have no objects. They are simply needs: physiological-psychological tensions or imbalances. Adaption, however, requires purposive behavior—including the turning toward objects or object relations capable of satisfying needs. Accordingly, the instinctual strivings, or aspects of the instinctual strivings, are organized by the psyche into drives: desires for need-satisfying relations with specific objects. Hence, as pointed out above, a drive has both an aim (need satisfaction), and an object (something with which a need-satisfying relationship is possible).

In psychoanalytic terminology, the word "drive" can be used in two senses, depending on whether the instinctual source of the drive or its object is referred to. In the first sense everyone has the same drives, and the aim of all drives is the same: need satisfaction. In the second sense, drives can find satisfaction in a wide range of objects or object relations.

While drives can become attached to the most varied objects, once the attachment has occurred it tends to be strongly fixed and can be changed only with difficulty. There is an important exception, however. When a drive is forced into the unconscious by repression it is often easily displaced onto another object which is associated with, and unconsciously identified with, the original (and unconsciously still retained) object. In this situation considerable instability and inconsistency of purpose may occur. Since rational action requires stability of purpose, such a process could lead to irrational behavior. On the other hand, such a derivative drive object itself can become strongly fixed. The pursuit of a derivative object can thus be rational in the sense developed earlier, although it might be irrational in the deeper sense that it might not result in need satisfaction because of the unconscious conflicts associated with the repression and subsequent displacement.

2. *Psychic organization and integration.* The development of a coherent idea of selfhood is essentially an organizing process. The world is divided into a "me" and a "not me" (although this distinction is far more subtle than might appear at first glance), and the various aspects and components of the self are organized into a more or less unified and harmonious whole. As the phrase "more or less" indicates, however, the process is never completely carried through. A considerable amount of internal psychic conflict is always present, and the identity problem, the task of setting the boundaries between the "me" and the "not me," and determining just what the "me" is, is never entirely resolved. Unless at least a reasonably adequate solution is found, however, the individual is headed for trouble in adapting to his environment.

3. *Reality orientation (assessment).* The ability to preceive reality in a relatively undistorted way is won hard and slowly. Although reality may in itself be difficult to grasp, especially on a theoretical level, a more general, pervasive, and obdurate problem springs from the workings of the psychic system. In the early stages of mental development perception of and judgments about the environment are dominated directly by need, and the individual tends to see what he wants to see, to substi-

tute pleasurable fantasy for hard reality, and to project outward onto the environment unwanted internal characteristics. These primitive "primary process" methods of thinking become strongly fixed because of the intense pleasure or reduction of pain which often accompanies their operation. Consequently, when the psyche develops to the stage where more realistic "secondary process" assessments are possible, earlier modes may be abandoned only reluctantly, if at all.

In the unconscious, the primitive and directly need-fulfilling methods of thought continue to operate; hence correct perception of reality always involves something of a psychic struggle. It is so much easier to rationalize, to invent an interpretation which fulfills the primitive tendency to see reality as we wish it to be, but which at the same time is sufficiently plausible to slip past that part of the psyche which knows that wishes are not horses and that beggars do not ride. To rationalize also means to make rational. One speaks of rationalizing the organization of a business firm, or the process of production, in order to reduce costs and to increase productivity; and this second sense of the word is closer to the first than might appear, for psychological rationalization reduces psychic costs. A clever rationalization can meet the strictest canons of rationality, hence the stamp "rational" may in a sense be genuine.

To pursue the matter somewhat deeper, according to psychoanalytic theory, all thought is unconsciously determined. From that point of view, the conscious motives are simply cloaks of respectability that allow the unconscious motives to slip past the censorship of the ego. The overt level of all behavior is a rationalization of unconscious motives.

The overt level can nevertheless have a validity of its own, in the sense of providing realistic ways of meeting genuine conscious needs and desires. The principle of the "overdetermination of behavior" asserts that instead of having one source or level of motivation, behavior regularly has several. This is in accordance with the economic principle of maximum drive satisfaction at least psychic cost and constitutes rationalization in the sense used, for example, by Weber as the organization of behavior to enable maximum goal achievement at minimum cost.

Due to the principle of overdetermination of behavior, rationalization in the sense of being determined by covert or unconscious motives is to be distinguished from rationalization in the sense of organization to produce maximum satisfaction at least cost only where the overt level is patently inadequate, either because it is not motivated by genuine overt needs or desires, or by not being realistically designed to serve such needs or desires.

The process of rationalization can be carried further. Suppose that we think, incorrectly, that a person is hostile toward us and that this is a rationalization. Suppose, further, that as a consequence we act so as to antagonize this person and that he in fact becomes hostile. Here the rationalization has been transformed into a correct perception of reality.

In sum, correct perceptions of reality may be even rarer than appears at first glance, because of the subtlety and ingenuity with which rationalizations may be formed, and because the line between rationalization and rationality is much thinner than is often thought. "To see life clear and see it whole" is not an easy task.

In general, the most effective method of achieving a good grasp of reality is through active interaction with the environment. Action based on an incorrect assessment of the situation regularly leads to unexpected and unpleasant results. Barking one's shins against painful reality provides one with an incentive for making a more correct estimate. The short-term psychic gain achieved through distortions of reality comes to be weighed against the longer-run consequences. A distinct advance is made by deliberate reality testing: undertaking a course of action designed to reveal, through examination of its consequences, which possible interpretation of the situation is correct. (In the intellectual sphere, such activity is known as research.) From this it is only a short step to the controlled experiment and scientific method.

4. *Motor control* (*execution*). To continue the list of the functions prerequisite to adaption, the psychic system must be able to direct voluntary activity toward drive satisfaction.

5. *Control over drive activity.* Impulses toward drive satisfaction commonly must be blocked, delayed, diverted, or adjusted because of the requirements imposed by reality and by the existence of a multiplicity of drive tendencies.

Just as the direct control of reality perception by need leads to a distorted view of the environment, and hence is maladaptive, so the direct translation of drive impulses into action often leads to trouble. Adaption requires that thought based on grasp of reality precede the translation of drive into action, and that action take this reality into account. Short-term satisfactions must be weighed against longer-run results. The needs of the individual are not one but many; they are present now, but they will also be present in the future. Hence adaption requires that behavior be directed toward the total satisfaction of the needs of the individual over a period of time, which often means that the primitive tendency toward direct and immediate action to satisfy whatever need is uppermost at the moment must be curbed. Furthermore, it is possible for a drive to be fixed on an object which is unattainable or inappropriate (not need satisfying even if obtained). Adaption requires that action toward the attainment of such an object be given up, and that the search for a new outlet for the drive be started. In a word, self-control is needed.

The idea of self-control is paradoxical unless it is assumed that the psyche contains more than one energy system, and that these energy systems have some degree of independence from each other. Hence the idea of a structural division of the psyche can be derived from an examination of the requirements of adaption, given the genetically determined nature of the primitive psychic apparatus and the reality which the individual faces. On the other hand, it is also necessary to assume that these energy systems are not completely independent, but influence each other in certain ways.

The striking similarities between the Platonic and the Freudian psychologies seem not to be a matter of direct influence but, rather, to spring from the fact that both adopted a functional approach. Starting with the idea of functional requirements, and a conception of the primitive psyche as consisting of a bundle of "appetites," Plato developed a tripartite division of the mind roughly corresponding to Freud's id, ego, and superego.[2] Even the idea of unconscious thought is suggested briefly.[3]

Plato's psychology is a tribute to the power of functional modes of analysis. The limitations of such an approach must also be understood, however. It is possible for quite different systems to be functionally equivalent. In navigation, for example, the use of compass, chronometer, speed gauge, and anometer to calculate position is functionally equivalent to the use of sextant and chronometer for the same purpose, even though the two systems rest on quite different principles. The range of possible systems which can perform a given function is broadened even further if one adopts the criterion of adequate, rather than perfect functioning.

A functional approach will often tell us where to look and give us some kind of broad idea of what to expect, but it is no substitute for detailed factual inquiry. This accounts for the differences between the Platonic and the Freudian psychologies, for while Plato's account makes use of only a few common-sense factual observations (notably the observed fact of psychic conflict), Freudian psychology rests on a massive accumulation of deep and detailed case studies, which provides the arena for hypothesis testing and the evidence for the conclusions drawn.

2. Plato, *Republic,* 434–91.

3. Ibid., 570.

B. *Psychic Structure*

The structural divisions of the psyche develop during the process of maturation. The first is the development of the ego from the undifferentiated psyche, which now becomes divided into ego and id. The psychoanalytic theory of the distinction between id and ego is both complex and subtle and does not lend itself to an easy or quick summary; so the following comments are perforce incomplete and somewhat one-sided.

The underlying distinction is functional: The ego is the subsystem within the psyche which performs certain functions. The distinction, however, is also structural. When fully developed, the ego constitutes a semi-independent energy system. The ego must not be understood as an "airtight compartment," but rather as merging gradually into the id. Two factors, however, separate it distinctly from the id. First, it is the center of consciousness and hence self-consciousness (whence the term "ego," or "I," as against the "id," or "it"). By no means all ego activity, however, is conscious. Second, to trace out the main lines of internal psychic conflict is to trace out the main division between ego and id. The conflicts between the two systems serve to make them distinct.

The function of the ego can be stated very simply: It is the mediator between the psychic system and external reality. It is the adaptive or adapting part of the psyche. Hence, the list above of the functions which the psychic system must perform in the process of adaption is, in fact, a list of the functions of the ego. Only the first function (formation of the drive apparatus) is something of an exception. The fixation of a drive on an object and other aspects of drive formation are processes in which the ego participates (for example, the psyche must be aware of the existence of an object before it can fix on it, which requires perception, an ego function), but which, the ego does not determine.

The ego thus faces two ways: toward the environment and

toward the rest of the psyche. It must be able to exert influence in both directions if the individual's needs are to be met. From this point of view its task is threefold:

1. The ego must be able to formulate, or participate in the formation of, a set of purposes which are at once realistic in the sense that these purposes have a reasonable hope of accomplishment, and adequate in the sense that the purposes, if accomplished, will satisfy the range of needs of the individual in a tolerable manner.

2. Having formed these purposes, the ego must be capable of organizing and directing the activities of the individual so as to maximize the expected utility of the results.

3. In doing so, the ego must be able to bring the rest of the psyche along with it. Psychic conflict, unconscious fixation on inappropriate drive objects, or the demand for immediate drive satisfaction may render the ego incapable of acting adaptively. These problems must be overcome. In addition, creative activity and problem solving require the use of the resources of the preconscious and, through this, the aid of the unconscious. Certain types of ego control may inhibit the development of this creative potential.

Modern treatments of rationality, and with them modern theories of power, have concentrated almost exclusively on the relation of the ego with the environment, what Hartmann has called the "alloplastic" aspect of adaption, and have ignored the internal, psychological dimensions, the "autoplastic" aspect.[4] This is one-sided and cannot lead to an adequate understanding of the processes whereby men are able to satisfy their needs and fulfill their natures, nor can it provide a solid basis for an inquiry into what kinds of social and political institutions are most likely to be useful to those who live within them.

4. Hartmann (1939), pp. 22–28. See also Piaget (1953), pp. 1–20. This section has been published in Rapaport (1951), pp. 176–92, where Rapaport's extensive notes relate Piaget's views to psychoanalytic theory.

C. *The Internal Power of the Ego*

At first glance it appears merely metaphorical to speak of the power of the ego over the "internal environment" (to use Jerome Frank's phrase) in the same sense as its power over the external social environment. Yet I think such an approach is valid if not pushed too far. It is of course fallacious to speak of the various components of the psyche as independent actors. But it is equally fallacious to treat actors within a social system as completely independent, for they are regularly joined by ties of identification and, as will be argued later, joined in participation in a real general will. It is going too far to treat society as a completely organic entity, as for example Durkheim at times seems to do, but still there is a sense and a degree to which it can be so treated. So, on the other hand, while the psychic components are not separate individuals, there is a sense and a degree to which they can be so treated. Thus, the concept of power developed in the previous chapter can be applied on the psychological level (although not in a quantifiable way).

Let a (a_1, a_2, a_3, etc.) be the class of all strategies *possible* for A to pursue. Let a' (a_1, a_3, a_5, etc.) be the class of all strategies which A is *capable* of pursuing. The closer a' is to a, the greater the internal power of A relative to his possible strategies. Notice that external power is defined by the relation of the class y (all possible values of a variable of the field) to y' (the values of y which A is capable of achieving), while for internal power, the relation is between possible strategies and strategies which the actor is capable of putting into effect.

A possible strategy is any course of action which can be perceived to be available if the actor's grasp of reality is correct. Capability of pursuing a strategy may be defined as follows: If a_n were the optimum strategy for A, and if, on that assumption, A were to choose and execute a_n, then, by definition, A is capable of a_n. In this case, should A not choose and execute a_n, he is not capable of choosing and executing a_n.

The relative internal power of a person depends on the level of capability of the ego in performing its functions of assessment, evaluation, choice, and execution. Perfect capability would insure that the rational strategy is always employed. To the extent that the ego is internally powerless, the range of strategies it can put into effect is limited, and hence its potentiality for adaptive responses is also limited. Limitations on internal power may be either organic or functional. Organic limits are those imposed by the innate intelligence, physical strength, coordination, etc., of the individual. The functional problems, which in general are more severe and extensive, have already received some discussion. Three closely related factors which bear on the power of the ego to choose strategies may be singled out for further mention: psychic integration, degree of psychic conflict, and the amount of "neutralized drive energy" at the disposal of the ego.

Although psychic integration and lack of psychic conflict are not the same thing, they tend to go together. Furthermore, the more solid the psychic integration, the easier it is for the ego to handle psychic conflict. The key to the ego's ability to work out and adopt adaptive courses of action lies in the degree of "neutralized drive energy" at the ego's disposal.[5] The language of Freudian theory is rather metaphorical at this point; we seem here to be dealing with an incompletely developed model, but the concept is clear enough. The energy at the ego's disposal is originally drawn from the libidinal and aggressive drives. As the ego develops, however, this energy becomes more or less detached from its original source (neutralized) and is thus freely at the disposal of the ego.

Three consequences of the progressive neutralization of the drive energy at the disposal of the ego may here be noted. First, it enables the development of realistic—as against fantastic and wish-directed—through processes and consequently improves the ego's ability to test and evaluate reality and to perceive ap-

5. Hartmann (1939), pp. 100–108.

propriate strategies. Second, it enables the ego to choose the more adaptive courses of action. Third, it improves the ego's ability to win out in the psychic conflicts that rage perpetually in the psyche of even the "best-adjusted" person. That is, the ego's power becomes increasingly independent. Only through such victories can the opportunities and the limitations presented by the environment be dealt with adaptively. Thus, neutralization of drive energy plays a key role in the ego's capabilities of assessment, relative power, and independent power. (In psychoanalytic terminology, the combination of relative and independent power is known as "ego autonomy.") In addition to the degree of neutralization of the drive energy at the disposal of the ego, the amount of energy so neutralized influences these capabilities, especially independent power.

D. *Internal Autonomy*

Internal autonomy bears the same relation to internal power as external autonomy bears to external power. Whereas external autonomy is measured by the degree to which the utility of the result obtained by the rational strategy approximates the maximum utility in the field, internal autonomy is measured by the degree to which the utility of the strategy actually adopted approximates the utility of the rational strategy. Where a_0 is the possible strategy which yields the lowest utility for A, and a_z is the possible strategy with the highest utility for A, and a_n is the strategy actually adopted, A's autonomy can be expressed by the ratio $(a_n - a_0)/(a_z - a_0)$, which can vary from one to zero.

Internal autonomy and internal power bear no necessary relation to each other. To take an extreme case, suppose the relative internal power of a person is zero, so that he is capable of only one strategy. There is no necessary reason why this one strategy might not be the one which maximizes his expected utility. This of course is unlikely, but a more general point has greater force. The degree to which a person is able to act adaptively depends in part on the severity of the challenge posed by the environment. Thus a person with little inner strength might fare better in a favorable environment than a person with considerable inner strength in an unfavorable one.

On the other hand, it must be pointed out that there is no such thing as an easy way to act rationally. The process of working out and adopting a rational course of action always involves, to some degree, an internal psychic struggle. To that extent there will be a positive correlation between independent internal power and internal autonomy.

We have now come a long way from the original mathematical theory of rational action. In that theory, the act of preference is posited and a utility scale is used to express the ranking of actual preferences mathematically. Choice must always be rational, because the theory amounts to a definition of rational action. Two considerations led to the broadening of this theory: First, the premise of consistency of preferences poses the question Under what circumstances will preferences actually be consistent? Answering this question in terms of psychoanalytic theory gave rise to the conclusion that actual preferences and actual choices may not be the best available, and that there may be potential or possible preferences and choices which, if made, will yield a higher utility than the one actually made. Hence, the idea of utility has been expanded from the idea of that which is to the idea of that which could be.

Second, it seems evident that a choice can hardly be termed rational unless there is some relation between anticipated utility (where the actor expects the result of a strategy to lie on his preference scale) and actual utility (how the event will, in fact, lie on his preference scale once it has happened). Such a relation must in part turn on the "correctness" of the aspects of rational action: grasp of reality, evaluation, choice, and the internal capabilities of executing a choice, once made. The psychological dimensions of these processes have been explored. Thus an examination of the ramifications and implications of a purely definitional theory of rational action has led to the outlining of a full-scale theory of action, which is capable of accounting for rational and irrational action, power and powerlessness, in both their behavioral and their psychological dimensions.

E. *Freedom*

One point about the relation of internal to external autonomy remains to be made. It will be recalled that internal autonomy is the extent to which the utility of the strategy employed approaches the utility of the best available strategy, and that external autonomy is the degree to which the utility of the best available strategy approximates the highest utility in the field.

From this it follows that high external autonomy requires high internal autonomy, but that high internal autonomy does not guarantee high external autonomy. The treatment of internal autonomy developed here simply serves to state the psychological preconditions of rational action and in no way bears on the results which rational action can achieve.

This concept of autonomy corresponds closely to one of the senses in which the term "freedom" is often used. Thus "inner freedom" refers to internal autonomy, while "full freedom" refers to external autonomy, with the understanding that inner freedom is a prerequisite to full freedom.

This formulation does not correspond with other, and perhaps nowadays more common, senses of "freedom." The term is often used synonymously with "power," or in a sense that implies that power is a necessary prerequisite to freedom.[6] The

6. Engels says, "Man's own social organization, hitherto confronting him as a necessity imposed by nature and history, now becomes the result of his own free action. The extraneous objective forces that have hitherto governed history pass under the control of man himself. Only from that time will man himself, more and more consciously, make his own history—only from that time will the social causes set in movement by him have, in the main and in a constantly growing measure, the results intended by him. It is the ascent of man from the kingdom of necessity to the kingdom of freedom." Engels (1880), p. 109. See also Oppenheim (1961).

point has already been made that freedom and power bear no necessary relationship to each other, although in practice they may often be connected, especially in their internal aspects.

Another idea frequently associated with freedom is that it is measured by the degree to which an individual thinks he is maximizing his utility. But this assumes that a person's judgment about himself is always correct, which is no more true than the assumption that a person's judgment about his external environment is always correct. Freedom may be a subjective mental state, but whether or not a person is free is a purely objective question. He is free when his internal psychic organization and the possibilities inherent in his environment combine to enable him to satisfy his needs. We will return to this question later.

7/

POWER AND

SOCIAL CONTROL

A. *Power and Identification as Social Interaction*

THE DEVELOPMENT OF our theory moves from action to interaction to social interaction to the human group as a pattern of social interaction. The previous chapters on action and interaction have laid the groundwork for our theory of social interaction.

Interaction occurs when the actions or utilities of one person influence the behavior or utilities of another. In general, but not necessarily always, the influence is mutual: that is, two-way. From the analysis in chapter 5, section *B*, above, it will be recalled that to influence the actions of another *(Cb,Eb)*, it is necessary to influence either the states of the field *(R)* or his process of evaluation *(Vb)*.

The first possibility has been examined in chapter 5 from the point of view of how a person goes about achieving his purposes; and influence over the behavior of others was considered only with regard to how it contributes to these purposes. As we move the focus from interaction to social interaction, from how each person goes about gaining his purposes in interaction to what forms of mutual influence on the behavior of others develop in this process, the conclusions of chapter 5 require some expansion.

Let y be a variable of the interaction field whose values (y_1, y_2, y_3), etc., are significant to the utilities of B. In that case y will be called a *sanction*.[1] When A has power relative to such a variable, he is said to control or possess a sanction over B's behavior. Since A has power over the value of the sanction, he is able to influence the outcome of various strategies for B, and hence his choice of strategy. Notice that we use the term "influence," rather than power, because we have not determined whether the influence is purposive.

Sanctions are often classified as positive (a benefit) or negative (a deprivation). This would imply a division of utilities into positive and negative, with a point of indifference at zero. This idea will not be worked out in a formal way, because of certain theoretical difficulties involved and because it is not necessary to the theory here presented to do so. The expression "negative sanction" will indicate that the sanction has a low utility compared with other significant utilities, while a positive sanction has a high utility compared with other significant utilities.

The great chess master Nimzovitch once remarked, "The threat is stronger than the execution." In general, the effectiveness of a negative sanction lies in the fact that its possible employment leads others to adopt strategies which avoid it. On the other hand, positive sanctions are inducements to others to adopt certain strategies, and hence their effectiveness implies their employment.

As translated into the language of our theory, the terms "threat" and "promise" are metaphorical ways of referring to the transmission of information about the interaction field and outcome matrix from one person to another. They are effective only if there is some reason to believe that they will be employed,

1. The intent is to follow the standard sociological usage of the term "sanction."

and one can expect an actor to use a sanction only if it is to his interest (will serve his utilities) to do so.

As a form of social interaction (as against a form of action), power is purposive influence over the actions of another through the use or potential use of sanctions. In general the "flow" of power is two-way—each person possesses sanctions over the other—whence the term "*interaction.*" Frequently, however, one person exercises more power than others in the interaction. This is measured by comparing the power of the actors, as outlined in chapter 5. It is only necessary to consider the strategies employed by the actors, and their outcomes, as variables of the field. One can then speak of relative, concrete, and independent power over these variables and compare their power in these respects. The point being emphasized here is that (ignoring identification for the time being) such influence will always operate intermediately, through power over the other variables of the field called sanctions.

We move now to the second possible form of influence, namely, over the process whereby others evaluate the state of the field. The groundwork for consideration of this process has been laid in the chapter on identification. When *A* identifies with *B*, then *A*'s utilities are influenced by *B*'s; that is, during the process of evaluation of the states of the field, *A*'s evaluation of a given state is influenced by *B*'s evaluation. This form of influence—involving simple identification—will be termed "personal influence." It is clearly common; in fact perhaps the very recognition of another as a fellow human being involves a certain amount of it. Our theory posits that persons who regularly interact identify with each other at least slightly.

Notice that personal influence is not a form of power, because the exercise of the influence need not be deliberate or purposive. True, people sometimes adopt a strategy designed to foster identification with themselves by others, but on balance this is exceptional. Normally, identification is something that just happens; indeed the process is usually more or less unconscious.

In this work, power and identification will form the two basic kinds of influence, and the typology of influence to be developed will consist of elaborations and combinations of these two. They are not, however, the only two basic kinds of influence, and all influence cannot be reduced to them. This point will be made later with respect to "rational authority," and it is doubtless true of other forms of influence. What is maintained, however, is that power and identification are the basic forms of influence which define and are indispensable to human society.

In this and the following chapters, a typology of social influence will be developed in the language of psychoanalysis and sociology. Later this material will be translated into the language of decision theory.

B. *Social Control and the Superego*

Social organization requires obedience: obedience to the commands of group leaders, and obedience to group rules. Why do men obey? In part, obedience springs from the use of sanctions: the exercise of power ensures compliance. In part, men obey because they regard the commands and rules to which they are subject as legitimate, quite apart from the sanctions employed or threatened. While it is possible for an individual to obey solely because of the sanctions on noncompliance, or solely because the rule is felt to be legitimate, in the general case the two forms of influence combine. The term "social control" will be used to refer to obedience which rests solely on legitimacy, or to the obedience-creating component of influence which rests on legitimacy.

Social control is the influence over the behavior of individuals exercised by group standards of behavior, or group norms. The individual adheres to the group standards voluntarily, because he considers them to be legitimate. Although the term "social control" is somewhat novel in this context, the idea itself is a familiar one in sociology. In this chapter, the term will be defined in psychoanalytic terms. In the following chapter it will be given an equivalent definition in the language of decision theory. An important linkage will thereby be established between psychoanalysis, decision theory, and sociology.

To understand what is meant by legitimacy it is necessary to summarize briefly some features of the psychoanalytic theory of the superego.[2] The superego develops as an attempt to handle a difficult internal conflict during the Oedipal period. At this time, the feelings toward both parents become strongly ambivalent. The negative side of these feelings, rage and jealousy, is experienced by the ego as strongly threatening. It must at all costs prevent these feelings from finding expression and is insecure about its ability to do so. The ego achieves reinforcement through identifying itself, or part of itself (the superego), with one or both of the parents. This does not eliminate the conflict—in fact to a certain extent it perpetuates it—but does help the ego to handle the situation. The development of the superego may, somewhat artificially, be summarized in the following typical stages:

1. The attitudes, feelings, commands, exhortations of the parent come from the outside; they are external.

2. The child identifies with the parent. The parental attitudes, feelings, commands, exhortations come from the inside, and hence are always present. The superego is a kind of portable parent. Although incorporated within the psyche, this self-parent is to a certain extent external to the ego. While it helps the ego handle the threatening drives, it also more or less conflicts with the ego.

3. The internalized parental image becomes an idealization of what the parent is actually like. For example, the super-

2. The following account is based on Freud (1921, 1923); Hartmann, Kris, and Lowenstein (1962); and Brenner (1955), pp. 108–40.

ego may be much stricter and more demanding than the actual parent. In effect, the child says, "I wish my parent were much stricter; it would help me control my threatening impulses." The superego commandments constitute a code of behavior originating from an idealized and internalized parental image.

4. As the ego develops, and the Oedipal conflicts subside somewhat in intensity, the way may be open for maturation of the superego, and its more successful integration with the ego. The demands of the superego may become less primitive and more reasonable. Eventually, the ego may be able to integrate to a considerable extent with the superego: that is, it may accept the moral requirements of the superego as its own—not as coming from an alien part of the psyche. The superego becomes incorporated within the self.[3]

5. Superego identifications may be extended to parent substitutes. The extension of these identifications normally widens progressively to include individuals and groups farther and farther removed from direct and frequent contact with the individual. Where such broader identifications occur, the commands of group leaders or the rules adopted by groups may have much of the force of the original internalized parental commands.

It is important to distinguish the psychological from the sociological functions of the superego. On the psychological level, social control may be defined as the influence exercised on behavior by the superego—to the extent that the superego code is drawn from, and reflects, existing social standards. It is the individual, however, who regulates his own behavior, and on the psychological level it must be understood that the superego is a means of handling internal psychological problems, not directly a way of adapting to the environment.

From the sociological point of view, the superego performs

3. And integrated with the ego. On the distinction between self, self-concept, identity, on the one hand, and the ego on the other, see Erikson (1950), pp. 203–31 et passim.

the function of linking individuals together, through bonds of mutual identification and feelings of mutual obligation, into coherent groups which can form the basis of social organization. In the sociological vocabulary, the group rules thus formed are called "norms," and the process whereby individual superego standards come to reflect the social norms is called "socialization."

Primary socialization occurs in the family, much of it through the process of superego formation. From the psychological point of view, later group attachments can be regarded as ramifications, extensions, and perhaps modifications of the original process. The sociological description of this process uses a somewhat different vocabulary and focuses on different aspects. The point is that a psychological description is centered around the functions of the process for the psychic system, while the sociological description is organized around the functions of the process for the operation of the social system. Hence the two descriptions are complementary but not identical. This is another way of saying that the psychological and sociological dimensions cannot be reduced one to the other. The aim must be the more modest one of translation.

C. *Patterns of Identification in Groups*

The psychoanalytic theory of groups has not gone far beyond the tentative and preliminary discussion to be found in Freud's *Group Psychology and the Analysis of the Ego*.[4] The following discussion is based on Freud's work, but goes beyond it by developing at greater length some of his brief and tentative remarks.

Human beings can be bound together in two ways—by ties of identification and by ties of libidinal object choice. In prac-

---

4. Freud (1921); also Scheidlinger (1952, 1955, 1964). But see Redl (1942) and Balint (1943) for development of the psychoanalytic idea of identification, as applied to groups.

tice the two intermingle and merge, but they may be separated for analytic purposes. Genetically, identification is the more primitive: indeed it would seem impossible to conceive of another being as a person, or to communicate with him in any way, without first identifying with him. Identification must be understood as being quite literal: "I am he"; the area of "me" includes and encompasses the area of "him." The self is, after all, not a material entity like the body, but a concept—a way of understanding and organizing things. At least after the onset of the Oedipal period, identification always involves a certain amount of idealization, as previously mentioned. Originally, the "ego ideal" incorporated within the superego is an idealized but still recognizable picture of a parent (normally the same sex as the child).

According to Freud, the basic relationship in all organized groups is between leader and led, and its emotional content is that of father to child.[5] The father is idealized, and his image internalized into the superegos of the members. His commands form the official code of conduct of the group: its social norms.[6]

A second identification occurs among the followers, the emotional content of which is of sibling to sibling. This identification springs from various interconnected sources: the biological relationship, the similarity (or identity) of status, the existence of a joint love (or hostility) toward the parents, the outgrowth of aim-inhibited libidinal feelings, and even the feelings of jealousy and rivalry among the brothers and sisters. Some of these sources will be described in greater detail later, but here the point is that while the peer identifications may have various sources and ramify in various ways, in the main it is the fatherhood of the leader that is the source of the brotherhood of the followers.

The whole configuration depends on a split within the self-concepts of the followers. It is the superego that is identified

5. Freud (1923), p. 86.
6. Parsons (1964).

with the father, while the sibling identifications are between the egos of the members. If we suppose that the egos of the members of the group are completely integrated, the characteristic dual identification of organized groups will not occur. In other words, the Freudian theory of the basic relations in groups presumes that the members are not entirely mature or "grown up."

This point can be put another way: From the Freudian point of view, to be a mature male is to be a father, in the emotional sense, and also, in a way, in the biological sense. The achievement of maturity occurs in a series of steps in the relationship of the son to his father or father image; for it is through identification with the father that the male reaches maturity. Correspondingly, the father's basic commandment to his son is: "Grow up to be a man, like me." (At least if this is not what the father communicates, the process of growing up will be much more difficult.) The problem is, however, that until full maturity is reached, identification with the father must be heavily conflicted. The child's central libidinal attachment is to his mother; hence for the son to be like his father is to usurp his father's place vis-à-vis his mother. Only when physiological maturity has been reached and the son shifts his libidinal attachment to another woman and carries the attachment through to consummation (which implies biological fatherhood) is a conflict-free identification with the father possible. Until this stage has been reached, adult behavior is at best acting a role—something that is put on, like a costume; a set of lines which have been memorized—rather than springing in an unambiguous way from the personality. Prior to this, a full ego identification with the father is impossible, and the identification is not only partial but full of ambivalent feelings. In the period of latency and adolescence a typical configuration is for ego identification to turn heavily toward siblings, and, by extension, toward peers of the same sex, while the identification with the father is heavily, if not largely, in the superego. It is this stage of development

that group organization represents. Group relations character-
istically represent arrested or regressive levels of emotional
development.

This raises the question why organizations of adults should
uniformly be built on essentially preadult levels. To this, two
mutually reinforcing answers may be given, one psychological,
and the other technical. From the psychological point of view,
it is relatively rare for full emotional maturity to be reached;
the final ego identification with the father does not become
established with complete firmness, and to a certain degree the
emotional level remains fixed at an earlier stage. Moreover, even
where the final stage is relatively well established, the earlier
formations by no means vanish. Freud made the point in the
simile of the architectural history of Rome. The new emotional
levels do not replace the old but are instead built over the old,
which still remain more or less actively in existence.[7]

From the technical point of view, group organization seems
to require a division of labor into the few who govern and the
many who are governed, as a matter of technical necessity. This
technical requirement fits into, and can be expected to evoke,
the emotional pattern of the father who commands and the son
who obeys. In an actual family, it is to be hoped, there comes a
time when the father says to the son, "You are a man now, and
I hereby set you free. I will no longer tell you how to behave—
you must follow your own standards, use your own strength instead of borrowing mine." With this, the father becomes a grand-
father, the son becomes a father, and the cycle of a generation
has been completed. For purely technical reasons, this is precisely what cannot happen in an organized group. The leader
must continue to lead and the follower to follow.

Freud draws the distinction between an army and a Christian church.[8] A good soldier is supposed to do what his com-

7. Freud (1930), pp. 69–71.
8. Freud (1921), pp. 93–95, 134–35.

mander says, but by no means to be entirely what he is like. The identification with the commander is essentially in the superego. The ego identification is quite limited. One should emulate the commander in bravery, and in diligence, but not carry the imitation to the point of threatening to overturn discipline and take his place. A very strong tie is instead established through ego identification among the comrades-at-arms of the same rank. Command and obedience are of course absolutely indispensable to the effective operation of an army. The technically necessary hierarchy of command, and the very strict authority relations, will, according to the theory here propounded, activate and utilize the emotional relations of the appropriate psychological level, providing there is a preexisting basis in the psyches of those involved.

Freud argues that the Catholic church is built on a different set of identifications. The central figure is Jesus Christ: the intermediary between God the father and man the son, with whom total identification is the ideal ("The imitation of Christ"). We would point out, however, that the technical requirements of church organization tend to push the group relations toward what one finds in an army ("the Church militant"). In the church organization, the equality of all, implicit in the religion, runs up against the need for a firm organizational hierarchy. The distinction between the elite and the rank and file, with different standards of conduct for each, is already explicit in the writings of the founder of Christian organization, Paul, and is carried through in the relationship of the ecclesiastical hierarchy (fathers) and the lay members (sons). Just as the soldier is not supposed to imitate his superior too closely, so the injunction "Don't be more pious than the Pope" holds for the laymen of the church.

It is possible to imagine a group made up wholly of emotionally mature people. Here, whatever the division of labor, on the emotional level there would be only one rank, no distinction between leader and led, and the members would identify with each other in their egos and superegos alike. There would be no coercive measures: power in the sense of the employment of negative sanctions would not be used, and the group rules would be obeyed voluntarily out of inner acceptance. Command and obedience, when it occurred, would be based entirely on rational authority (to be defined presently).

It would be interesting to observe and analyze the behavior of such a group, but apparently there are none in existence. In actual practice, the emotional basis of organized groups seems to conform to Freud's description:

> A primary group of this kind is a number of individuals who have substituted one and the same object for their ego ideal and have consequently identified themselves with one another in their ego. This condition admits of graphic representation. [See fig. 15.][9]

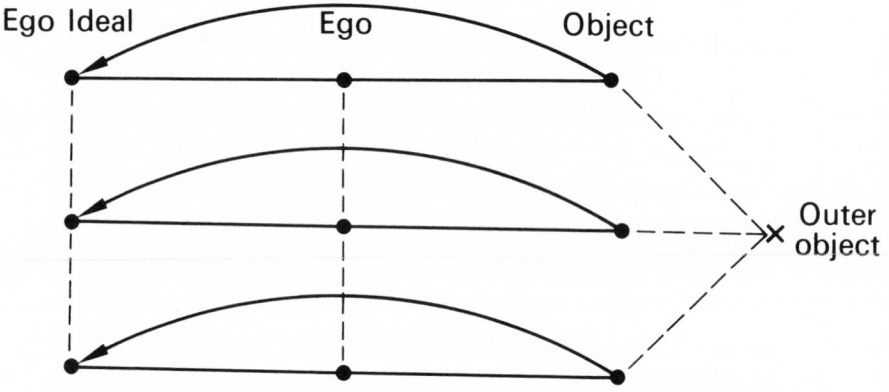

Fig. 15. Identifications in a social group (Freud)

Source: Sigmund Freud, *Group Psychology and the Analysis of the Ego* (1921), in *Collected Works of Sigmund Freud* (London: Hogarth Press, 1955), vol. 18, p. 116.

9. Ibid., p. 116. The idea of the "ego ideal" developed in this work was later extended (and somewhat altered) by Freud into the theory of the superego, in Freud (1923) and elsewhere.

This is not to say that organized groups are nothing but extended families—or at least this is true only in the sense that a cathedral is nothing but a pile of stones and glass. It is not possible to predict the nature of group relations simply from a knowledge of the psychology of the individual members. The technical requirements of organization will have a fundamental impact, as will the historical context, not only in its present configuration, but with its residue of attitudes and techniques, and the momentum of events, which come from the past. In this part of the analysis the underlying psychological forces in group relations are in the forefront, but in later treatments the other factors will be given their due.

We may note a first distinction between the family and other groups springing from the quotation above. In a family, the superegos of the members are internalized and idealized images of the parents. With other groups, the process is reversed; the group leader is identified with the internalized image that is already there. In primary socialization, the internalized image replaces the object (the parent) through identification. In later group formations, the object (the leader) replaces the internalized image.

The nature of the relationship between leader and led will depend on the level and type of superego development of the group members. At a primitive level, whatever the leader says or does or commands is automatically right. This has been termed "authoritarian" leadership. At a more advanced stage of superego development, the ego ideal has become more fully internalized and generalized into principles, and the distinction between the ideal object of identification and the actual leader may begin to emerge. This corresponds to the situation, common in adolescence, where children begin critically to apply to their parents the very standards they have learned from them. Here a more critical attitude toward leadership may develop. The leader is required to live up to the standards which the followers have set for him. Institutional devices may be set up to insure that he does so, and from here it is only a step to representative government. But this is to run ahead of the argument.

The prevailing idea among the followers of the leader is equality, but again this may take many forms, depending on the actual psychic formation. The idea may be quite literal, demanding complete uniformity of thought and action, or it may develop sophisticated forms, such as equality before the law. All this of course becomes vastly more complicated as the members assume differentiated roles and a coherent social organization develops. It is important to note, however, that in this type of group formation the idea of equality has its roots in the existence of a common leader whose word is law.

The foregoing preliminary account of the basic psychological dynamics of group leadership fits in well with Max Weber's typology of legitimacy, and it is possible to characterize charismatic, traditional, and rational-legal authority in terms of the level and type of superego formation involved.[10] The Weberian typology, however, is incomplete. It arises in response to the question "Why do men obey the commands of their leaders?" and hence focuses solely on the leader-follower relation, without going into the correlative relations among the followers.

D. *Leadership*

It was stated earlier that the two basic human relations are those of identification and libidinal object choice, and that both relations are to be found in groups. The two, in fact, interweave very closely. Consider two individuals without emotional ties with each other who are thrown together in regular interaction, whether of common work, or simply social in nature. Gradually, unless there are predisposing factors to the contrary, they will form a mutual libidinal attachment. Except for the most direct

10. This idea is briefly developed in McIntosh (1963).

and intimate relationships, this mutual attachment is "aim inhibited": there is no question of overt sexual relations; rather, the bonds are of friendship or affection. Suppose further that the ego ideal (superego) of each has become more or less internalized, more or less detached from its original parental source. As Freud points out, it is characteristic of such aim-inhibited libidinal relationships that the partners idealize each other to a certain extent.[11] The good points of each are brought out and exaggerated. Perhaps each attributes some to the other which he in fact does not possess. What others may consider vices become transformed by a mental alchemy into virtues.

In other words, aim-inhibited libidinal ties lead to identification of one's partner with one's ego ideal. This process has two aspects. In the first place, the other person is felt to live up to the standards of one's own ego ideal. In the second place, the actual characteristics of the other person's ego ideal are accepted as valid and incorporated into one's own at least as far as the friendship is concerned. Hence, by a process of mutual interaction of the two ego ideals, a jointly accepted, idealized picture of the relationship will emerge in the superego of each. Although our hypothetical case has so far concerned only two individuals, the same process operates in groups with more members. On the basis of Freud's *Group Psychology and the Analysis of the Ego*, it is to be expected that unless there are predisposing factors to the contrary, when a group of individuals interact regularly there will gradually emerge a commonly accepted "ideal group member," with which each of the individuals identifies both himself and the other members of the group in their superegos. This theory seems to be confirmed by modern sociological research, most notably perhaps by the well-known Hawthorne study of the "bank wiring observation room."[12]

11. Freud (1921), pp. 111–12.

12. This study is described in Homans (1950), chap. 3.

Further consequences follow from this analysis. For an individual, when the actions of the ego run contrary to the expectations of the superego, the superego reacts punitively, with feelings of self-hostility (guilt). Since the members of a group identify with each other, a deviation from the requirements of the ideal group member will likewise produce hostile and punitive reactions from the other members. Just as the superego will attempt to bring the ego into line by hostile feelings, so the members of the group will exercise sanctions on each other in order to secure compliance with the group expectations.

As a further consequence, those group members whose behavior most closely corresponds to the ideal will have the highest esteem. The others will identify with such individuals most closely, and, in turn, the standards of such persons will be the most influential in shaping the group ideal. In this way leadership may emerge. For example, in the bank wiring observation room study, Taylor, the individual who adhered most closely to the group norms, gradually began to emerge as the group leader.[13]

The frequency and type of group interaction seem to bear on the question under what circumstances group leadership will or will not emerge. For example, as an occupational group, physicians have clearly defined group standards of behavior, which are quite strictly enforced, but, at least in many communities, there is little leadership. It may be significant that a physician may interact with patients more than with other physicians, or, even where this is not true—for example, with interns in a hospital—the official role concerns mainly his relations with patients, not other doctors. To take another example, the quarterback of a football team at the outset is given a command position (calling the signals), and it seems likely that he will emerge as the leader of the team; indeed this appears indispensable to the successful performance of his assigned task. In a college

13. Ibid., pp. 78–79.

football team, with frequent and close interaction over several years, one expects a strong pattern of leadership to emerge, usually around the quarterback. On the other hand, anyone on the defensive team can call defensive signals, and we expect exactly the reverse trend to exhibit itself here: appointment as defensive captain will devolve on the player who has already established a position of leadership.

E. *Conclusion*

In sum, any set of individuals who interact regularly and co-operatively will in the process of time form themselves into a social group in the sense defined here. Aim-inhibited libidinal attachments will form and lead to superego identification and the emergence of a joint conception of an ideal group member. In turn, individuals will emerge with whom these superego identifications are especially strong, and these individuals may become group leaders.

It is not, however, necessary for a group to have an actual leader. The internalized superego identifications in a group may to a certain extent operate independently of the actual presence of the leader. They may spring from the common life and common identifications among the members of the group, and the presence or emergence of an actual leader may be the effect rather than the cause of the existence of these norms. When the group norms are defined as the commands of the group leader, it must be understood that the real leader may be the internalized superego image, rather than the person who occupies the position of leadership. By the same token, the identification of the internalized image with the external object is a matter of degree. This point is especially important for groups other than the family because of the difference, pointed out above, that while in a family the internal image is derived from the actual parent, with other groups the leader is identified with an already existing image.

F. *The Relationship between Power and*
   Social Control

From the psychological point of view, social control is the
influence on individual behavior by an internalized group ideal.
This ideal may be embodied in the figure of an authoritative
leader, or it may be a commonly accepted "ideal group member"
with which each identifies.

Social control may operate in two ways. In the first place it
may operate *directly* when the individual obeys the group standards because they have become his own internalized standards.
Social control operates *indirectly* when compliance is forced on
a member by sanctions or the threat of sanctions by others.
Here the voluntary exercise of sanctions represents direct social
control on those who exercise them, and indirect social control
on those over whom they are exercised. Since purposive control
over the behavior of others is power, indirect social control has
a power aspect. This raises the question of the interrelations
between social control and power as forms of influence.

Power and social control are radically different kinds of influence. Power involves the purposive regulation of the behavior of one actor by another actor and operates through the
use or threat of sanctions which affect the utilities of the possible courses of action open to the other in such a way that he
will choose the course of action that the other desires him to.

When we ask, What regulates the choices of the actor in
the case of social control? we will get three differing answers,
depending on whether we answer at the level of action, interaction, or social interaction.

On the psychological level (i.e., the level of individual action), social control represents the power of the superego in
determining behavior, often more or less in competition with the
ego. Internal sanctions (feelings of guilt, self-hostility, or shame)
are brought to bear by the superego to enforce its will. Social
control is thus a form of internal influence, operating entirely

within the psyche. On the other hand, there is also an external influence in the form of sanctions from outside the psyche which influence the choice of the ego. Bailey makes this distinction in speaking of the legislative behavior of Senator Buck of Delaware. He says that Buck's consistent support of the interests of the Dupont family, into which he had married, represented the influence of the Duponts not *on* Buck, but *in* Buck.[14]

On the level of interaction, in the case of social control an individual acts freely, according to his own desires and standards; on the other hand, when external power is exercised, only the winner is free, while the loser is constrained by sanctions to act otherwise than as he wishes.

From the point of view of social interaction, we must answer that society itself, rather than any specific actor, does the regulating. Group norms arise spontaneously, almost always in an unplanned way, out of the interactions of individuals. The normative order is the internal system of self-regulation of a social group and is no more purposive than the system of forces whereby an atom or a solar system maintains itself in stable equilibrium. It stands in antithesis to the idea of the social order as the product of rational, purposive action on the part of the members of society. From this point of view there is something ironic about the spectacle of the clash of purposes in society, the power struggle which perhaps leads to the victory of one side, which then imposes its purposes on the social whole; for these victorious purposes themselves are the blind product of the social system.

Someone has said that a chicken is an egg's way of making another egg; so, from the point of view of the flow of human purposes, power is simply one of the means by which a non-purposive society maintains itself. Purposive influence is an epi-phenomenom; power is really powerless. This point, which may be labeled the sociological insight, received its classic

14. Bailey (1950), p. 192.

expression in the writings of Hegel and Marx, but it is, of course, as old as Plato. Plato and, following him, Rousseau sought to dissolve the dilemma by calling for political leadership which can exert purposive and rational control (i.e., power) over the social norms themselves. While we are not yet in a position to treat this question in its full range, there is an aspect to which the theory developed so far provides an answer. This is the relation between power, social control, and freedom.

G. *Power, Social Control, and Freedom*

In chapter 1 we pointed out that the idea of power has its roots in the belief that men are potentially capable of mastering their own destinies through rational thought and action: that the cosmos is formed, in Erikson's phrase, of verifiable reality and modifiable actuality. Ideally man can be autonomous, not in terms of omnipotence, but in terms of utilizing the resources at his disposal in order to achieve a reasonable purpose.

This notion was carried through in the definition of autonomy: the capability of achieving the most desirable possible state, where a possible state is one which will occur if interacting individuals choose certain lines of action which are in fact open to them. Later, the idea of psychic autonomy was developed. This idea is more complex, because it cannot automatically be assumed that an individual actor is psychologically a single entity. Rather the psyche is divided into partly conflicting elements, and a situation which will satisfy one element might not satisfy another. If the ego is taken as the "actor," then psychic autonomy has two closely interrelated features. First it requires that the ego be capable of acting in a way relatively unimpeded by internal conflicts and competing demands from the rest of the psyche. To achieve this, however, it is necessary to attain psychic integration: the ego cannot be victorious *over* the rest of the psyche, but only *with* the rest of the psyche. The demands of the superego and of the instinctual drives of the id, as both are modified by ego activity, must be accepted as the ego's own. It must be emphasized that both internal and external autonomy are not defined as the best of all possible worlds, but as the best possible in *this* world. Even this more limited goal is of course always unattainable, but it measures the success or failure of an individual's efforts: the degree of his autonomy.

The problem thus arises: If the superego's values reflect the standards of the social environment, does not the acceptance of these values, even in modified form, infringe on the autonomy of the ego? To this it may be replied that to the degree that these values are internalized and integrated within the psyche, they become the ego's own purposes and hence constitute no impairment of autonomy. There is no necessary conflict between man and society, between socially accepted values and individual freedom. Nevertheless, such a conflict may regularly occur.

In any normative system there is a latitude of what is permitted between what is prescribed and what is proscribed. For example, a whole range of permissible strategies might be available toward a given purpose. In this case the selection of the appropriate strategy (within the prescribed limits) is an ego function, and the way is opened for rational action. It is precisely this situation which creates the possibility for the exercise of power within the framework of a social system. (See the discussion of social power in the following chapter.) If no latitude of action is allowed—if there is always only one strategy permitted—then behavior becomes ritualized, the ego plays no role in choosing the course of action, and power and rationality disappear.

The influence of superego over ego may be counterbalanced to a certain extent by the rationalization inherent in the process of psychic integration. For example, the Roman Catholic church distinguishes between mortal and venial sins. On the other hand, traditional Calvinist morality tends to regard the slightest infraction of the rules in the gravest light. This corresponds to a primitive level of superego development, where integration of the superego into the psyche has not occurred. The difficulty of rationalizing a normative order is well illustrated by the process of rationalization of the law (a characteristic feature of modern legal development). Law can be rationalized only by drawing a sharp distinction between what is illegal and what is considered to be immoral, a distinction which even trained jurists can have trouble observing in practice and which is beyond most laymen.

In sum, social control both enlarges and limits the scope of human power. It advances human power through the development of a culture which not only enables control over nature (technology), but also, through social organization, enables individuals greatly to increase their power, both absolutely and relative to others. On the other hand, limits within which power over others must operate are established by internalized norms, and—where these fail—through socially legitimate sanctions. Thus, in organized societies power is always limited. These limitations need not, however, constitute restrictions on individual autonomy, provided that the social values from which they spring are internalized and integrated within the psyche. In that case, the limitations imposed by the normative system do not impose limitations on autonomy.

George Homans expresses part of this point as follows:

> The moralists recognize that liberty means neither isolation nor absence of restraint. Men do not live in isolation from one another; in fact they will do any mad thing, even submit to a tyrant, in order to escape from freedom of this kind. They get their satisfactions, including liberty, from collaboration with others, and we know that all collaboration implies norms and that departures from norms are punished. The individual is constrained to obey, and, some would ask, if there is constraint, where has liberty gone? Nor is liberty in collaborative groups always a matter of particular "freedoms"; of speech, or religion, *habeas corpus*, and

the rest. They are dear to us, being what we are. The savage has none of them; indeed he is said to be tyrannized by custom, and yet when we see him in the bush he does not *look* oppressed. Apparently what custom requires him to do he also deeply wants to do. A man, then, is free if he feels free . . . a society is free so far as the behavior it makes appropriate and natural for its citizens— the behavior they feel is good—is also the behavior its controls demand of them.[15]

While this passage well expresses the point that autonomy of action depends on a harmony between the social and physical conditions imposed by external reality on the one hand, and the goals formulated by the individual on the other, we have some misgivings about Homans's claim that his happy savage is truly free.

In the first place, primitive societies often require a great deal of ritualization of behavior, leaving less that is permitted between what is required and what is forbidden, thus limiting the scope of power.

Second, and more fundamentally, we should like to know more about what is going on in the mind of Homans's savage. For, as has been argued previously, autonomy has two faces, internal and external. Internally, autonomy depends on the development of an ego which can integrate, control, and work to fulfill the complex drive system. I wonder at what cost to the potential internal autonomy of the savage is the process of socialization whereby he becomes content with his lot. The above passage from Homans must be balanced by a passage from Rousseau.

Nothing is more certain: those borne in slavery are born for slavery. Slaves lose everything within their chains, even the desire to unchain themselves: they love their servitude as the companions of Ulysses loved their brutishness.[16]

15. Homans (1950), pp. 332–33.
16. Rousseau (1762), bk. 1, chap. 2.

Or, to put it another way, freedom involves both internal and external autonomy, worked together in a harmonious way. A person who is internally but not externally autonomous is a slave to his environment, while a person who is externally but not internally autonomous is a slave to himself. Freedom is to cast off both sets of shackles. To cast off one set only is fruitless and perhaps impossible, for the two are linked together.

8/

A TYPOLOGY

OF INFLUENCE

A. *Power and Social Control as Pure Types*

WHILE POWER AND social control are conceptually distinct, they commonly intermingle in practice, as has already been seen in the case of indirect social control. Especially within a social system, relations between individuals which are purely those of power are rare, for power relations are normally infused with and bounded by the influence of social norms and personal influence.

It is true that the idea of relationships which are purely those of power occurs often in writings on politics. Machiavelli's Prince, for example, seems to rule entirely by the artful use of power (although this is possibly a superficial interpretation). Hobbes's *Leviathan* draws a picture of a political system which includes only power relations. The work as a consequence has little or no descriptive force, although it tells us a great deal about the concept of power.

The idea of pure power is most nearly descriptive of international politics, but even here reservations of the most fundamental kind must be made. To treat the nation-state as an actor ignores the influence of both subnational and supranational groupings. The idea of a given interaction having a value to a nation-state as a whole ignores the fact that the value might be different for different groups or individuals within the nation-state. Finally, not only do nation-states often act irrationally, but the very idea of rationality as a standard of national action is not at all clear.[1] If we abandon the idea of the nation-state as actor, but instead concentrate on groups or individuals within a nation, then the social system of which they are a part will modify the purely power aspect of their behavior. Pure power seems to be a polar type, not often encountered in practice, except during total war.

B. *Authority*

Social control has been defined as the action of conforming to group norms because they are legitimate. A rule may of course be accepted as legitimate and still not be obeyed. This may occur because a conflicting norm has higher priority, or because the ego has ignored the superego commandment. Pure social control is relatively far more common a form of influence than pure power. It is simply a fact that people often behave in certain ways solely because they believe it to be right to do so. Still, it is normal for power and social control to be admixed.

In the previous chapter, two types of social control were distinguished. In the first place, the control may be exercised by the group norm, considered as a commandment, not of any group member, or of the whole group, but of an "ideal group member" or "idealized parental image" incorporated within the superego. Second, the control may be exercised by a member of the group (group leader), whose commands are regarded as legitimate. The leader is able to exercise influence because he

---

1. Schilling (1962) graphically illustrates how slippery the idea of rationality can get when applied to questions of national policy.

is identified with an ideal parental image incorporated within the superego.

Commands may be obeyed for one of two reasons. First, the command may be obeyed because its contents are accepted as legitimate. In that sense, any member of a group may act as a leader, since the function of the leadership is simply to articulate and call to attention what is already latently accepted as legitimate. Second, the command may be obeyed, not because of its contents, but because the leader has a recognized right to command. This is leadership proper. The legitimacy of the leader may spring from personal attributes which he possesses, or is thought to possess, or it may spring from the position which he occupies in the social order. This leads to the distinction between two types of authority, personal and institutional.

In common with general usage, authority will here be defined as legitimate power.[2] It is a relationship between persons who occupy more or less clearly defined positions in social groups. To say, for example, that the law possesses authority is to say, first, that it is legitimate; second, that it is the commandment of a specific body of men, the government; and third, that these commandments are obeyed. To put it another way, it is to say that the authority of the government is defined by law. The influence is in principle always intended, that is, purposive.

C. *Personal Influence*

Personal influence is to be distinguished from authority on two counts. It will be recalled that personal influence occurs when *A* identifies with *B*, and, as a consequence, *B*'s utilities influence *A*'s utilities, and hence *A*'s actions. For this to occur, it is not even necessary for *B* to be aware of *A*'s existence, much less for

---

2. For example we here use authority in the same sense as Homans (1950), p. 418. Notice, however, that our definition of "social control" differs slightly from that of Homans. See Homans (1950), pp. 281–92. See also Friedrich (1958).

him to exercise deliberate direction over A's behavior. Second, authority always occurs in a group context. We shall see that, at a minimum, a social group must contain three members, while personal influence can operate between two individuals, and quite apart from their group relations. (In contrast, for a person to exercise authority he must occupy a definite position in a group.) Since all legitimacy is built on identification, however, authority will always contain a strong element of personal influence. What marks it off is the presence of purposive control and the group context.

D. *Personal Authority*

Two main types of authority may be distinguished, personal and institutional. In personal authority, the superego identification is with the person of the leader. This identification is completely uncritical: the leader's commands are accepted, not because they are right, but because they issue from him. He defines what is right. As such, personal authority represents a rather primitive level of superego development. Nevertheless, the more advanced forms of authority, including institutional authority, which will be treated below, are always more or less admixed with a certain element of personal authority. We have already mentioned Freud's point, that in the process of maturation, the more primitive modes of relating to the world are not so much superseded as overlaid by the more advanced and continue to operate to some degree.[3] Institutional authority is regularly accompanied by more or less personal authority.

In the modern state, the most significant form of personal authority is charismatic authority. Charismatic authority is often confused with personal authority, for example, when it is said that all leadership contains a charismatic element, but in fact not all personal authority is charismatic. This point is worth a short discussion.

3. Page 143 above.

E. *Charismatic Authority*

According to Weber, charismatic authority rests on a "belief in the extraordinary quality of the specific person," who is felt to possess "magical" or "supernatural" powers.[4] This of course is the way in which the father is perceived in childhood, and in general, charismatic authority seems to spring from a transferal of a primitive identification with the magical father. Indeed the process may represent such an early level that it cannot be sharply distinguished as pertaining to the superego, rather than the ego. So far, charismatic authority is not to be distinguished from personal authority in general.

The process appears to be complex. For example, in the development of the charisma of the religious prophet, which Weber saw as the prototype of charismatic authority in general, there seem to be at least two stages or aspects: first, the investiture of a deity with supernatural paternal powers; second, the dual nature of the prophet, who is a mortal specially chosen and possessed by God, who speaks and acts through him. The prophet is at once divine and mortal. Hence the authority of the charismatic leader may not be directly paternal—at one extreme he may be a kind of older brother who speaks for the father. The ultimate source of charismatic authority, however, seems to rest on a reactivation and transference of early identifications with the father.[5]

In Weber's account, another distinctive feature of charismatic authority is that it stands in opposition to existing institutional authority.[6] This is a distinguishing point between personal authority in general and charismatic authority in particular. For example, Winston Churchill's leadership of Britain during World War II had a strong element of personal authority, with the uncanny, magical element attributed to the father in child-

4. Weber (1925*a*), pp. 358-59.

5. Erikson (1950), pp. 284–302.

6. Weber (1925*b*), p. 250.

hood, but, far from standing in opposition to the established institutions of British authority, Churchill was their very personification. Personal and institutional authority were in perfect harmony. In a way the question is a purely semantic one, but it seems appropriate to reserve the term "charismatic authority" for the sense on which Weber laid the most stress: that of a leader who arises at a time when the established institutions of authority have become weakened, takes the mantle of authority on his own shoulders, stands in opposition to the older system, and, if successful, serves as a transitional figure between one form of institutionalized authority and another.

So defined, charismatic leaders typically arise when the existing social norms no longer wholly reflect the superego formations among certain sectors of society. This must not be understood, however, as a case of the individual versus society, but rather of a strain within the social system, and also within the psychic systems of the members of society. For example, Erikson has emphasized the ambivalence of the identifications on which Hitler's appeal was based.[7]

Normally superego formation occurs within the family. When social changes produce a change in family relations, the pattern of superego formation may change. These widespread new superego patterns, however, have no social or institutional expression. The consequence is a strain within family relations, where superego patterns are inconsistent and conflicting, and a loss of legitimacy of the official norms. From the sociological point of view, charismatic leadership is the means by which the official norms are brought into correspondence with the superego formations of the members of society (sort of the obverse of socialization). Its function is the mitigation of social strain. From the psychological point of view, charismatic leadership is a way of resolving an "identity crisis," or, more accurately, an identification crisis, on the part of members of society.

7. Erikson (1950), pp. 284–315. The following paragraph draws on Erikson's treatment but generalizes and extends it.

Superego controls are regularly somewhat insecure, and the resultant anxiety is greatly lessened if an external authority figure or group can reinforce these controls by providing a firm basis for identification and thus reinforce the superego.

F. *Institutional Authority*

In contrast to personal authority, institutional authority springs from the status which an individual occupies in a group. Personal authority validates the position of a person in a group, while group position creates institutional authority. Consequently, institutional authority is transferable, while personal authority is not. When a person leaves a position for any reason, his institutional authority is conferred onto his successor. The line between personal and institutional authority is not sharp, and either may flow out of the other. For example, while the original authority of the father normally has a strongly personal character, as maturation proceeds the parental code becomes internalized and is then projected outward, onto an individual or social group. The exact process will be analyzed presently. The consequence is a more critical attitude toward authority. The group leader is expected to conform to the group standards, which in turn are the individual's own. The father and, by extension, other leaders will be seen as in a literal sense embodying family or group norms. Thus, the leader is not given carte blanche. If his behavior and commands do not correspond to the normative expectations of the group, he will lose authority. The social code, and not the magical individual, is the source of the authority.

Authority, whether personal or institutional, combines power and social control. On the one hand, the person in authority is able purposively to influence the behavior of others, and hence to exercise power. On the other hand, the effectiveness of his power rests on the fact that it is legitimate, that the norms, whether personal or institutional, support his right to command, and often the substantive content of the command. Hence the definition of authority as legitimate power. The ability of the authoritative figure to bring sanctions to bear to ensure conformity also rests on the legitimacy of the sanctions. Their effectiveness springs from their inner acceptance by the group members—often including those over whom they are exercised—as rightful.

Max Weber distinguished two types of what is here called "institutional authority," traditional and rational-legal. This distinction will be treated in a later volume.

At this point, it may be useful to put in outline form the typology of influence which is here being developed. (See table 1.)

TABLE 1

A Typology of Influence

Action		Influence	
	Interaction	Social Interaction	
		Polar Types	Combined Forms
Rational Action	Power over → the Field	Power over → Other Actors	1. Personal Authority Charismatic Authority Etc. 2. Institutional Authority Political Authority Economic Authority Religious Authority Etc.
Identification	Personal → Influence	Social → Control	3. Social Power Political Power Economic Power Religious Power Etc.

Note: Not included in typology: Rational Persuasion → Rational Authority.

G. *Social Power*

Before developing the idea of social power as a combination of power and social control, it is necessary to introduce a further discussion of the role of sanctions in exercising influence. A sanction has been defined as a variable of the field which is significant for the utilities of one actor and over which another actor has relative power. As has been pointed out, the mere possession of a sanction—its potential use as distinguished from its actual use—will typically influence the behavior of others.

Sanctions may be of three types: legitimate, nonlegitimate, and illegitimate. In pure power relations, sanctions are nonlegitimate, since the influence of social control has by definition been ruled out. In the context of a normative system, sanctions assume a somewhat different form. A legitimate sanction is (or is the result of) an action recognized as legitimate, which is designed to ensure or reestablish conformity to group norms, or to punish deviance from the norms.

Legitimate sanctions have both social and psychological functions. The social need for sanctions springs from the fact that voluntary conformity to norms cannot be counted on in all cases. On the social level, deviance may occur as a consequence of a contradiction within the normative system, either between subsystems (cross-pressure) or within a given system or subsystem, for example, between normatively defined goals and normatively defined means.

On the psychological level, legitimate sanctions may serve to reinforce insecure internal superego controls. Deviant behavior may nevertheless occur, and it can take several forms:

1. Crime: The norm is regarded as legitimate, but not obeyed. (Failure of superego control.)

2. Rebellion or retreatism: The whole normative system is rejected. (Failure to incorporate the norms within the superego.)

3. Innovation: Rejection of a particular normative element, while attempting to maintain the overall bonds of group identification. (The superego partly conflicts with social norms.)

In deviant behavior in the form of crime, both the criminal

and society accept the sanction as legitimate. In the other two forms, the sanctions are not regarded as legitimate by those over whom they are exercised. A truly retreatist individual regards group sanctions as nonlegitimate—he has withdrawn psychologically from membership in the group. A rebellious or innovative individual may regard sanctions as illegitimate. He may still identify with the group but have a different perception of the group identity.[8]

We have introduced this very brief and incomplete discussion of sanctions in order to distinguish a particular situation—where the sanction itself is regarded as nonlegitimate by all actors, but the possession of the sanction springs from status or office within a group. Perhaps an example will make this clear.[9] Consider the office of the United States presidency. This office carries with it a very substantial grant of constitutionally defined right to command, all or most of which is generally regarded as legitimate. Yet these constitutional "powers" are by no means as influential as might appear at first glance. The president has the recognized right, for example, to direct the official actions of members of his own administration but regularly finds it extremely difficult to do so. The legitimate sanctions at his disposal, such as reprimand, demotion, or dismissal, regularly result in such disadvantageous consequences as to be not utilizable. His actual authority is, in general, less than the formal definition of his authority.

In addition, the president commonly needs to be able to exercise influence beyond (but not in violation of) his legitimate authority. For example, he must normally be able to exercise considerable influence over Congress in order to achieve his objectives. While his role as chief legislator is perhaps now fully legitimate in the sense that his right to propose legislation is widely accepted, it is clear that in no sense does he possess

8. Compare and contrast the above discussion with Merton (1949).

9. The following account draws heavily on Neustadt (1960), pp. 1–57.

the authority to require compliance with his wishes from Congress or individual congressmen.

In this situation, however, where his legitimate right to command seems insufficient to enable him to carry out his purposes, the President is not without resources. It is often possible for him to make artful use of the authority that he does possess in order to secure compliance either where he has the recognized right to secure compliance but finds his official sanctions to be inadequate to the task, or where he has no recognized right to command obedience.

For example, the president's right to appoint federal judges is normally "self-enforcing"—his choice is usually approved without serious question or opposition. This authority is potentially capable of being used as a lever to secure the cooperation of an influential congressman with some aspect of the president's program. To take another example, the president has no authority to forbid a company to raise the price of its products. He does, however, through such offices as the secretary of defense, have the authority to decide which companies shall receive lucrative federal contracts. The artful use, or threat of use, of this authority is potentially capable of influencing the price policies of some companies.

In short, the influence of an office often exceeds its authority, because the authority of the office can itself be used as a nonlegitimate sanction or used to create such a sanction. Such influence involves an amalgamation of power and authority. The authority not only rests on legitimate sanctions—in addition, it itself constitutes a nonlegitimate sanction. The influence partakes of power because it represents the conscious influence of one person by another, and because it rests on sanctions. It partakes of authority because, first, the status or office is the source of the power, and, second, the use of such power is limited and directed by the normative order in which the actions are imbedded. Hence, social power may be defined as the use of authority itself as a sanction (or to create a sanction). Social power is the artful use of authority to extend influence beyond its legitimated bounds. Such power is non-legitimate—neither rightful nor wrongful—and is hence permitted.

As Hobbes has remarked, in the state of nature, without society or government, the power of one individual does not differ greatly from the power of another.[10] As Rousseau has pointed out, it is the existence of social institutions which enables one man to be greatly more powerful than another.[11] In organized societies, the use of pure power is rare; power normally takes the form of authority or social power. Sociologists tend to concentrate on the first, and political scientists on the second. We are here adopting an approach which utilizes both ideas in an integrated way.

H. *Rational Authority*

When an individual possesses a skill or talent which enables him to perform a given task with competence, his role in performing such a task is often accepted as authoritative. This is what we mean when we say, for example, that "Smith is an authority on the Peloponnesian War." If Smith tells us that the battle of Cyzicus occurred in 410 B.C., we are inclined to believe him. Smith influences our opinions because of his recognized competence. Rational authority rests on evidence. We believe Smith's statements, not because we have in our possession evidence that the battle of Cyzicus occurred in 410 B.C., but because we have evidence that Smith knows what he is talking about on the subject and is not in the habit of lying. This evidence may be that we have read several impressive articles by Smith on the Peloponnesian War, or that he has a

10. Hobbes (1651), chap. 13, par. 1.
11. Rousseau (1754), pp. 70–71.

high reputation among scholars whom we know by experience to be good judges of other scholars, etc. If the evidence is insufficient, but Smith is still regarded as an authority, then his authority is not rational, but pseudorational. The artful use of propaganda (a type of power) can create such pseudorational authority.

If we do not credit Smith's authority, then in order to persuade us he must show us the evidence on which his conclusion is based. This is rational persuasion. In general, rational authority is directly or indirectly based on rational persuasion. Scholarly authority possesses to an especial degree the somewhat paradoxical character of rational authority—that the less it is used as a method of influence, the stronger it is. The most respected and authoritative scholar is (or should be) the one who habitually relies on persuading us by carefully showing the evidence on which his conclusions rest, rather than asking us to accept his views simply because his competence is already proved.

The legitimacy on which rational authority rests is distinct from the legitimacy involved in social control and hence has a place outside the main typology developed here. That it does not receive much attention in this volume reflects my conviction that, however desirable it may be as a form of influence, it does not play an indispensable role in stable social organization. The idea will, however, be used in a later volume in connection with a discussion of Max Weber's treatment of bureaucratic authority.

9/

THE GENERAL WILL

A. *Introduction*

WE NOW TURN TO working some of the content of the previous chapters into the language of decision theory. From a purely formal point of view, this chapter will consist of a description of a certain type of outcome matrix which yields a solution, and its only unusual feature will be that the utility scales of the actors will be assumed to be sums of other scales. The operating ideas will be preference, choice, and interaction pair; all other properties of the matrix will be defined in terms of these three. The meaning of these terms is simply the sum of the formal properties of each in the theory. For example, the formal meaning of "preference" is defined as follows: "There is a class **S**, such that for any two members of the class, s_n and s_m, either s_n has relation P to s_m; s_m has relation P to s_n; or s_n and s_m have relation E to each other.

This formal pattern becomes interpreted when we say that P means "is preferred to," and E means "is indifferent to," etc., so that the interpretation becomes, "for any two interaction pairs, an actor will either prefer the first to the second or the second to the first, or be indifferent between them." But other interpretations of this formal relation are possible. For example, suppose **S** is the class of people, *P* means older than, and *E* means the same age as. Then the interpretation is, "For any two people, either the first is older than the second, the second is older than the first, or their ages are equal."

Both of these interpretations make sense as sets of concepts; they are intelligible. The concepts "is preferred to," and "is older than," are formally identical concepts. (Although the introduction of further postulates would result in formal differences, for example, age is measured on a ratio scale while preference is measured on an interval scale.) From a purely formal point of view the differences between the concepts "is preferred to" and "is older than" have no epistemological standing; they are, at most, devices to help the mind grasp the formal relation.

However, the interpretation of the formal structure here presented contains more than the formal structure itself. While the interpretation uses the language of decision theory, the conceptual content has been drawn from psychoanalytic theory and traditional political theory, especially the theories of Jean-Jacques Rousseau. The thought of both Freud and Rousseau has often been accused of being vague and metaphysical. It is hoped that these objections will be met by the present formulation, which aims at precision of expression (though not full formalization) in a manner which will lend itself to the introduction of translation rules and, through this, of empirical testing.

It will be recalled that in our previous treatment the process of identification was described as follows:

1. Actor *A* perceives *B*'s preferences and hence knows his utility scale.

2. Actor *A* compares *B*'s scale to his own: he measures *B*'s scale in his own units.

3. Actor *A* forms a new utility scale, which is a weighted sum of his scale and *B*'s. The weight will depend on the degree of identification.

This describes simple identification, but in the light of our development of psychoanalytic theory it has been seen that a more complex process characterizes the identifications in social groups.

B. *Primary Identification*

The superego formations characteristic of social groups develop in two stages, the first of which will be called *primary identification*.

1. Actor A forms an idealized conception of the utility scale of a person significant to him (a parent or parent substitute).

2. Actor A transforms this scale into his own units.

3. Actor A internalizes this scale; that is, he takes it over as the utility scale of his own superego. This is the first critical point of difference from simple identification.

4. This internalized scale will be an idealization of the scale of the object of identification. This is the second critical difference from simple identification.

5. The internalized and idealized scale in the superego will have a dual relationship with the utility scale of the ego. In part, it will be integrated with the ego's scale by the process described under simple identification; that is, in working out its preferences the ego will take account of, and to some degree accept as its own, the idealized scale internalized in the superego. To that extent—that is, to the extent that psychic integration has been effected—the identification is in both ego and superego.

In part, however, ego and superego will remain in conflict. Here, the process of choice will involve a struggle between ego and superego. The actual choice will be a result of the interaction, decided by the comparative power of the two. Whatever the result, however, the cost will be high. The conflict between ego and superego does not suddenly activate itself when a choice arises and subside when the choice is made; rather it rages perpetually in the psyche. The assumption on which the theory here being developed rests is that important conflicts of this kind exist in the psyches of nearly every member of every social group.

Nevertheless, it is still possible to speak of the particular wills (or actual wills) of the group members. Utility scales are built on preferences, and a preference is an intended choice. Whether these choices arise (or would arise if the occasion presented itself) out of either the integration or the struggle of ego and superego, they define the particular wills of the group members. Notice that the utility scale of the particular will does not necessarily measure psychic satisfaction, pleasure, happiness, or anything of the kind. We are engaged here in a theory of *action*, and the scale simply measures degree of preference, and a preference is nothing but an intention to choose. The process of primary identification may be represented graphically as in table 2.

TABLE 2

PROCESS OF PRIMARY IDENTIFICATION

OUTER OBJECT		PSYCHE						
			Object		Superego		Ego	Actual Will
s_1 u_1			$u_{1.1}$		$u_{1.2}$		$u_{1.3}$	$u_{1.4}$
s_2 u_2		Stage I	$u_{2.1}$	Stage II	$u_{2.2}$	Stage III	$u_{2.3}$	$u_{2.4}$
s_3 u_3		Idealization	$u_{3.1}$	Internalization	$u_{3.2}$	Integration	$u_{3.3}$	Stage IV	$u_{3.4}$
s_4 u_4		$\longrightarrow$	$u_{4.1}$	$\longrightarrow$	$u_{4.2}$	$\overleftarrow{\text{Conflict}}$	$u_{4.3}$	Summation $\longrightarrow$	$u_{4.4}$
$\vdots$ $\vdots$			$\vdots$		$\vdots$		$\vdots$	$\vdots$
s_n u_n			$u_{n.1}$		$u_{n.2}$		$u_{n.3}$	$u_{n.4}$

C. *Secondary Identification*

Secondary identification assumes that the superego identifications are already formed, and it involves a transferal of identification from the original object to a new object. In principle, the process is as follows:

First, the superego image becomes more or less detached from its original object. This detachment is in part the result of the process of internalization, but it goes further. This can be illustrated by the changed status of a simple rule, such as "Obey your parents' instructions." Before the process of identification begins, when this rule is obeyed it will be out of a varying mixture of trust, respect, fear, and awe of the parent. When primary identification has been completed, the command "Do what your parents say" comes from the inner voice of the superego. At the next stage, by displacement, a new person is identified with the original object, and the command then becomes, "Do what your teacher (boss, commander, president) says." This is the underlying psychological formation behind personal authority.

A variant occurs when an institution, rather than a person, is the object of the displacement. The institution becomes, from a psychological point of view, personified. Although psychologically this is quite close to displacement onto an individual, politically the difference is large. The central point of difference is that when displacement has occurred onto an institution, it is the legitimacy of the office, rather than the resemblance of the office holder to the original object, which determines the matter. Displacement onto an institution is the psychological basis of political absolutism. The distinction may be illustrated by the difference between charismatic leadership and royal absolutism. The charismatic leader possesses authority because of his magical personal qualities (displacement of internalized identification from parent to charismatic leader). In contrast, the authority of an absolute monarch depends on the fact that he has attained the throne by legitimate means. This assumes that the individual already has internalized standards of legitimacy, and the monarch is granted authority (i.e., is considered legitimate) only if his mode of acquiring the throne meets these standards. Although the two types may stand in the sharpest contradiction, as when the charismatic leader challenges established authority, they also may be closely allied; for example, a legitimate monarch will normally be endowed by his subjects with the qualities of the idealized image of the original object.

Third, internalization and the detachment of the superego from the original object may become complete. Instead of the simple commandment "Do what your parents say," the superego generalizes the idealized parental commandments into a code of conduct, which is binding regardless of what the actual parents may say. Thus, if the parent orders the son or daughter to do something that he or she regards as illegitimate, or wrongful, the order will be refused. Here displacement onto another object (individual or institution) occurs when the new object is felt to embody the superego code. This displacement may be quite conditional; the new object will possess authority only as long as it in fact lives up to the code of the superego. Discrepancies may, however, be rationalized away. In addition, this formation may be admixed with one of the previous two, and as a result the original superego code may be modified toward acceptance of the rules advanced by the authoritative leader or institution.

It is possible to develop further the various ways in which group authority rests on the superego formations of the members, but here we are emphasizing what they have in common. For the time being, we will not stress the differences between the three types just developed, or any other types that might arise from a further elaboration; rather we will be content to point out that all three types exemplify the second stage in identification, whereby, by displacement and superego identification, a group leader acquires authority. He has authority because the superego codes of his followers dictate that his commands be obeyed, whether because of identification with the original object or identification of the institution with the original object, or because his commands express the contents of these codes.

These superego codes may be expressed as utility scales, inasmuch as they contain directions concerning the proper choices in various circumstances, and, in principle, a utility scale can be constructed from these preferences.

D. *Ego Identification*

The central lateral identification (as opposed to the vertical identifications involved in authority) among members of a group is a straightforward case of simple identification (not primary identification), as treated earlier. The situation becomes considerably more complex, however, when ego-superego relations are taken into account. It has been pointed out that simple identification does not involve the introjection of the other's image into a separate component of one's own ego. Rather, the utility scale of the other is compared, weighed, and then summed within the ego, as indicated in table 3.

TABLE 3

PROCESS OF EGO IDENTIFICATION

	COMPARISON		WEIGHING (Degree of Identification)		SUMMATION (Ego after Identification)
	Ego	Alter	Ego	Alter	Ego
s_1	u_1	v_1	$u_1 \times N$	$v_1 \times (1-N)$	$(u_1 \times N) + [v_1 \times (1-N)]$
s_2	u_2	v_2	$u_2 \times N$	$v_2 \times (1-N)$	$(u_2 \times N) + [v_2 \times (1-N)]$
s_3	u_3	v_3	$u_3 \times N$	$v_3 \times (1-N)$	$(u_3 \times N) + [v_3 \times (1-N)]$
s_4	u_4	v_4	$u_4 \times N$	$v_4 \times (1-N)$	$(u_4 \times N) + [v_4 \times (1-N)]$
..	..	..	..	..	..
s_n	u_m	v_n	$u_m \times N$	$v_n \times (1-N)$	$(u_m \times N) + [v_n \times (1-N)]$

The new ego scale so formed then enters into relations with the superego, as outlined above. This may result in a very complex situation. For example, suppose that the ego identification is primarily negative (e.g., assuming sibling rivalry, or a derivative, as the predominant relation between the egos of the group members). This might run into sharp conflict with the preferences of the superego code concerning how the members should behave toward each other. On the other hand, the underlying rivalry might turn into a fierce demand for equality, by a mechanism to be outlined below, and so harmonize with the superego code. In addition, aim-inhibited libidinal relations among the group members will in general lead to idealized identification among the members. These idealizations may fit into and reinforce the superego code. On the other hand, they may produce a split within the superego. An example is the conflict of loyalty experienced by students in colleges which have honor codes. On the one hand, one set of norms, built around displaced parental identifications, requires that violators be reported. On the other hand, another set of norms, built around idealized peer identifications, may require silence, and refusal to "squeal" even under heavy duress. This is not a conflict between ego and superego, but within the superego, although the conflict has been produced by the divergent consequences of ego and superego identifications. These brief considerations are only a sample of the great complexity of the psychological relations which may obtain within even the simplest group.

E. *The General Will*

We are now in a position to advance our theory about the dynamics of the operation of the normative system of a social group:

PROPOSITION 1. *As far as they concern group interactions, the superego utility scales of the group members will under normal circumstances (unspecified boundary conditions) be closely similar.* This proposition rests on several arguments. In the first place, the members of most groups are drawn from persons occupying similar social positions (similar social and technical circumstances of life). As a consequence, their psychic formations will be similar, including their superego formations. For example, when one speaks of a "middle class ethos," presumably the similarity of superego contents of the members of the middle class is partly due to the fact that most of them face similar material conditions of life. Second, the object of superego identifications among the members will be the same, and hence the superego contents will be similar. Third, the idealized ego identifications among the group members will tend to bring their superego codes into conformity and iron out discrepancies and divergencies.

PROPOSITION 2. *These similar superego utility scales do not necessarily bear any close resemblance to the actual will of any actor.* The actual will of every group member is the product of the interaction of his ego and superego scales, and, if a conflict exists and the ego carries the day, there will be a divergence of the actual will from the superego code. As a matter of common observation, the degree to which the actual will reflects the superego code varies widely from person to person.

PROPOSITION 3. *The similar superego codes of the members may, however, be visualized as representations of the actual will of an ideal group member.* When the members of a social group are questioned, they will usually be able to describe in considerable detail how a group member is supposed to behave under varying circumstances. They will be able to define a set of preferences, and hence the utility scale, of someone who always obeys group standards. These accounts often differ little from each other, as would be expected from proposition 1 above. The behavior of this ideal group member will be dictated solely by his superego, and thus there will be an exact correspondence between his actual will and his superego scale.

In other words, while the similar superego scales of the group members will likely not be the actual will of anybody, these scales define the actual will of an imaginary (and ideal) person, and in fact the members of a group will to a certain degree look at the matter in this light.

PROPOSITION 4 (DEFINITION). *The utility scale of this imag-*

inary ideal group member will be called the "general will of the group."

The actual influence of the general will over the members of the group will depend on a number of factors:

1. The members of the group may not have exactly the same picture of what constitutes the general will, that is, the images with which they identify may not be exactly the same. This situation may be presented diagrammatically, as in figure 16. The three circles represent the concepts which the members

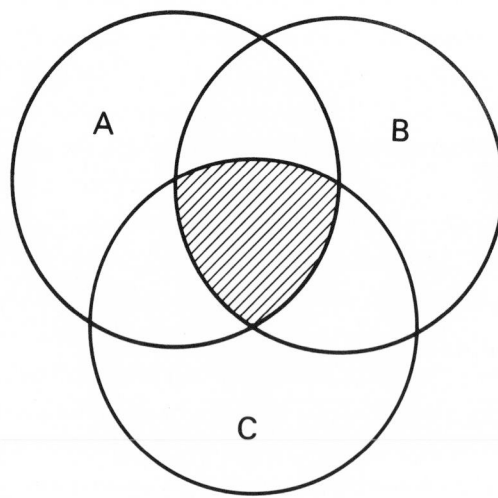

Fig. 16. The general wills of *A*, *B*, and *C* create
a single real general will.

have of the general will (what they think the actual will of the ideal group member is like). The shaded area of overlap among all three circles represents the area where all three are in agreement concerning the nature of the general will. For this area it is correct to speak of a single general will which influences each of the members. This area of overlapping image will be termed the *real general will*.

Outside this overlap each member may have a conception of a general will which influences his behavior, but since this conception is unique to him or only to some of the members, it does not constitute a true general will—simply an "incorrect" idea that he has of the general will.

2. The real general will normally constitutes only a part of the superego formation of the members of the group, with the exception perhaps of the general will of the family before the individual has moved on to form other group ties. In the first place, the displacement of superego identifications will never be total. Much of the original constellation centered around the family can be expected to remain except in the most extreme cases where the individual's whole life is swallowed up by his allegiance to a group. In addition, a number of distinct group attachments will normally be formed, even within a monolithic totalitarian society. From this point of view the superego is splintered into a series of discrete group attachments. Opposing this is the tendency toward integration, an attempt to maintain a single, ideal self-concept, of which the various group roles played by the individual form harmonious parts. Often the original superego formation, before the addition of broader group attachments, will provide the focus for such an integration.

Hence as it operates in the minds of its members in the course of working through to actual behavior, the general will of a particular group is subjected to two forces: first, the conflicting claims of other group attachments; second, the attempt on the part of the psyche to integrate this general will with the rest of the superego.

3. A third factor which has already been discussed is the relation between the superego and the ego. This relation is always more or less conflicted, and the influence of the superego over actual behavior may be more or less substantial, more or less direct, more or less transformed by the alchemy of unconscious forces.

Other considerations could be mentioned, but perhaps these three points will be sufficient to show that while the general will of a group influences the behavior of its members, it normally does not completely determine this behavior, and the influence may be highly indirect. In other words, if we express the general will as a utility scale and then examine the actual utility scale of the individual (his particular will), the two scales will normally differ to some extent. In sociological terms, it is one thing for a social norm to be internalized, and another for it to determine behavior.

To sum up the discussion so far:

1. It appears to be impossible to explain the existence of cooperative groups on the assumption that individuals behave rationally to maximize their expected utilities without regard to the utilities of the other actors. In fact, the modern theory of games and decisions seems to indicate that far less cooperative behavior is possible on these assumptions than has usually been supposed.

2. Dropping the assumption of impersonality of relations, the possible consequences of simple identification were explored. In simple identification, the utilities of each actor are influenced by the utilities of the others. If mutual full identification occurs, that is, if the utilities of the other actors count equally with each individual's own private utility, then total harmony will prevail. Otherwise, mutual identification will enable cooperation in some instances but not in others.

3. Following Freud, and extending his analysis, actual group ties involve a dual identification: first, a superego identification with the image of a parent or parental surrogate; and second, ego identifications with the other members of the group. Insofar as it is internalized by the members, the utility scale of the image of the ideal group member constitutes a real general will, which tends to influence the members toward cooperative behavior. However, the process of the translation of this general will into actual behavior by the group members is complex and is subject to a variety of influences. Hence it is hazardous to assume that even the existence of a real general will is suffi-

cient to establish stable social interaction. There is, however, a mechanism which greatly increases the tendency to conform to group norms, which will now be developed.

F. *The Enforcement of the General Will*

The degree of influence exercised by the general will over the particular wills of the members of a group will vary according to three factors:

1. The relative intensity of the values of the general will as against the private will. For example, if the difference in utility between two states is slight for the private will and major for the general will, the influence of the general will upon a choice between the two will be comparatively great.

2. The degree of identification with the general will. This point has been treated at some length.

3. The degree of conflict between the general and private wills. If the general and private wills are in complete accord on the relative desirability of the various states—that is, if one can be expressed as a linear transformation of the other—then the actual decision will be the same, whatever the variation of factors 1 and 2 above. It will indeed be impossible to tell which was the more important in determining the decision. Some writers have held that rational self interest is completely in accord with the principles of morality.[1] This amounts to saying that the conflict between ego and superego does not exist, or would not exist if the ego were rational. In the light of Freudian theory this view appears doubtful to say the least.

In point of fact, compliance with group norms regularly requires substantial instinctual renunciations on the part of the individual. From prohibition of various kinds of sexual and aggressive behavior, to insistence that taxes be paid, society regu-

1. Hobbes is an example. The reader cannot help feeling that something has been lost when the golden rule is derived from the laws of rational self-interest. Hobbes (1651), p. 130.

larly imposes demands that are felt by at least part of the psyche to be onerous. Insofar as the social norms have been internalized, this conflict goes on within the individual, not between the individual and society. Successful social organization hence requires compliance with social norms even where these norms conflict sharply with the private wills of the members. The stronger the superego (i.e., the greater its power over the ego) the greater the likelihood of compliance, but, as a common-sense observation, many successful social systems are not characterized by especially strong superegos on the part of most of their members.

Since the actual identifications involved in group membership are highly complex and varied, it will aid the exposition to examine a simplified situation. Assume a three-person group, with a general will fully internalized in the superego of each.

As far as the general will is concerned, of course, compliance with its commands is obligatory. Assume, however, that if some members of the group do not obey, then as far as the other members are concerned obedience is still obligatory, but not as highly valued as when everyone else obeys. (This premise is used because, as will be seen, it is the least favorable to stable obedience to the general will. It also accounts for the apparent fact that under some circumstances disobedience is contagious. Nevertheless, we will argue that in other circumstances it is the opposite; that is, disobedience tends to produce conformity.)

For example, let the general will of the group (superego scale) composed of *A*, *B*, and *C* consist of one commandment, with utilities, as in figure 17, the same for all three actors. This

	Both Others Obey	One Other Obeys	Both Others Disobey
Obey	10	9	7
Disobey	0	1	2

Fig. 17. General will of group *ABC*

matrix may be interpreted as follows: It is always right to obey, regardless of what the others do. But obedience is slightly less important and disobedience is a slightly less serious infraction if others disobey.

The private will (ego scale before identifications) of each actor is represented in figure 18. Assume that none of the actors

	Both Others Obey	One Other Obeys	Both Others Disobey
Obey	5	4	2
Disobey	10	8	4

Fig. 18. Private wills of *A*, *B*, and *C*

is in a position to exercise sanctions on the others except for those already implicit in the matrix. The matrix may now be interpreted as follows: Crime always pays: it is always the most advantageous course to disobey the commandment of the general will. Both obedience and disobedience are relatively most advantageous when others obey. The criminal is best off in a law-abiding community, while those who abide by the law are best off if there are no criminals. The situation where all disobey, however, is more advantageous than where all obey.

Now let us adopt the undoubtedly overoptimistic assumption that all three members have strong superegos which are integrated with the ego in a conflict-free way producing an actual will for each actor, as given in figure 19. This matrix was formed

	Both Others Obey	One Other Obeys	Both Others Disobey
Obey	7.5	6.5	4.5
Disobey	5.0	4.5	3.0

Fig. 19. Actual wills of *A*, *B*, and *C*, after 0.5 identification with general will.

by counting ego and superego scales equally (i.e., a 0.5 identification with each). Here, the force of the internal superego controls of the group members is sufficient by itself to insure conformity. All will obey the general will voluntarily without the need for additional sanctions.

We have not as yet considered the impact of the ego identifications among the members. If we assume a 0.125 total positive identification, which is the average of a 0.125 identification of each actor with every other actor, then the ego scale for each is as indicated in figure 20. The effect, as with all cases of

	Both Others Obey	One Other Obeys	Both Others Disobey
Obey	5.000	4.375	2.750
Disobey	9.250	7.625	4.000

Fig. 20. Figure 18 after positive ego identifications

positive identification, is to mitigate the conflicts of interest among the members. Since disobedience is a disadvantage to others, and obedience an advantage, the net effect is to raise the utility of obedience and to lower that of disobedience. As a result, the superego is reinforced by the ego identifications of the members. It would be otherwise if it were to the advantage of each for the others to disobey, for in this case the net effect of the identifications would be to weaken the general will.

Suppose, further, that the ego identifications among the members are negative rather than positive (that is, group relations are competitive rather than cooperative). Specifically, for every interaction pair (dyad), let us take 0.125 of the absolute difference between the utilities for the two actors and add this figure to the higher utility and subtract it from the lower utility. Then let us form the triads by averaging each actor's two dyads for each case. Our private-will matrix (fig. 18), after such negative identifications, is shown in figure 21.

	Both Others Obey	One Other Obeys	Both Others Disobey
Obey	5.000	3.625	1.250
Disobey	10.750	8.375	4.000

Fig. 21. Figure 18 after negative ego identifications

Here the net effect will be to weaken the influence of the general will. On the other hand, if it is to the private interest of each that the others do not obey, then negative identifications will strengthen the influence of the general will.

In summary, where the ego and the superego have conflicting interests, but where the psyche is well integrated, then—if it is to the interest of each, while disobeying the general will, to have the others obey—the general will is aided by positive identifications and hindered by negative identifications; but if general disobedience to the general will is to the interest of the group members, the general will is aided by negative identifications and hindered by positive identifications. The last case seems the most disadvantageous from the point of view of the general will.

As has been pointed out, the weaker the superego, and the sharper its conflicts with the ego, the less likely it is for the general will to be obeyed, unless sanctions are employed. This brings us to the second means by which the general will is enforced: the use or threat of sanctions against those who would otherwise be violators. For the sake of the analysis, let us assume the following situation:

Actors *A*, *B*, and *C* are comparatively about equally powerful in their ability to bring effective sanctions to bear; that is, no one is much more powerful than another. To be effective, then, the use of sanctions must normally involve a coalition of two against one. Sanctions by one against two, or one against one, with the third neutral, can by supposition be ruled out as ineffective. Finally, suppose that the use of, or threat of, sanctions by two against one is always effective in enforcing compliance with the general will. The question is, given these conditions, Under what circumstances will the general will be enforced by sanctions?

At first glance it seems to be a simple matter of the law-abiding versus the would-be violators. If those with strong superegos are sufficiently numerous and powerful, they will gang up on the others to ensure that everyone obeys the general will. While this possibility is not to be discounted entirely, we are not inclined to give great weight to it, for three reasons.

In the first place, on the basis of my intuitive conclusions drawn from general observation, I am inclined to doubt whether there is any substantial coincidence of those with the strongest superegos and those most eager to enforce social norms. To take a single example, the police—the group charged by society with the enforcement of the law—have, throughout history, been one of the most corrupt and least law-abiding groups in society. Exceptions to this generalization appear to be quite few. The point becomes more persuasive when it is noted that the rare instances of relatively law-abiding police forces seem to be accompanied by sharp restraints on the use of violence as a sanction, as, for example, the British police, which are reputed to be among the best in the world, and who are not normally permitted to carry firearms.

The second reason is purely theoretical. We have argued that the psychic formations of the members of a social group will tend to be similar. It therefore appears arbitrary to divide the members of a group into the law-abiding and the potential lawbreakers, and to see the enforcement of the general will as springing from a preponderance of power of the former over the latter. It is more in accord with our theory to develop the idea of norm enforcement from a group with similar psyches and similar utility scales.

Third, in line with the previous discussion, it seems to be too severe a condition to require that a group have either a high proportion of its members with strong superegos, or a low level of conflict between ego and superego, for norms to become operative. Many—perhaps most—stable groups do not appear to meet either of these conditions.

It must be noted that the idea of conflict between ego and superego has been used in two senses, first as a divergence of preference, as expressed in their utility scales (theory of decisions), and second as an actual struggle between the two (psychoanalytic theory). That the two do not necessarily go together can perhaps be illustrated by an analogy. It is possible, for example, for two people to have strong differences in preferences and still not enter into a struggle with each other. For example, suppose that a husband strongly prefers to vacation in the mountains, while his wife equally strongly prefers the seashore. It is conceivable that their difference could be settled amicably, without bitterness or dispute on either side. On the other hand, a married couple can engage in the most bitter dispute about the most trifling difference of preference. Everything depends on the basic relations between the two. It is the same for the relation between ego and superego. In fact, as has been pointed out, differences in preference between ego and superego regularly lead to a rather bitter internal struggle, even in well-integrated psyches. In these circumstances, any choice will have a relatively low utility because of the substantial psychic costs involved.

In short, our illustrative matrices (figs. 17–21) have not yet taken into account two conditions which psychoanalytic theory tells us will be very common: weak superegos and sharp internal struggles between ego and superego. We will allow for these factors by taking the illustrative ego and superego scales, introduced earlier, and forming an actual will, first by assigning less weight to the superego scale (0.2), and second by lowering the utility of the result in accordance with the degree of conflict between the two scales (assuming, for simplicity, that actual psychic conflict is commensurate with this). Arbitrarily, we will subtract 0.2 units from the utility of each state for each unit of divergence between ego and superego preferences. Assuming, as before, a 0.125 positive identification among the members, their actual wills will then be as given in figure 22.

	Both Others Obey	One Other Obeys	Both Others Disobey
Obey	5.000	4.375	2.750
Disobey	5.550	4.975	3.200

Fig. 22. Actual wills of A, B, and C: Solution is disobedience

In contrast to figure 19, which, it will be recalled, was produced by giving a weight of 0.5 to both the private-will matrix in figure 18 and the general-will matrix in figure 17, the dominant strategy in figure 22 is disobedience. This difference is accounted for as follows: The positive ego identifications among the members and the costs of psychic conflict both tend to reinforce the general will. These factors, however, are overbalanced by the reduction of the weight of the general will (superego strength) to 0.2. The result is disobedience to the general will.

Having introduced assumptions that are more realistic in principle (although arbitrary in actual numerical value), we are now in a position to consider the possibility of sanctions. Following the previous discussion, assume that any two members will be able to apply a sanction of −4 utility units on the third. In figure 22, it is to the interest of each that the others obey the rule; hence it is reasonable to assume that an attempt by one member to disobey will be met by a coalition of the other two, enforcing obedience. Or suppose that A and B enter into a coalition to disobey and force C to obey. This coalition will provide a result with utilities of $A = 4.75$, $B = 4.75$, $C = 2.4$. At that point, C can arrange a coalition with A to enforce the rule on B, since both will gain thereby. The outcome will be $A = 5.1$, $B = 4.15$, and $C = 4.15$. But at that point, B and C

will form a coalition against *A*, so that all three must now obey, with an outcome of 5 for each.

Such a process may produce conformity to norms in matrices where *every* member of the group would, apart from sanctions, prefer to disobey than to obey. What is required is that the members prefer that others conform. This factor does not seem sufficiently general, however, to provide a full theoretical explanation for social conformity. It is possible to think of many matrices where the required coalition formation would not occur, or where the outcome is not clear. For example, take the actual will for all three members to be as represented in figure 23.

	Both Others Obey	One Other Obeys	Both Others Disobey
Obey	3	2	1
Disobey	6	5	4

Fig. 23. Actual wills of *A*, *B*, and *C*: Sanctions produce obedience

Assuming that each adopts his dominant strategy (i.e., disobedience), the outcome will be $A = 4, B = 4, C = 4$. Now *A* and *B* might form a sanctioning coalition against *C*, producing an outcome of $A = 5, B = 5, C = 1$. Next, *C* would band with *A* against *B* (since both would gain), producing the outcome $A = 6, B = 2, C = 2$. Finally, *B* and *C* would turn against *A*, producing the outcome $A = 3, B = 3, C = 3$, which presumably would be stable, since disobedience would produce a counter coalition. Still, the result appears rather paradoxical; all three would be better off with the original solution of 4, 4, 4. Matrices of this kind have received considerable study.

The above mechanism fails entirely where each is indifferent to whether the others obey the rule, or prefers that the others disobey. What is needed is a theory which will explain general conformity to norms in a wide range of circumstances—from strong to weak, or integrated to nonintegrated superegos, and from high to low ego-superego conflict—for a wide range of different matrix configurations; that is, it is desirable to find the most general possible explanation.

Such a solution emerges if we apply the psychoanalytic theory of identification in a more thorough way to the matrices under consideration.

It will be recalled that it was assumed, first, that the group members identify with each other in their egos, and, second, that rather sharp ego-superego conflicts exist in their psyches, which substantially reduce the utility of *any* course of action. Let us now look at the relation of A to B. The superego of A is in rather sharp conflict with his ego. It reacts punitively toward the ego. Since A identifies in his ego with B, his superego will have the same feelings toward B that it has toward himself. Hence, the identification with B is ambivalent. On the one hand, A's ego sides with B's ego in its wish to evade the oppressive superego code, while, on the other hand, A's superego is filled with anger at what he believes to be B's wishes.

From a psychological point of view, an excellent solution to A's internal psychic conflict will occur if B in his actions violates the general will and A reacts punitively by applying sanctions. In the first place, B's violation will produce vicarious satisfaction to A's ego. By identification, he participates in the forbidden act. Second, the punishment satisfies the superego's need for punitive action. As a consequence, A's internal psychic conflict is sharply reduced, and the utility of any course of action increased. This is the well-known mechanism of the externalization of psychic conflict. It has often been adduced as an explanation for the hostility that exists between members of different groups. In such instances, repressed desires of the members of one group are attributed to the members of the other group and hence find, through identification, a vicarious outlet. At the same time, on the conscious level, an angry, aggressive, punitive attitude is taken toward the members of the other group, allowing internal self-aggression to be displaced outward. Internal psychic conflict is thereby reduced. There appears to be no reason why such a mechanism cannot operate within a social group, as well as between members of different groups.

In short, the violation of a group norm, followed by the application of a negative sanction (punishment) on the violator may result in a sharp gain of utility for the sanctioner. This gain can come from several sources:

1. the pleasure felt by the superego in enforcing its standards

2. the gratification achieved by the direct outlet afforded the aggressive instincts

3. the gain to the ego by the displacement of the punitive thrust of the superego outward

4. the vicarious pleasure (through identification) to the ego at the sight of the violation

5. the lessening of internal psychic conflict, and hence the lessening of the anxiety created by this conflict

The psychic gain produced by the exercise of sanctions can be expected to vary according to two factors:

1. The closer the identification the higher the gain. If the application of a sanction results in a gain of utility for a given degree of identification, the gain will be higher for a closer identification. But if the application of sanctions results in a net loss of utility to the sanctioner, the loss might be greater for a closer identification. This would be so, for example, if the utility loss largely resulted (by identification) from the loss imposed by the sanction on the one sanctioned.

2. The greater the conflict between the private will and the general will, the greater the gain. The punishment of social transgressions committed by others permits the conflicted psyche to have its cake and eat it too. The greater the conflict, the greater the relief afforded by the punishment of others.

At first glance it may appear that we will find the most reliable obedience to the general will in groups whose members have the strongest and most securely internalized superegos, coupled with a high degree of harmony and integration between ego and superego. Our theory indicates that this need not be true, and that, on the contrary, stricter conformity may occur where the very opposite conditions prevail. The only psychological requirements for stable social organization are that the ego identifications among the group members be relatively strong, and that their superegos be sufficiently developed to produce a high psychic cost for internal conflict. Within these very broad boundaries, stable social organization can occur among groups between which and within which the members exhibit the greatest diversity of psychological constellations. In human groups, stable social organization should be expected as a matter of course. It is social *dis*organization and social change which require explanation.

Note that it is not being argued here that crime is automatically prevented by fear of punishment. On the contrary, it seems that the existence of crime is most helpful in creating the bonds which hold groups together. We may even expect to find social devices for encouraging deviation.[2] It is not the deterrence of punishment which holds groups together, but the cohesion of the punishers, and the inner acceptance by all of the validity of the norms and the rightfulness of the punishment. There is a saying that to lock one's door is to protect oneself from honest men only.

In conclusion, if we examine the psychological ties that bind groups into cooperative units, we are presented with a continuum. At one pole we have a group whose members have relatively strong superegos, relatively well integrated with their egos. Here it is the force of the general will alone, and its harmony with the individual's ego, which secures compliance. At the other pole, we have a group with relatively weak superegos, rela-

2. Menninger (1968); Dentler (1959).

tively poorly integrated with their egos. Here cooperation is secured through the psychic gains which result from banding together against real or imagined violations of the group code.

If the foregoing speculative account of the basis of social cohesion is granted, a number of conclusions follow:

1. The distinction developed in the previous chapter between social control and authority has been placed on a firmer basis. Social control may now be defined as the influence of the general will. Authority, as legitimate power, is a form of influence in which the legitimacy of the group norm in the superegos of the group members, and the impulse to employ sanctions on others, even by those on whom themselves the influence of the general will is not strong, combine to produce conformity.

2. The strength (degree of influence) of the group norms is not measured by the comparative strength of the superegos, nor by the lack of psychic conflict between the superegos and the egos of the group members, nor finally by the lack of conflict between the private wills of the group members. As long as the group norm is fully internalized, the mechanism described here is sufficient to produce high social conformity even when—

a. the superego is only moderately powerful in influencing behavior;

b. there is a relatively sharp conflict between superego and ego;

c. there is a relatively sharp conflict of interest among the private wills of the group members.

Social conformity is thus no measure of psychic health (integration of superego and ego), nor of an underlying harmony of interest between group members. Perhaps a better index of the psychic health of a group system could be found in the rationality and humaneness of the criminal code (whether formal or informal) and the absence of scapegoats.

3. Individual deviance from group norms presents an ambivalent picture. It would oversimplify the matter to look to incompletely carried through superego formation, incompletely

internalized norms, or sharp superego-ego conflicts as the main causes of violation of group norms. While such factors might be expected to operate, it should not be overlooked that the presence or threat of criminal action serves to tie the group together. Hence, there may be social devices which encourage criminal behavior as long as such behavior can be kept within bounds. The individual deviant represents on the one hand a threat to the social fabric, and on the other hand a means of maintaining it.

4. The principal threat to the successful operation of cooperative groups thus seems, not to be the individual violation of the norm, but the generation of subgroups, whose conflicts with each other might endanger the overall unity. The problem of successful social organization (as against beneficent social organization) is thus not the problem of the individual versus society—the problem of how the individual is to be motivated to do what his society requires—but rather the sociological and political problem of how a complex social system can be organized so that its subgroups cooperate with one another sufficiently to maintain the social whole. It does not deny the importance of psychological modes of explanation to assert that the basic unit of sociological and political analysis is the group, not the individual.

G. *Role Differentiation and the General Will*

1. While a full treatment of role differentiation must await the next volume, some preliminary considerations will be undertaken here in order to clarify the nature of the underlying relationships involved in stable groups.

There are three basic *human* relations: love, hate, and identification. Far from being mutually exclusive, these three elements are normally intermingled in various and often complex ways. Love and hate regularly involve identification; indeed it seems to be an essential part of the process whereby these attachments are formed. In addition, identification normally carries with it a libidinal or aggressive attachment, often both together.

These three elements do not of course form the exclusive content of relations between persons. Love is not the only libidinal relation, nor hate the only aggressive one. A libidinal or aggressive attachment need not involve identification; for example, such relations can be established purely, or at least partly, for the pleasure that attends the object relation. In this case the relation is that of person to object, as distinct from person to person. It is impersonal. In addition, relations between persons may have a purely instrumental component, where the meaning of the relationship is that the other person serves as a means, and to this extent there is no object relation at all. It may be doubted that a purely impersonal or instrumental relation between persons actually exists. Still, this component may be large. In formal organizations, where the interactions are not frequent and not intense, the human relations may be diluted, and the impersonal and instrumental aspects play a large role. Yet in all groups love, hate, and identification are always present, making up the basic relations, even if at certain times and for the purpose of certain analyses they may recede into the background.

Such, in any event, is my thesis, which rests not only on psychoanalytic theory but also on an examination of the modern mathematical theory of human interaction. The latter point rests on three main arguments: first, that utility theory presupposes that the actor is a person with a coherent self, and that such a person can only develop through a social process in which identification with others is an indispensable element; second, that stable cooperation presupposes a real general will, which develops from a network of identifications; third, that hate can bind men as strongly together as love.

It is important to understand that all three relationships—love, hate, and identification—hold groups together. Love and hate, of course, do not always bring men together—the exclusiveness of love and the bitterness of hate often drive men apart. Still, taken together, they form the glue of social cohesion.

It follows from the above arguments that not only cooperative groups but also the roles which persons play in these groups are to be defined and understood in terms of their basic human relations. I will here treat only two broad categories of social roles, peer relationships and authority relationships, which spring from sibling and parent-child relations, respectively.

2. As Aristotle already saw clearly, the central idea in peer relations is that of equality. "Equal," he says, "but equal with respect to what?" That is a large question, but here we are concerned only with the psychological origin of the idea, rather than with an exploration of its varieties. In the family, the equality of the siblings arises from their common relationship to the parents. They spring from the same flesh and blood and hence are bound to identify with each other. If the parents apply the same treatment to each of the children, their superego formations are likely to be similar: they share the same values. If the parents love and esteem the children equally, they will tend, through parental identification, to love and esteem each other equally. Brotherhood has its roots in common parenthood; that much is obvious.

Yet siblings are always jealous of each other; they are natural and inevitable rivals for parental affection and esteem. Freud describes how this jealousy is transformed into mutual identification and the passion for equality.

> The elder child would certainly like to put his successor jealously aside, to keep it away from the parents and to rob it of all its privileges; but in face of the fact that this child (like all that come later) is loved by the parents in just the same way, and in consequence of the impossibility of maintaining its hostile attitude without damaging itself, it is forced into identifying itself with the other children. So there grows up in the troop of children a communal or group feeling, which is then further developed at school. The first demand made by this reaction-formulation is

for justice, for equal treatment for all. . . . If one cannot be the favorite oneself in all events nobody else shall be the favorite. This transformation—the replacing of jealousy by a group feeling in the nursery and the classroom—might be considered impossible, if the same process could not later on be observed again in other circumstances. . . .

What appears later on in society in the shape of *Gemeingeist*, *esprit de corps* "group spirit," etc., does not belie its derivation from what was originally envy. No one must want to put himself forward, everyone must be the same and have the same. Social justice means that we deny ourselves many things so that others may have to do without them as well, or, what is the same thing, may not be able to ask for them. This demand for equality is the root of social consciousness and the sense of duty. . . .

Thus social feeling is based upon the reversal of what was first a hostile feeling into a positively-toned tie of the nature of an identification. . . . Many equals who can identify themselves with one another, and a single person superior to them all—that is the situation that we find realized in groups which are capable of subsisting.[3]

The fact that identification can have its source in hostile feelings throws additional light on why a leaderless group must be regarded as a transient polar type. A group of peers, ungoverned by a parent, will be impelled to create a common parental authority. The necessity springs from the anxieties attendant upon the aggressive feelings that peer relationships create. The individual's own superego reacts strongly against the aggressive feelings; it is necessary to overcome them. In this situation, the formation of superego identifications within the group reinforces the individual's own superego by opposing these aggressive tendencies and replacing them with the demand for equality.

There is, however, a difficulty. The peer-group situation is especially susceptible to factionalism, because this is psychologically a very economical way of handling the conflicts endemic

3. Freud (1921), pp. 120–21.

to peer relations. Within the faction, the strongest bonds of solidarity can be observed, precisely because the sentiments of hostility can be diverted onto the opposing faction or factions. The conflicting sentiments of love and hate can thus be separated and channeled in different and nonconflicting directions. When the father is absent, the brothers will start fighting; not, as Hobbes would have it, each with all, but rather one faction against the other. (This reinforces the previous point—that the group, not the individual, is the main unit of political and social analysis.) As a consequence, quite apart from environmental pressures, the successful organization of a peer group seems to require the establishment of authority relations within the group: Leadership must emerge. Yet the authoritative leader *within* the peer group appears to be a contradiction in terms, for the leader is no longer a peer. A logical solution is for leadership to emerge in the image of the older brother. The older brother possesses, more than the others, the mantle of parental authority. He is, in Freud's phrase, a "father surrogate,"[4] especially if he exemplifies the ideal group member in his behavior. He is the equal brother charged with maintaining the absent parental authority. The common image of the ideal group member now has a particular individual around which it can coalesce and from whom it can gain support.

The authority of the elder brother in the peer group, however, is never fully that of the father. He must remain a peer. His methods of securing compliance are those of example, cajolery, friendship, persuasion; he cannot simply command and expect obedience, for to do so would be not only to accept the mantle but to usurp the throne.

As evidence of this view of the relations involved in peer groups and the nature of the authority system which develops within them, we submit the history of legislative organization in general, and the seniority system in the United States Congress in particular.

4. Ibid., p. 94.

3. The authority relationship, that of superior to subordinate, ruler to ruled, has its psychological origins in the relationship of father to son. The bulk of the psychoanalytically oriented
literature on such authority relations has been hostile to them.
The word "authority" slides easily into "authoritarian," which
is implicitly or explicitly rejected as "unhealthy," or "imma-
ture."[5] This is opposed to "democratic" relationships, where no
one exercises authority over anyone else, and a "healthy" political system is held to be composed of peers only, who set policy
in a brotherly way by mutual discussion and compromise. We do
not propose to undertake a critique of this view, except to point
out that in actual group relations, especially political ones, we
almost always find that the few rule and the many are ruled, and
that this is just as true of democratic groups as of authoritarian
ones. Indeed, even if in some distant future authority relations
become no longer psychologically necessary, the complex requirements of social organization seem to dictate some cen-
tralization of decision making in organized groups, and hence
the need for the relationship of ruler to ruled. It is thus a question, not of whether this relationship is justified, but rather what
form it shall take.

In its pure form, the authority relation of subordinate to
superior is one of superego identification. The follower seeks not
so much to be like the leader but to do what he says. This point
must not be carried too far, of course. The original identification with the father normally takes place in the pre-Oedipal
period, when ego and superego are not yet differentiated, and
the relationship is regularly one of a kind of idealized ego identification. To a certain extent the leader is not only to be obeyed,
but imitated, and the line between the two ideas may not always
be sharp. Still, it is an essential feature of the authority relation
that the distinction between leader and led be sharply drawn; a
certain emotional distance must be maintained. The ranking

5. For example, this idea creeps into the Adorno (1950) study.

order must be clear and firm; privilege and prerogative are essential attributes of office.

While the son identifies with the father in his superego, the father identifies with his son in his ego. This means that his attitude toward his son replicates the relation within his psyche of ego to superego. He wishes the son to behave according to his own standards and rewards obedience with love and approval, disobedience with anger and punishment. There may be a more or less strong subsidiary theme; the father may secretly encourage in the son the rebelliousness against authority which he himself (perhaps unconsciously) feels but does not allow himself to express.[6]

These patterns of subordination and superordination may of course take a thousand different forms, depending on the particular shape that the psyches of the individuals take. What has been outlined is only the central core of a common configuration.

When transferred from the family onto broader group connections, this authority relation works out as follows: The superego formations of both leader and followers will be more or less similar. These superego contents define the general will of the group, which dictates how the members are to behave and establishes different behavior patterns for leader and led. The leader is strong, decisive; his word is law. He treats his subordinates firmly but fairly and equally, showing no favoritism. Behavior according to his standards is rewarded; disobedience or nonperformance punished. He can show warmth both in affection and in anger, but this is tempered by his insistence on a certain emotional distance, for his superior rank and privileges must at all times be respected. The follower is obedient, respectful. He imitates his leader, but moderately, so as not to challenge the underlying difference of rank. The leader is idealized —his strengths emphasized, his weaknesses minimized or over-

6. Erikson (1950), p. 293.

looked. The follower shows only as much initiative as is allowed.

The above description assumes well-internalized and strong superego formations on the part of both leader and led, and a relative lack of integration between ego and superego. Where this is not the case, the relationship will be different. For example, insecurity of ego controls can give a harsh, angry, and demeaning quality to the behavior of the leader, who demands utter servility by the led, and perhaps secretly encourages its opposite, outright rebellion. This is typical of the so-called authoritarian character. Or, through a holdover of the original Oedipal conflict, the leader may have difficulty in accepting his role and may seek to deny his position by belittling, covering over, or minimizing his difference of rank. Since he is hesitant about asserting his leadership, he will be slow to move, sensitive to opposition. His guilt feelings about the exercise of power will lead him to deny its existence and to try to dissolve political relations into good feeling and consensus. This is the so-called democratic leader, singled out as particularly healthy by some writers,[7] but whose behavior in fact rests on an incomplete resolution of the Oedipal conflict.

Thus, according to the psychological content of the relationship, one can distinguish three types of leadership, which might be termed paternalistic, authoritarian, and democratic. It is doubtless possible to distinguish other types. Attempts to label one or another of these types as psychologically better, more mature, or healthier than another must be viewed with caution. In fact, as has been pointed out, all forms of social authority rest on pregenital emotional levels.

This preliminary discussion of social organization has been

7. The most solid work in the field, the Adorno study, is careful not to label a definite personality type as "democratic." But the use of the term "anti-democratic" to designate high scorers on their scales invites the term "pro-democratic" for the low scorers. Adorno (1950), pp. 771–83. Note the idealization of the "genuine liberal," ibid., pp. 781–83. This type, the authors say, "may be conceived in terms of that balance between superego, ego and id which Freud deemed ideal." No citation is given.

introduced to show how the general will not only supplies the overall moral code of the social group but also assigns specific roles to different positions within the group, and to indicate how the psychological content of the resulting relations is derived from earlier constellations within the family.

We do not wish to leave the impression that social groups and organizations are nothing but extended families. As will be explained presently, in its broadest outlines our theory will seek to explain social and political behavior as the result of the interactions of two basic sets of independent variables, psychological and technical or material. At present we are exploring the former set, and by necessity the latter is temporarily in the background.

IO

ECONOMIC AUTHORITY

AND ECONOMIC POWER

W E MOVE NOW to the further development of our typology
of influence by distinguishing kinds of authority and social power. The treatment of economic authority and economic
power will be brief, serving mainly to distinguish the political
realm from the economic and to amplify and illustrate the distinction between authority and social power.[1]

Economic activity is often defined as the production and
distribution of goods and services, a good or service being anything which has value and is scarce. The term "scarcity," however, does not constitute much of a restriction over and above
the term "value," while value may in the vocabulary employed
here be taken to mean utility. Thus economic action, as the production and distribution of utilities, seems difficult to distinguish
from human action in general; and, correspondingly, the economic system of society seems to comprise nearly the entire
social system. "Economics" has sometimes been used in this
broad sense, like the older term "political economy" and modern
theories of action which have been derived from economic
theory, such as the theory of games, econometrics, and praxiol-

1. The following discussion owes much to Davis (1948), pp. 451–76.

ogy. This is of course purely a question of nomenclature, and since we are here concerned with delimiting subsystems within society, such a broad usage will not be employed.

Examination of the question when a human being is considered a good or service (a commodity) in the economic sense leads to the definitions adopted here. A slave is generally considered a commodity, while a free person is not. The distinction lies in the fact that a slave is owned by someone; he is the property of someone, while a freeman is not. This suggests the definition of economic action as the production, distribution, and use of property (as against commodities). It is by now generally accepted that persons should not constitute property; that there is a moral difference between the relation of a person to another person and a person to a thing. The distinction between persons and things is central to the theory being developed here, for only a person is capable of action, and the central relations of love, hate, and identification have been defined as uniquely human. Slavery is thus to be condemned because its foundation is the false assumption that a human being is not a person.

Property is a right of use or disposition of a commodity (a thing which possesses utility). What distinguishes a property right from other rights is its unilateral nature—the thing which is owned has, in turn, no rights. In contrast to a right over a thing, a right over another person is always reciprocal; the other person has rights of his own. There is no right over a person without obligations to him.[2]

It must quickly be added that property rights are actually relations between persons with respect to a commodity. They hence involve reciprocity, like any other right. We may express this by saying that persons are the subjects of property rights (as with any other rights), while commodities (not persons) are the objects of such rights. For example, ownership of a commodity defines a set of rights and obligations between the owner and other persons, with respect to the commodity.

2. This point is associated with Green (1895), pp. 29–48.

This distinction between economic and noneconomic relations may be illustrated by the example of a wage contract between an entrepreneur and a worker. The contract is clearly economic in that it involves the transferal of money from the entrepreneur to the worker; in addition, by virtue of the contract and the laws of property, the entrepreneur owns the product of the worker's labor. But the contract seems to have a noneconomic element in that, although the worker is a person, the entrepreneur has the right to direct the activity of the worker in certain ways. This, however, is handled by making the distinction between the worker as a person, and his labor as a commodity. By the contract, the entrepreneur owns this commodity (the worker's labor) and may direct its use. To this, it may be objected that any right or obligation can be so treated, and hence the distinction between rights over things and rights over persons is lost. But this is just the point; it is possible for persons themselves to be treated as commodities, as in slavery. It is precisely whether someone or something is treated as a subject or as an object of rights that marks the distinction between noneconomic and economic rights.

This principle allows us to determine when an exchange is an economic act, although the line may be thin at times. For example, suppose two senators trade votes. The exchange is economic only if votes are treated as property. If that is so, then Senator A has in some sense acquired the vote of Senator B, and vice versa. But this is illegal—the right of voting cannot be transferred—hence according to law the trade is not an economic exchange, because the vote is not property. Suppose, however, that the informal organization of the Senate has created a real general will, specific to that body, whose operation can be discerned in the informal organization. If one of the rules of this informally organized general will is that vote-trading agreements must be honored, and if mechanisms of enforcement exist, then trading votes becomes an economic transaction, at least in an extended sense.

Property as a set of rights and obligations among persons with respect to the production, distribution, or use of commodities rests on the general will of the group in which the system of property exists. In primitive societies, the relationship is direct: the social norms define property relations. For societies with highly developed legal systems, the relations between the general will and the law of property are more complex. In general, the law of property is supported by the general will, and much of its content may reflect the general will. Clarification of this point must await a fuller treatment of the relations between the general will and the legal system.

Economic authority is the power to exercise economic right. When A has economic authority with respect to a commodity, he has available a strategy which if chosen will result in the exercise of the right he has with respect to the commodity. Here, however, we must make a distinction. Assume that the right in question is the right to sell. Normally this does not mean that A has the right to require B to buy (although that could be the case, for example, if they had signed a contract to that effect), but rather that, if someone wishes to buy, A has the right to transfer ownership. In this instance, when we say that there is a strategy whereby A can sell, we do not imply that there must be a buyer, but rather that if there is a buyer, then A will be able to exercise his right to sell.

Economic activity rests on two factors: first, the recognition of the right as legitimate by society; and second, the sanctions that society (or the State or both) will bring to bear in support of the right.

The common-sense statement "X is the property of A" can mean one of two things: first, that A has economic rights with respect to X; or second, that A has economic authority with respect to X. The ideas of right and authority are sometimes used interchangeably, as if right automatically leads to authority. This is the same confusion that arises when one speaks of the "powers" of the presidency defined by the constitution; the president may not have the power to put these "powers" into effect. It is important to distinguish, for example, between the right to keep trespassers off one's property and the actual ability to enforce this right (the authority to keep trespassers off).

Another confusion may arise with respect to the value (or utility) of a commodity and the utility of the authority over the commodity. A commodity has been defined as any valuable scarce thing; that is, its use or possession (in the physical sense) has utility. As a consequence, the authority to use the commodity also has a utility, as will the right of use, to the extent that the right confers authority. What authority confers is the option of use, and the utility of a fully secure authority to use seems in general to be at least as great if not greater than the utility of the use itself.

The critical and defining aspect of economic exchange is the exchange of economic right. The transfer of actual possession is secondary and indeed may not occur. Hence, the price of a commodity is the price of the right of use. We are not here drawing the well-known distinction between use value and exchange value of a commodity, at least as the terms are used by modern economists. A little reflection will show that the exchange value of a commodity is the price of the right to use a commodity—that is, the price of ownership—while the use value is the utility of ownership. The theory of marginal utility asserts a relationship between the price and the utility of ownership, namely, that within certain boundary conditions, for a small increment of the commodity, the price of ownership (exchange value) will equal the utility of ownership (use value).

We are after a different point here: that, as one can distinguish between a commodity and the right to use (ownership of) a commodity, so one can also distinguish between the utility of a commodity and the utility of ownership of a commodity. Further, we are suggesting that the utility of ownership may be greater than the utility of the use of the commodity itself, because the right itself can sometimes be put to uses which the commodity cannot. A clear example is paper money, which as a commodity has little or no value. The value of money springs from the fact that its ownership confers the authority to exchange it for the ownership of valuable commodities.[3]

Economic authority rests on sanctions. In addition, such authority can in certain interactions *be* a sanction. The use of economic authority as a sanction constitutes an exercise of economic power.

Perhaps some examples will make these points clear. Suppose that a farmer owns a field and a tractor and, by using them, grows corn. The process of the production of corn is not economic but agricultural. We are here in the technical or technological level. The process is described in terms of the organic composition of the soil, the biology of plants, the mechanics of internal combustion engines, etc. We are on the same level if the farmer makes bread with the corn and eats it; here we describe the chemistry of baking and the biology of digestion. We are describing the production and use of a commodity.

Now suppose that the farmer sells his corn at the market. The process whereby the corn is transported to the market, stored, shipped to the baker, baked, and eaten by the consumer remains on the technical level. But something has been added—the technical process of shipping the corn to the market has been accompanied by an economic interaction, namely, transferal of ownership of the corn. We now notice that the earlier agricultural activity was also accompanied by an economic event, the process whereby the farmer acquired ownership of the corn. This ownership was not totally unrelated to the technical process, for the fact that this tractor and this land were used is indispensable. The critical factor, however, was not the technical process but the legal relationship between the farmer and the tractor and the land, for, by law, since he owns them, he owns

3. While the distinction developed here is not the modern distinction between use value and exchange value, we feel it may be not far from the original distinction drawn by Smith (1776), p. 28.

their product. In the same way, the sale of the corn had only a secondary (and in some cases dispensable) relation to the transportation of the corn to the market. It was not the corn which was exchanged, but the ownership of the corn.

We are in effect asserting that Robinson Crusoe's island had no economy. Crusoe possessed certain things, but he did not own them, because ownership is a relation between persons with respect to a commodity, and there was no one with whom such a relationship could exist. Only when Friday arrived could an economy be established. For this to occur, Friday and Robinson Crusoe must form a social group with a real general will which states who owns what, and in what circumstances.

To return to our farmer, if someone asks his permission to cross his field, he may rightfully refuse. If someone is on his field, he may rightfully order him off. This right is validated by the law, and behind the law the general will of society. In a contest of power with a trespasser, the farmer can call the police to his aid, and behind the police stands the entire organized might of society. All this involves an exercise or use of authority which the farmer possesses over a trespasser relative to his land. Notice that the authority itself does not constitute a sanction; rather it is backed by sanctions.

On the other hand, suppose that the farmer negotiates a contract to plow his neighbor's field with his tractor. In the process of this negotiation, the terms will be influenced not only by the technical properties of the tractor (how effective it is in plowing the field) but also by the fact of his ownership. Presumably he would not be able to negotiate the contract if he did not own the tractor. In this instance, the ownership (authority to use) is a sanction which enables the farmer to influence the other to enter into the contract. Hence the farmer exercises economic power (as distinct from economic authority) over the other person while negotiating the contract.

Or assume that the farmer has proposed marriage to a woman, and she wishes to know if he will be able to support her.

The farmer replies, "I own this field and this tractor and will be able to use them to support us." The farmer has no economic authority over the woman at all. His ownership of the field and the tractor do not create any rights or obligations between them, except that she may not cross his field without his permission, etc. His ownership, however, gives him a lever which he can use in his attempt to persuade her to marry him. If this lever (sanction) influences her choice, then he has exercised economic power over her.

Finally, to take a more typical and theoretically crucial instance, suppose that the farmer is engaged in the sale of the tractor. The price he will get will depend on the technical capabilities of the tractor. But he will not be able to sell it at all if he does not own it. What is exchanged is ownership of the tractor for ownership of a sum of money. The farmer wants money, and in order to induce the buyer to give him the money he offers the ownership of the tractor in return. The farmer's ownership of the tractor and its potential transfer constitute a positive sanction over the buyer, which induces him to give the farmer the money in exchange. The transaction is thus an exchange of ownership of tractor for ownership of money which takes place because each constitutes a positive sanction to the other. The transaction is hence an interaction of economic power between the farmer and the buyer. To generalize, while the lawyer and the sociologist study economic authority, the economist studies economic power.

In most instances, the scope of economic authority is rather sharply defined. The owner of a commodity may do only certain things with respect to the commodity; he has only certain specific rights over others with respect to the commodity. Especially in societies with a well developed legal system, it is possible to state the contents of economic authority with precision. In contrast, the scope of economic power, especially in capitalist or semicapitalist societies, can be indefinitely broad. In general, it appears to have the widest range of application of any of the forms of social power.

In conclusion, it may help the reader to understand the views presented here if they are briefly compared with those of Marx. Our term "technical level," or "technological capabilities," corresponds to Marx's "forces of production," but it is broader, including distribution and use. Our term "economic authority" corresponds to Marx's "production relations." Marx was not entirely clear on this point, but we take his "relations of production" to refer at least primarily to the legal relations that men enter into in production, and hence to designate economic authority. As the course of the argument of this work indicates, we would deny that economic authority springs solely from the technological system, although the influence is undoubtedly very great.

Finally, Marx's view that power in society springs from the relations of production asserts, in the language of our theory, that all social power springs from economic authority. Our own view is that economic power springs from economic authority, political power from political authority, military power from military authority, etc. So far, we have not advanced any views on whether one or another of these forms of authority is basic, in the sense that the others derive from it.

11/

GOVERNMENT

A. *Definition*

SINCE POLITICS IS an aspect of government, our treatment of political authority and political power must be postponed until we have examined what constitutes government of a group and distinguished various types of government.

The term "government" has two distinct meanings. The first and most familiar meaning refers to the direction or regulation of any process according to the purposive intelligence of an actor or set of actors. In other words, we are dealing with a system of action, and the influence of the actors on the field of interaction constitutes the government of that field.

The second sense of the term asserts that the activity of a system exhibits regularity which can be stated in terms of some general principle which is then said to "govern" the system. Thus the activity of the solar system is "governed" by the laws of celestial mechanics.

The two senses appear quite distinct, but they were not always felt to be so, and there is indeed a connection. The word "government" has its roots in the Greek *kybernan* ("to steer," or, broadly, "to govern"). This is also the root of the term

"cybernetics."[1] A cybernetic system is "self-governing" in that
its behavior is regulated by devices internal to the system. Although this government is nonpurposive, a cybernetic system
acts "as if" it were regulated by a purpose, as do many systems
in nature—a colony of bees, for example, or indeed anything
at all that can be described as an equilibrium system.[2]

We can preserve the similarity of meaning of the two senses
of government, while retaining the distinction, by designating
the purpose or seeming purpose of the system as its *function*
and then distinguishing two kinds of functioning, purposive
and nonpurposive, teleological and nonteleological, or, to use
Merton's phrase, manifest and latent function.[3] For reasons
set out in the introductory chapter, we will in this volume take
"government" to mean a form of purposive regulation.

What is distinctive about government, and sets it off from
other forms of action, is that what is chosen is not a strategy,
but a strategy set. Up to now our theory of action has assumed
that each individual chooses only his own strategy. His choice
or possible choices may influence the choices of others, but
each individual chooses his own strategy.

It should be intuitively evident that this idea is not sufficient to account for the activity of deliberately organized
groups. In such groups, choice occurs in two stages. First there
is a choice which prescribes a strategy for each member of the
group. This choice is a *governmental decision*, and the prescribed set of strategies constitutes a *governmental program*.
Second, each member chooses (or does not choose) the strategy
defined for him by the governmental decision.

For the process of government to occur, governmental decisions must be effective, that is, the individual choices must be
in accord with the governmental choices. Our theory so far

1. Santillana stresses the fundamental importance of this idea of "government" to all science. Santillana (1961), chap. 2, esp. p. 39.

2. Wiener (1948), pp. 113–36.

3. Merton (1949), pp. 21–81.

has laid the groundwork for an examination of the question of how and when government is effective.

It is obvious that governmental organization can often make possible an enormous increment of utility for every member of a group. In practice, however, government often (perhaps almost always) benefits some members more than others, and different governmental programs may have highly different consequences in this respect. Indeed, the net impact of government may be harmful to some group members. Hobbes's point, that the absence of any government is worst of all for everyone, loses force if we take into account the possibility of the informal (not deliberately planned) regulation of group activity by a general will. In this volume we are concerned, however, with an assessment, not an evaluation, of the institutions of government.

B. *Self-government*

The question is, whose purpose regulates the activity of a group which is governed? In the first instance, the purpose may be common to the entire group, that is, in principle, to every member. Such regulation by, or according to, a common purpose will be called "self-government." When self-government occurs, the group itself, as distinct from an individual or set of individuals, can be said to be the actor. We are hence moving on to a new stage in our theory of action, from individual action to group action. The reasons why the idea of a group acting is not metaphorical, but must be taken in a literal sense, will emerge from the following discussion.

Earlier it was pointed out that "purpose" contains two ideas, "aim" and "object." The aim of any action is always the same, the satisfaction of the actor. By definition, two actors cannot have a common aim. The term "common purpose," then, must refer to a common object of action or choice, that is, to common preferences among states or variables of the field.

Let y_n and y_m be any two values of a variable (**y**) of the field. If two actors both prefer y_n to y_m, their purposes will be said to be identical with respect to these two values of this variable. If one prefers y_m to y_n, while the other prefers y_n to y_m, their purposes will be said to be conflicting with respect to these two values, while if one has no preference or both have no preference (are indifferent), their purposes will be said to be "independent."

This definition expresses the theoretical link between preference and purpose already established by Bernouli's law, which states that a person will always act (with the purpose) to maximize his expected utility. Since we are now examining the purposes of A and B, we can specify their power relations more fully than in the earlier chapter, where the treatment was confined to an examination of the capabilities of A and B, without regard to their purposes.

Suppose that y_n and y_m are the only two aspects of the field which are significant to the utilities of A and B. Suppose, further, that A prefers y_n and B prefers y_m. If y_n is in the range of A's relative power, then, being rational, he will choose y_n, which will then be the result. On the other hand, if y_m is within the range of B's power, he will choose it, and y_m will occur. If their purposes conflict, therefore, it cannot be simultaneously true that y_n is in the range of A's power, and y_m in the range of B's. It may be, of course, that neither has power relative to his preferred alternative. Barring that, the result depends on the comparative power of the two. We will express this by saying that if y_n is the result, A has power over B with respect to their conflict of purpose relative to the value of **y**.

Suppose now that their interests coincide; that both prefer y_n. In that case, if y_n is in the range of power of either, it is in the range of power of both. We are therefore in doubt about whose strategy is decisive and who merely rides along on the coattails of the other. Theoretically, however, there is a procedure whereby we can determine whose influence was decisive.

It will be recalled that the properties of the interaction field are independent of the values of the actors. Hence we can change our assumption about their values without altering the properties of the field. Suppose we take a field where A and B both prefer y_n, and both have power relative to y_n. Now let us examine what would have happened if their purposes had conflicted. Suppose that if A had preferred y_n (and B had not), y_n would have occurred. If this is true, then when their purposes coincide it is A's choice of strategy which is decisive and B is lucky that A prefers y_n; in fact B can now adopt any strategy he wishes, secure in the knowledge that A's strategy will produce his preferred alternative y_n. We can express this by saying that B's power is dependent on A's. If, on the other hand, it is true that should their interests conflict it will be B's preferred alternative, not A's, which results, then A's power is dependent on B's.

But suppose that y_n will not occur if *either* A or B prefers another alternative (for example y_m). In that case, y_n is a joint product. Neither has power over the other with respect to y_n. Rather, together they have joint relative power over y_n, and we can say that y_n is the result of joint action toward a common purpose.

Now, continuing the assumption that both prefer y_n, suppose we have the interaction field given in figure 24. It is clear that y_n will occur as the result of their choices, since A will

	b_1	b_2	b_3
a_1	y_l 6,7	y_m 7,8	y_n 8,9
a_2	y_o 4,6	y_p 5,7	y_q 6,8
a_3	y_r 2,5	y_s 3,6	y_t 4,7

Fig. 24. Interaction field and output matrix
with respect to variable **y**.

choose a_1 and B will choose b_3 (their respective dominant strategies).

But now suppose we have the matrix in figure 25, under conditions where each must choose simultaneously with the other, or without knowledge of the choice of the other (i.e., the

	b_1	b_2
a_1	y_n	y_m
a_2	y_m	y_n

Fig. 25. Interaction field requiring a choice of joint strategy

normal form). Here, in order for y_n to occur with more than a probability of 0.5, actors A and B must consult with each other and decide on a joint strategy, in this case either a_1b_1 or a_2b_2. The object of choice is not a strategy, but a strategy pair.

This leads us to our definition of self-government. While action is the process whereby an individual chooses a strategy and puts it into effect, self-government is the process whereby a *group* jointly chooses a strategy set (a strategy for each actor) which serves a common purpose, and puts this strategy set into effect. Such a strategy set will be called a self-governmental program.

In the example, one can think of a number of ways in which the self-governmental program could be decided. For example, A could say to B (or B to A), "You decide." Or "I propose that I decide." Or they could decide to flip a coin over the choice between the two equally desirable alternatives, or they could decide to vote and continue to vote until unanimity has been achieved for one strategy pair or the other. We will undertake an examination of the processes whereby governmental decisions are made in later chapters.

C. *Rule*

If there is no common purpose, there can be no self-government. There can, however, be purposive regulation of group behavior as follows: Suppose that one member of a group (A) prefers y_n to y_m, while the others (B and C) prefer y_m to y_n. Suppose, further, that the result of y_n requires coordinated strategies by A, B, and C, and, finally, that A has power relative to both y_n and y_m. In this case there will be one or more strategies by A which, in conjunction with the strategies employed by B and C in maximizing their own utilities, will result in y_n. Where A chooses such a strategy, he will be said to *rule* the group ABC with respect to the values y_n and y_m of the variable y. Notice that although rule involves a decision about the joint strategies (strategy set) to be employed by the three members, the process of making the decision is the process of A's choice alone. Hence, A has made the governmental choice, and it is his purposes which regulate the group behavior.

Self-government and rule are thus mutually exclusive ideas. Self-government is regulation for a common purpose while rule is regulation for one purpose against others. The antithesis, however, is purely conceptual. Indeed, as we shall see, the establishment of a system of self-government in a group may enable a massive expansion of rule by a subgroup.

D. *Politics*

In practice, if we examine the preferences of the members of most groups, it will be found that their purposes are partly identical, partly conflicting, and partly independent. (The latter case presents no great theoretical problems, and will not be examined.) This creates the political situation, which presupposes neither complete identity nor complete conflict of purpose. A political system is a system of purposive regulation which combines elements of self-government and rule.

So far we have defined common and conflicting purposes, self-government and rule, with respect to only one or two values of a single variable. The same principles hold for aggregates of values, as follows:

1. Suppose that y_n is causally related to other values of

the variables of the field, for example, if y_n, then v_n, w_n, x_n, z_n, (as a nomic universal). A preference for y_n must then be understood to be a preference for this entire set. Suppose also that if y_m, then v_m, w_m, x_m, and z_m, and that A prefers y_n to y_m but is indifferent to w_n and w_m, while B prefers w_m to w_n but is indifferent to y_n and y_m. Because of the causal relations involved, the purposes of A and B are conflicting with respect to y_n and y_m (and w_m and w_n).

2. One can generalize about preferences with respect to the whole range of values of a given variable. For example, suppose that **y** can be quantified, and that A's purpose is to maximize, and B's is to minimize, the value of **y**. Thus A's and B's purposes conflict with respect to the *variable* **y** (i.e., all pairs of values of **y**).

3. A state is a set of values of the variables of the field. Hence from the idea of purpose with respect to values of a variable, one can derive the idea of identical or conflicting purposes with respect to pairs of states of the field. The states of the field can be divided into two sets, such that every actor prefers every member of the first set (called the negotiation set) to every member of the second set (called the nonnegotiation set), but that for every pair of states in the negotiation set, not every person prefers the same state. Here, there is identity of purpose with respect to the two sets (i.e., everyone prefers that the result of the field be in the negotiation set), but conflicting purposes with respect to every pair within the negotiation set. If the negotiation set is empty, then there can be no self-government. If the negotiation set has only one state (i.e., if there is one state which everyone prefers to all others), then self-government is the purely technical ("administrative," in the narrow sense of the term) process of working out and coordinating strategies so as to produce this state. As a matter of practical convenience, or labor saving, one or more members of the group might be charged with the task of creating and directing the self-governmental program, that is, of calculating

the correct strategies for everyone, reducing these to rules, communicating these rules, checking to see that the various strategies are properly coordinated, etc. This self-governmental apparatus would be perfectly conflict-free and hence nonpolitical. When the negotiation set has more than one state, we have the political problem: how to choose and successfully execute a governmental program which lies within the negotiation set.

Here we have an apparent paradox. If we suppose that in the general case, where there is a negotiation set which taken as a whole represents the common interest, but which taken one by one represents divergent interests, the arrival at a coordinated strategy will represent at once self-government and rule. It is self-government to the extent that the process results in a decision within the negotiation set; it is rule in the sense that the particular set chosen within the negotiation set represents the victory, through superior power, of the purposes of one member or set of members over another member or set of members. This, however, is precisely our point. While self-government and rule are conceptually antithetical, in practice the purposive regulation of group action commonly partakes of both.

Aristotle distinguished between States which are regulated for the interests of all and States which are regulated according to the interests of some. The position adopted here is that most processes of group decision making combine both elements in an indivisible way. Self-government and rule are thus relative terms. The same process can be termed either, depending on which aspect one is examining. In the polar cases, pure self-government is the technical process of administration, while pure rule is the outcome of an unadmixed power struggle, not to be distinguished from war, unless the latter is defined solely in terms of the use of the instrumentalities of violence. Between administration and war lies *politics*, in which self-government and rule can be used to describe the same process, although from a different point of view. Politics, then, is the process of purposive regulation of group action which combines self-government and rule. In the normal case, government—the purposive regulation of group action—is a political process, in that it involves such a combination. Unless otherwise qualified, this is the sense in which the term "government" will be used.

E. *Summary*

At this point it might be useful to the reader to review the steps whereby our theory of government has been developed and to give some indication of the direction in which we are moving.

1. We started with the mathematical theory of rational action in situations of strategic choice and partial conflict, which seem to present in a precise and formal way the situation of social interaction. Von Neumann and Morgenstern presented the solution of matrices as "imputation sets": large classes of strategy pairs (or triads, quatrads, etc.). Granted that each member of the set is a rational solution compared with those not in the set, the imputation sets themselves are much too large. We wish to know which single imputation will occur among rational actors, and the theory supplies no answer to this question.

2. We did not seek to find the answer by a more refined mathematical analysis (as much subsequent decision theory has tried to do, with very limited success) but, instead, followed the suggestion of Von Neumann and Morgenstern themselves and sought the answer in special social arrangements. The chain of theoretical reasoning led through comparison of utilities, identification, and the formation of a social group governed by a real general will. Within such a group, members will predictably follow group rules in their behavior. Hence individual action can be chosen on a probabilistic, as against a strategic, basis. While contemporary decision theory has followed the modern tradition from Hobbes to Marx of seeing organized society as the outcome of rational action, we have returned to the

formulation of Plato and Aristotle (and Rousseau), which views organized society as the precondition of rational action.

3. Government (in the broad sense) has been defined as the process of choosing group strategy (as against individual strategies). What is chosen is a set of coordinated strategies, one for each group member. A social group without a formal government is informally governed by its general will. However, the general will, being general, usually defines a broad range of governmental decisions, not a specific decision. Hence, in such a group without a formal government, the actual course of events is governed in the sense that the general will dictates that it fall within a given range, but ungoverned within this range because the strategies are chosen unilaterally by the members.

A governmental decision (one strategy for each member) will occur within a "negotiation set." This idea of a negotiation set has two connected sources. First, in a group without a real general will it is the Von Neumann imputation set for games of imperfect competition where communication between the actors occurs. This set has two properties: (*a*) The actors unanimously prefer every member of the set to every member not in the set. (*b*) Within the imputation set there are no unanimous preferences; that is, if someone prefers A to B, then someone else is sure to prefer B to A. We have already examined this idea in connection with the "rowboat" problem in chapter 4.

Second, for a group with a real general will, the negotiation set is the same as—or in any event within—the set of strategy sets determined by the general will.

4. It is already implied, and will be further argued, that in general only a group with a real general will is capable of developing a government (i.e., capable of developing a process whereby strategy *sets* are chosen). As a possible exception, it seems that certain forms of the most primitive type of governmental organization (alliances) may occur among actors not bound together by a real general will.

5. It also follows from the argument so far that the process

of government is hence *political* in that it involves a mixture of concord and conflict. Insofar as the governmental decision falls within the negotiation set, it involves concord. But, unless the negotiation set has only one member, the process of deciding on a particular member of this set must also involve conflict. By definition (this is not a factual proposition) the selection of a particular governmental strategy within the negotiation set is determined by the configuration of relative power. Furthermore (and this is, in principle, an assertion of fact), this power will almost entirely take the form of authority and social power.

6. In the future course of the argument we will devote considerable attention to the impact of the structure and scope of government on the structure of power.

7. Table 4 outlines the classification of government developed in this chapter.

TABLE 4

A Typology of Purposive Group Regulation

I. According to *Whose Purpose* Governs

    A. Self-government (regulation by the group purpose)
        1. Pure Democracy (no specific governmental organization)
        2. Representative Government (government organized and delegated)

    B. Rule (regulation by other than group purpose)
        1. Regulation by the purpose of an outside individual or group
        2. Regulation by the purpose of a subset of the group

    C. Government (the political process)
        (A mixed form, combining elements of self-government and rule. The normal form combines A2 with B2, and unless qualified, the term "government" is used in this sense.)

II. According to *Who* Governs (requirements for making governmental decisions) [See chapter 12]

A. Alliance (unanimous assent of all group members required)

B. Democracy (unanimous assent of a majority of group members required)

C. Oligarchy (unanimous assent of a minority of group members required)

D. Monarchy (assent of only one group member required)

F. *The Organization of Government*

On the highest level of abstraction, a political solution to a field will occur when each actor has a rational strategy, and the resulting state involves an effective governmental choice of a strategy set which lies within the negotiation set. We have argued that in general such a political solution requires the existence of a real general will, with its patterns of identification and legitimate coercion. We are now operating under the assumption that such a solution exists, and moving to the next lower level of abstraction, with the question What arrangements and devices can (or must) be brought into effect in order to enable the assessment, choice, and execution of the strategy set requisite to the solution; in other words, by what means is the regulatory program to be worked out and put into effect? This is the level of the general theory of group organization. We will proceed by developing a typology of organization and then describe several of the types in some detail. The typology will turn on the way the choices of governmental programs are organized, although considerations of assessment and execution will not be entirely ignored.

In governmental action, as has been stated, the process of choice is not carried out independently by each member, but rather a strategy set is chosen: a decision is made about how each member is to choose. The individual member (as for every individual action) of course has the option of complying or not and can be expected to comply only if he believes that the strategy assigned him will in fact maximize his utility, but the organization presumes that he will comply. The point is that a given purpose is taken as self-governing (if it is a common purpose) or ruling (if it is not), and the individual strategies required for serving this purpose are worked out in a coordinated way as a single choice or decision.

Formal organization represents the "rationalization" of group organization in the sense of the term developed by Weber.[4] This is not the place to develop this idea in full detail, but two of its characteristics may here be mentioned. First, the process of making the group decision is defined in a set of explicit written general rules. Also, the decisions themselves, where feasible, are stated in the same form. Second, the overall task of making and executing group decisions is divided into subtasks which are performed by different persons; that is, there is a division of the labor of regulation.

On the other hand, in informal organization the agreed process of decision making may not even be a matter of conscious definition in the minds of the actors. Instead it may be defined only by their actions, as, for example, in the implicit alliance which historians point out existed between Great Britain and the United States for much of the nineteenth century, and of which the statesmen themselves were by no means always aware. In addition, the division of labor in informal organization is not well developed, if it exists at all.

Formality of organization is a matter of degree and can never be fully carried through. There will always be some informal elements, and in fact formal organization itself breeds informal organization.[5] At this juncture the point we wish to make is that as organization becomes increasingly formal, a

4. Weber (1925a), pp. 196–97. The idea of the rationalization of behavior runs like a lietmotif through almost all of Weber's writings. See Bendix (1960), pp. 49–79 et passim.

5. Homans (1950), pp. 108–30; Blau and Scott (1962), pp. 89–100; Selznick (1949, 1957).

consequence of organization which is of the greatest theoretical importance becomes increasingly evident. This point, which was first (as far as I know) clearly grasped by Rousseau, and worked out in a detailed way by Weber and Michels,[6] may be stated briefly as follows:

Suppose that a group has a purpose (either a common purpose or the purpose of a ruler). Suppose further that the accomplishment of this purpose, or at least the more efficient accomplishment of this purpose, requires government. The institution of governmental organization will have two consequences: First, it will alter the structure of power in the group; and second, it will alter the utility scales of the group members, especially those to whom the task of governing has been delegated. As a consequence it will not suffice for the political theorist to proceed (as so many have done), according to the analytic schema of ends and means, first to treat of the purposes which men have, or ought to have, and then to consider what kind of organization, from a purely technical point of view (i.e., purely as a means), will best serve these ends.

In this respect, Weber and Michels stand at the watershed. (Rousseau is a precursor, whose insights were both historically premature and incompletely followed through.) They analyze group action according to the conceptual distinction between ends and means. The substance of their analysis, however, breaks through this distinction. The conclusion they both drew is that the results of organization (and of action in general) regularly stand in a paradoxical relationship to the purposes which motivated the organization.[7] The paradox, however, springs from the employment of the ends-means distinction to analyze a subject matter to which the distinction is not appropriate.

In this work we have approached the problem through the distinction between an interaction field and its outcome matrix

6. Rousseau (1762), bk. 3, chap. 15; Weber (1925a), pp. 224–35; Michels (1915).

7. Weber (1925a), pp. 102–6; Michels (1915), p. 408.

(the evaluation of this field by the actors). The field itself contains, as component elements, the various possible strategies, as well as the consequences of these strategies. A strategy, hence, is both a means and an end, or rather the distinction does not apply. What government organizes is strategies: it is a process in which the strategies of the actors assume coherent interrelationships. Hence, governmental organization is neither ends nor means, but simply a property of the process of interaction.

12/

GOVERNMENTAL

ORGANIZATION

A. *Preliminary Classification*

THE FOLLOWING classification of government assumes that
there is a set of group purposes, partly of the whole group,
partly of some members of the group, according to which policy
(strategy sets) for the whole group is chosen. Without denying
the possiblity of disobedience to these decisions by those who
are governed, it is assumed that normally the governmental decisions are obeyed, for otherwise the government does not in
fact govern.

All government requires a unanimous agreement on policy
by some set of individuals (or one individual as a limiting case).
Governments vary according to who these individuals are. An
alliance is a government which decides by unanimous vote or
assent of all members of the group. A *democracy*, or *radical
democracy*, decides by unanimous vote of a majority of the
group members. An *oligarchy* requires the unanimous agreement of a subset of individuals drawn from the overall group,
while a *monarchy* requires the decision of only one particular
member of the group.

With the exception of alliances, this typology is hoary with
antiquity, and indeed is somewhat antique. It serves, however,

as a useful starting point, later to be replaced by a more detailed typology depending, not on who governs, but on how government is organized. Despite its preliminary nature, a few remarks about this classification are in order.

While pure examples of these types exist, especially in small groups, normally actual governments are mixed types. The government of the United States may be taken as an example. The constitution defines the structure of governmental decision making. In principle, although this is perhaps a fiction in practice, certain kinds of decisions about the constitution itself require more than majority assent. (We define *assent* as an act of favorable choice, *consent* as lack of unfavorable choice.) The original document required assent by more than a majority of states, and amendments require a process that is clearly more than majoritarian. The process seems to lie between radical democracy and alliance. (Calhoun's doctrine was that the constitution provides for decisions by essentially an alliance of states.)[1] On the other hand, some aspects of the constitution can be amended or altered by the act of five men only (a majority of the Supreme Court), a highly oligarchic principle. Certain governmental officials are elected by majority vote or something not far from this. These decisions, which vest these men with office, are made democratically. Legislative decisions are oligarchic, executive, a combination of oligarchic and monarchic, etc. Confining our focus to subgroups within the government: The Supreme Court and many governmental agencies operate democratically, Congress is basically democratic with some oligarchic features; the relations between Congress and the president have many features of an alliance, etc. The use of these categories is not empty playing with words. Examining the internal workings of Congress: The fact that most legislative decisions must receive a majority vote has the most profound effect on the process of decision making; and, with respect to the relationship of Congress to the nation, if

1. Calhoun (1853).

congressional legislation had to be submitted to the citizens for acceptance or rejection by majority vote, the legislative process would be revolutionized. While the present classification does not get at the actual dynamics of government (i.e., the classification is not based on political considerations), it is not thereby of minor significance. The point is, for example, that when decisions are made by a majority of a committee of twelve, both the process of decision making and the content of the decision can be expected to differ in major respects from the case where the decision is made by one person, or by a minority of the twelve. While the influence of such structural features can be exaggerated, their importance must not be underestimated.

To the extent that the decisions of an oligarchy or monarchy carry out the purposes of the whole group, the government will be said to be *representative*. Representative government can be of two kinds. First, the correspondence of the governmental policy to the group purpose may be due to influence exercised over the formal government by nongovernmental members acting to achieve the general purpose. This will be called direct representation. On the other hand, governmental policy may serve a group purpose, not because of any influence brought to bear on the government, but simply because the members of the government share the general purpose and act to achieve it. This will be called indirect representation. There is a third possibility: the governmental policy may serve a group purpose even though neither the government nor anyone outside the government acts towards this purpose. This idea, that the interplay of partial interests can serve the general welfare, apparently originated with Mandeville and has been much used from Adam Smith to David Truman. Although such a process may occur, it constitutes representation without government, for government has been defined as purposive regulation, and if a purpose is not intended, its achievement is not government.

Direct representation implies the existence of three sets of individuals: first, a group, the great majority of which share a common purpose; second, a government (as a subgroup) which has its own purposes which may or may not be the same as the purposes of the first group; and third, a set of individuals who exercise influence over the government. Direct representation means that the governmental policy represents the first group with respect to purpose, and the third group with respect to power. The third group in turn may indirectly represent the first. The first group will be called the public, and the third the constituency, in the representative process. Normally, the constituency is a subgroup of the public. It is clear that representative relations may vary from issue to issue and from decision to decision.

Both alliances and democracies seem technically feasible only for small groups, or for small subgroups. Larger groups seem to require the introduction of oligarchic or monarchic principles into government. Here the distinction between self-government and rule becomes the distinction between representation and rule. In part the purposive regulation of groups expresses a common purpose, and in part it involves the imposition of a particular purpose on the whole group. Politics consists of the interplay between these two factors. Hence the distinction between representation and rule will play a central part in our treatment of the concept of a political system, which will be undertaken in the final chapter.

B. *Alliances*

We now proceed to examine government not in terms of who governs but according to how government is organized. Our first type is the alliance. In an alliance, the members unanimously adopt certain coordinated strategies, which often can be stated in terms of general rules. The idea is not far from a "coalition," as defined in game and decision theory. The distinction between a coalition and an alliance turns on a point already made. Alliances arise from a situation where explicit consultation and agreement is necessary to produce the coordination of strategy necessary to carry out a common purpose. In other words, in an alliance a *strategy set* is unanimously chosen, while in a coalition each member acts independently, although in coordination with the others. The difference can be one of degree, since it is possible to speak of implicit alliances. In each case the solution is the result where each member acts rationally. What differs is the process of choice. The literature on coalitions in game and decision theory, which is large and developing rapidly, thus bears directly on the theory of alliances, but no attempt at a treatment of this literature will here be made.[2] Rather we will be content to explain and illustrate some of the basic ideas and locate them in the context of our theory.

In contrast to other forms of government, there need be no ties of identification among allies. It was noted earlier that by its premises, the existing theory of decisions precludes such identifications. This, we think, explains why coalitions (alliances) have received such heavy attention by this theory. On the other hand, the attempt to explain more integrated forms of government as essentially complex alliances is bound to fail, for as we shall see these forms require identifications among the participants and turn on different principles.

Since the incidence of identification between members of different nation-states is almost invariably sharply lower than among members within a nation-state, and, as a connected point, since the higher governmental forms are largely lacking in the international arena, the typical governmental form among States is that of alliance. Of course alliances are also common among groups and individuals within integral governments, but here they are themselves typically governed by the formal and

2. Almost all games where *n* equals 2 plus have coalition possibilities. Cf. Shubik (1964), pp. 44–45, for a brief discussion of some of the literature. See also Riker (1962).

informal rules of that society, and hence alliances do not generally occur in a pure form. To take a trivial but clear example, in the game of bridge the rules whereby the partners act cooperatively in communicating information during bidding and play are essentially of an alliance nature. But many possible signals, for example, scratching one's left ear if one's strong suit is hearts, constitute cheating and are strictly forbidden. The laws of bridge are a whole set of rules of this kind which regulate the ways in which an alliance between partners may and may not coordinate strategy. These rules, within the confines of which the partnership alliances must operate, cannot themselves be regarded as of an alliance nature. In general, alliances within an integral governmental system operate within the confines of legal and social norms; indeed, as has already been suggested, many alliances can be formed only under such conditions— for example, when the social code eliminates the double-cross possibility.

The existence of an alliance, like all governmental forms, presupposes that the interaction field has a solution. In such a field, the differences between the interactions if an explicit alliance is formed and if it is not may be insignificant and, in general, will not be large. For example, suppose two States both fear a third, but not each other. If the third State were to conquer either of the other two, the position of the remaining State would be all the more vulnerable. Hence a defensive alliance between the two States who fear the third is "built into" the interaction. Each will defend the other if it is attacked, alliance or no alliance. The formal negotiation of the alliance might however, be expected to include the working out of joint contingency plans and to produce cooperative behavior which would strengthen both States against the contingency of a war. For example they might agree to install railroads of the same gauge, but different from the gauge of the third State, to facilitate troop movements between the two allies and hinder movements from the third State. This is the kind of "difference" which an alliance makes; it may in some cases be fairly substantial, especially if a war is actually in progress, but it rarely if ever approaches the kind of impact of other and tighter forms of governmental organization. The principle of unanimity and the consequent lack of any well-developed governmental apparatus precludes this.

An alliance also presupposes a common interest among the members. There must be at least one state in the negotiation set. If the configuration of the negotiation set changes, the terms of the alliance will change. If the negotiation set ceases to have any states, the alliance will cease to exist. As Bismarck said, all alliances are binding *res sic stantibus.*

Another remark attributed to Bismarck is that in every alliance one state is the horse and the other the rider, and that before entering into an alliance, a statesman must consider carefully which role his country will play. This reflects the fact that while the common interest ensures that the result, if any, will be within the negotiation set, the particular state within this set which is the result is the product of the power relations between the parties, specifically of their comparative power against each other relative to the variables over which their purposes are opposed. In a pure alliance—that is, not within the framework of a social or larger governmental system—this power will be technical and material. For example, in the negotiation of alliances between States, the form of power which may influence the result regularly includes existing or potential military power, strategic position, diplomatic skill, etc. In this case while the interaction is the product of the interplay of common and divergent purposes, the process will be political only in an extended sense, since political power will be defined as a form of social power, as against technical or material power. Within the confines of a larger social or governmental system, however, alliances may be highly political, and in fact they often play a central role in the political process—for example, alliances between political parties for electoral or governmental purposes.

C. *Voluntary Association*

Voluntary associations, along with a closely similar form, contractual associations, have become very prominent in the modern State and have received a great deal of theoretical analysis.
The utilitarian theorists, from Hobbes to J. S. Mill, have by and
large regarded the State as a voluntary association and pro-
ceeded to wrestle with the problem of why, then, its jurisdiction
is compulsory. Hegel sees civil society as a voluntary association. Following Sir Henry Maine, Weber and Tönnies distinguished two basic types of social organization, *Gemeinschaft*
and *Gesellschaft* (community and association), and subjected
the two to a profound analysis. This literature, especially the
works of Hobbes, Hume, Hegel, Weber, and Parsons, has
strongly influenced the treatment adopted here.[3] Nevertheless
the special angle from which we approach the problem, namely,
from the point of view of our theory of action, may enable us to
say something new on this much-discussed topic.

Traditionally, the central theoretical issue is whether one is
prepared to distinguish sharply beween a community and an
association, as theorists following Hegel have tended to do. To
make a long story short, roughly this amounts to the question,
in the language of this essay, whether an association is to be
distinguished from more integral forms of organization by the
fact that it does not have, or in any event need not have, a real
general will.

Although we will not attempt to shut the door on this question, if only to avoid the error of Galileo's critics in refusing to
look through the telescope of the empirical testing that would
seem potentially possible in this case, we are inclined to believe
that in general, and perhaps always, the effective operation of
a voluntary association requires that it have a real general will,

3. Maine (1861); Tönnies (1926); Weber (1925*b*); Hobbes (1651); Hume
(1739); Hegel (1831), Introduction, pp. 1–102. Parsons (1937), pp. 686–94,
contains an excellent short discussion of the distinction between Gemeinschaft
and Gesellschaft.

and that the only possible form of "pure" association is an alliance. We have already pointed out that on the premise that a set of actors has no general will, it is by no means clear that there is always a cooperative solution for cases typical of actual social cooperation, and hence that social cooperation may regularly or even always require a real general will. This point seems to apply not only to associations but also to alliances, but it will be waived for the sake of the discussion.

We will approach the problem by assuming that voluntary associations are specialized alliances, then argue that this is an insufficient basis on which to account for or describe them. From this point of approach, what distinguishes a voluntary organization is that there is a unanimous agreement, not on substantive group policy, but on the rules which shall govern policy decisions. In other words, there are rules for making rules; the government itself has a government, and it is this second government which is negotiated exactly as is an alliance.[4]

There is also normally an understanding on the purposes of the association, often explicitly stated. This statement, however, will be more or less deliberately vague, in the sense that it will have no clear-cut policy implications. Rather, the statement of purpose will serve to define the negotiation set, the area where the purposes of the members overlap, while remaining silent about the differences of purpose among the members. This may be carried to the extent of a rather clear-cut definition of the negotiation set by incorporating among the association's rules explicit prohibitions against solutions which lie outside of the negotiation set. In other words, the agreement may include a statement of purpose, which can be expected to be vague, and a statement of prohibition on governmental choice which can be quite precise. In the literature of political theory

4. Note the similarity to the idea of the "second contract," widely held to be implicit in Locke's theory of the origin of government and explicitly developed by other contract theorists. Locke (1690) Second Treatise, pars. 95–99, 123–133; and Sabine (1937), pp. 531–34.

this agreement is called the social compact (as distinct from contract), and a well-thought-out compact theory of government can be found as early as Plato's *Republic*.[5]

As the word "voluntary" in "voluntary association" indicates, an individual may leave a voluntary association at any time he wishes, without penalty. While a member of the association, he agrees to abide by the rules and may be subject to penalties if he does not, but all such provisions are void if at any time he chooses to leave. For example, suppose an organizational rule is that violation of a certain ordinance will be punished by a ten-dollar fine. Suppose a member violates this ordinance and is asked to pay the ten dollars. He may instead, if he wishes, leave the organization, in which case he no longer owes the money. Alternatively, if he refuses to obey the ordinance without leaving the organization, the maximum enforceable penalty is expulsion. In this circumstance, the rules of the organization are binding only as long as the individual chooses to obey them. This property a voluntary association shares with an alliance. The only significant difference between an alliance and a voluntary association thus appears to be that while in the former it is the joint strategies that are negotiated, in the latter it is the rules by which joint strategies are to be decided which are negotiated. In a sense this is true; but there is more to be said.

The decisive advantage of a voluntary association over an alliance is technical: it enables a rationalization of group action in terms of an orderly division of labor, central cost accounting, supervision of execution, etc. These and related points have been tellingly made by Weber. An alliance is essentially a question of coordination of individual strategies. A voluntary association enables group strategies that are far in advance of the set of unanimously agreed on individual strategies involved in an alliance. The possibility of centralized government produces a whole new interaction field, and a new negotiation set, wherein

5. Plato, *The Republic*, 357–59.

the utility of each state may be higher for each member than that of the previous set.

For example, assume that there are three farms in a valley, each with different soil and terrain, and consequently each with its own agricultural potentialities and limitations. Each farmer grows crops and sells them at the market as best he can. Now assume that they negotiate an agreement to sell their crops at a certain price at the market, each agreeing not to undercut the others. Since reneging on the agreement would lead to a price war, it might reasonably be supposed that once an agreement is reached it will be kept. Such a mutually beneficial arrangement would be an alliance. Suppose, however, that they decide to form an association, and for the purposes of agricultural production to treat the three farms as a single unit. This would result in a much higher production per unit cost and produce a higher income for each of the three farmers.

Such a program, however, would not require a single decision, as in the alliance, but a series of decisions, perhaps many each day, according to which the joint agricultural effort would be directed. Unanimous choice by each of the three farmers on each of these decisions would be out of the question, since a deadlock or, in any event, time-consuming negotiations would seem likely to occur constantly. Better to have the decisions made by majority vote; better yet to hire an agronomist to direct their joint activity. His decisions would be made on purely technical grounds (rather than on the quasi-political grounds that might motivate the farmers) and hence maximize the total product per unit cost.

The above argument, which has been sketched only in barest outline, is as old as political theory. In contrast, the following point has been fully appreciated only very recently, mainly as a result of the influence of Michels's *Political Parties*: that the establishment of a distinct and specialized government radically alters the configuration of power in a group. Those who hold the reins of government, especially at certain key points, acquire greatly enhanced power by virtue of their positions. Under the traditional premises of the theory of association, and under the premises adopted so far here, they can be expected to use this power to their own advantage, and, since we are here dealing with the range within the negotiation set, this must be to the relative disadvantage of those who have the lesser power.

A continuation of our example will perhaps make the force of this point clear. Assume that the utility of agricultural activity is directly proportional to annual income, and that without any cooperation the optimum strategies of farmers A, B, and C will produce incomes of $2,000, $2,500, and $3,000, respectively, per year.

Now let us take into account the results of possible alliances among the three farmers. Many such alliances would be possible. The negotiation set would consist of all alliances wherein each of the three farmers would do better than in all other alliances not in the set, and better than with no alliance. The specific alliance formed will depend on the comparative power of the three farmers. Assume that as a result of the negotiations (the result of the interaction) a solution is arrived at wherein the incomes of the three are, for A, $3,000 (versus $2,000 formerly); for B, $3,400 (versus $2,500); and for C, $3,600 (versus $3,000). It is clear that C is the least powerful member of the alliance, since his increment of income is less than that of A or B, both absolutely and as a percentage. By the same token, A is more powerful than B.

To continue the example, suppose the farmers now explore the possibility of forming an association. The floor of the negotiation set for the association would be at A equals $3,000, B equals $3,400, C equals $3,600; for none of the farmers will be willing to enter into the association unless he can do better than in an alliance. Suppose that they agree unanimously on the following rules: (1) Income will be distributed in the ratio of 30 to 34 to 36 (as in the alliance). (2) All other basic decisions will be made by majority vote. (3) An agronomist will be hired to make the day-to-day and hour-to-hour decisions. Suppose, further, that after a few years of operation, the income of the three farmers is $6,000, $6,800, and $7,200, respectively (twice the result of the alliance). Holding the association together is the knowledge that if it is changed back to an alliance, the income of each will be halved. Had an alliance been formed, holding it together would be the knowledge that if it were dissolved, the income of the three would be reduced to $2,000, $2,500, and $3,000, respectively. The exact terms of both the alliance and the association (the position of the result within the negotiation set) is determined by the comparative power of the three farmers.

The operation of the association can be expected to produce major changes, however. Where each had a small tractor, there is now one large tractor. The configuration of the fields has been altered, the course of a stream changed, reforestation instituted in certain areas, etc.; all with an idea of the maximization of the *total* output—not the maximization of the output of any of the three sectors. These developments will alter the amount each section will produce should the association be dissolved. Suppose that *C*'s section now would produce an income of only $2,000 yearly if the association were dissolved. This produces an opportunity for *A* and *B* to ally against *C*, demanding a larger portion of the association's income. Farmer *C*'s bargaining power will be greatly diminished, because he cannot now leave the association with impunity. Hence, *A* and *B* may be able to force a renegotiation of the terms of the association, such that the distribution is *A* equals $7,500, *B* equals $8,000, *C* equals $3,000. Farmer *C* is now worse off than if he had never entered into the association! The force of this kind of consideration becomes enhanced when we move from agricultural and mercantilistic societies to industrial civilization, with its vastly higher level of technical efficiency and interdependence. The relative power of a group of individuals who enter into a technically advanced and complex association is certain

to be radically altered by the position which the members occupy within the association. In terms of our example, as the
firm becomes industrialized, it will turn out to be, not *A* or
B who become masters of the association and run it to their
benefit at the expense of *C*, but rather the agronomist they have
hired, who with his technical skill and strategic position will
eventually become the master of the association and turn its
operation to his own benefit.

Not even Michels has put this point more forcefully than
Rousseau. The social compact, he says, was a plot of the rich
man, when,

> . . . after having represented to his neighbors the horror of a
> situation which armed every man against the rest, and made their
> possessions as burdensome to them as their wants, and in which
> no safety could be expected either in riches or in poverty, he
> readily devised plausible arguments to make them close with his
> design. "Let us join," said he, "to guard the weak from oppres-
> sion, to restrain the ambitious, and secure to every man the pos-
> session of what belongs to him: let us institute rules of justice and
> peace, to which all without exception may be obliged to conform;
> rules that may in some measure make amends for the caprices of
> fortune, by subjecting equally the powerful and the weak to the
> observance of reciprocal obligations. Let us, in a word, instead of
> turning our forces against ourselves, collect them in a supreme
> power which may govern us by wise laws, protect and defend all
> the members of the association, repulse their common enemies,
> and maintain eternal harmony among us."
>   . . . All ran headlong to their chains, in hopes of securing their
> liberty; for they had just wit enough to perceive the advantages
> of political institutions, without experience enough to enable
> them to foresee the dangers. The most capable of foreseeing the
> dangers were the very persons who expected to benefit by them;
> and even the most prudent judged it not inexpedient to sacrifice
> one part of their freedom to ensure the rest; as a wounded man has
> his arm cut off to save the rest of his body.

Such was or may well have been, the origin of society and law, which bound new fetters on the poor, and gave new powers to the rich; which irretrievably destroyed natural liberty, eternally fixed the law of property and inequality, converted clever usurpation into unalterable right, and, for the advantage of a few ambitious individuals, subjected all mankind to perpetual labor, slavery and wretchedness.[6]

Or, as Plato argues, Glaucon's social compact, which seems to grant equal rights and safety to all, in fact will become the iron rule of the weak by the strong.[7] The force of this point becomes redoubled when we take into account the vastly increased means of exercising power inherent in modern forms of organization. As a consequence it does not appear plausible to adopt the theoretical position that a voluntary association is essentially an alliance without abandoning either the premise of rationality or the premise of nonidentification. In other words, people can be expected to enter into a voluntary association only if they are fools, or if they have a real general will which provides guarantees against exploitation.

There is an additional argument. We have held that when people enter into regular interaction with each other, bonds of identification quickly spring up and lead to the formation of a real general will, as embodied in a code of social norms which are binding in a far deeper sense than the rules of an alliance or association as defined above. Hence, even if an association can be conceived of as an alliance at its inception, it will very shortly become something else altogether. Even if the "social compact" theory accounts for the inception of voluntary organizations, it does not account for their operation.

For all these reasons, we conclude that a voluntary association will come into being and continue to exist only within a social order governed by a real general will. It is the mutual trust and predictability created by the normative system of this social whole which enables voluntary associations to operate

6. Rousseau (1754), pp. 78–79.

7. Plato, *The Republic*, 360–67.

effectively. The importance of the surrounding culture becomes clear when it is noted that in different cultures associations take quite different forms. Some cultures favor their development, as in the United States, where already Tocqueville laid great stress on their importance.[8] In contrast, this development in France was very slow and did not get fully under way until after World War II.[9]

We will pass swiftly by some important features of voluntary associations in order to concentrate on a single point. Associations, both voluntary and contractual (the latter will be treated shortly), appear to assume importance in society as the family ceases to occupy a pervasive role, although it may still be the basic unit. This movement has been traced with respect to political parties by Weber. A similar movement has occurred for economic organizations. Weber's central point here is the inappropriateness of family organization and attitudes for the technical rationalization of behavior which he sees as the hallmark of associational organization. The relation between cultural norms and organizational forms is a vast subject which we must here pass by with the single remark that a crucial factor is whether the content of the prevailing social norms encourages and fits in with the development of associations, as in the United States and England, or discourages and acts against this development, as in many non-European countries, and formerly in France.

In the normative order of associations, one may distinguish between what Homans calls the "external" and the "internal" systems.[10] The external system includes those norms which the individuals bring in from outside the group, reflecting their nationality, locality, social class, profession, etc. Members of voluntary associations tend to be drawn from the same ranks

8. Tocqueville (1840), pt. 2, bk. 2, chaps. 2–7.

9. Rose (1954); Ehrmann (1957); Wright (1964); Hoffman et al. (1963).

10. Homans (1950), chaps. 4, 5. This book has had considerable influence on the theory of groups developed in the present work.

of society and hence from the start to identify with each other more than with the average member of society and to share common attitudes and values. Norms which dictate standards of behavior of the members of the association toward each other, obedience to organizational rules, and, in particular, a code setting up what constitutes fair bargaining procedure and a fair bargain are not only useful to the successful operation of an association, but, as we have argued, indispensable to it.

The *internal* system is the set of norms specific to the group which arises out of the group interaction.[11] These norms hence constitute the general will of the association and are based on the identifications of the members with each other, and with the association itself. This general will may be regarded as the product of three factors: the psychological predispositions of the members, the norms they bring in from the outside, and the specific structure of interaction of the group. The structure of group interaction, in turn, is the product of the technical imperatives of achieving the group purpose, the relative power relations of the members as reflected in the agreement on rules of decision making, and the norms of the cultural environment.

The net effect of the normative system of the association— both the norms brought in from the outside and the general will of the association—will be to create a system of authority which partly reinforces and perhaps partly alters the official structure of decision making. In addition, the organizational goals may be altered.[12] The new bonds of identification may narrow the range of conflict of interest defined by the negotiation set.[13] Once the organizational strategy has been arrived at, possibly after an intense conflict, a marked alteration of attitude will frequently occur on the part of those previously opposed to the adopted strategy, who now, through their identification

11. Ibid., chap. 15.

12. Michels (1915), pt. 6, chap. 1.

13. That is, informal organization often promotes social cohesion. Barnard (1938).

with the organization, suddenly embrace what they had so vigorously opposed.[14] This effect, for example, is often quite striking in political parties after a candidate for office has been chosen. On the other hand, negative identifications may aggravate existing conflicts, and the organization may break apart.

In sum, approaching voluntary associations as specialized alliances, we have been led to conclude, first, that the existence of a voluntary association presupposes an overall society with a real general will; second, that the operation of an association will likely alter the power relations on which it was originally based; and third, that they will, indeed must, develop their own normative systems, including a general will, which will profoundly alter the field of the original association.

It is possible to approach the idea of voluntary association from another direction, starting with the idea of a social group without a government. By definition, a social group has a real general will, but it does not necessarily have a government. Nevertheless, the general will often prescribes, not individual strategies, but strategy sets. Furthermore, the strategy sets dictated by the general will regularly involve highly coordinated action. This is true, for example, for the general will of a family. The duties and rights of the father, mother, and children form a highly articulate, coherent, and coordinated strategy set.[15] It follows that any group which obeys its general will is self-governed. It is impossible to assume that each person figured out his strategy independently, for this cannot account for the clear-cut fact that what is chosen is a strategy set, not a set of strategies. The question is, Chosen by whom? Whose purpose governs? For we have already seen that the general will cannot be identified with the particular will, and hence with the purposes of any given member or set of members of the group. If the group has no leader and no governmental structure, the government can be purposive only in a metaphorical sense—it is the purpose of the ideal group member which governs. If the

14. Coser (1956).

15. Davis (1948), pp. 392–414.

group has a leader with personal authority, the general will becomes identified with the particular will of this leader, and his purpose then governs. If the authority which regulates the group behavior is institutionalized, that is, if there are explicit governmental institutions, then the purposes of the institution become identified with the general will, and these purposes govern. In the latter two cases an overt government exists whose commands are authoritative in the sense that they are the dictates of the general will. We will term such a government an *integral* government, and the group which is governed an *organized community*.

Usually, however, the general will does not dictate a unique strategy set, but a range of strategy sets, within which the decision is up to the particular wills of the individuals. The range of strategy sets permitted by the general will constitutes a negotiation set for the group. The general will insures that the result of the field will occur within the negotiation set which it defines. Hence if a social group has no explicit governmental apparatus, it can possess only a quasi-government, in the first place because what is chosen is a range of strategy sets, and in the second place because the chooser is an imaginary ideal group member.

We are left with the question What state within this negotiation set will be the result of the field for a social group? There are several possibilities. First, each actor may independently choose his rational strategy; hence the group will be ungoverned except in the sense already indicated. Second, the members may form an alliance; that is, they may decide unanimously on a given strategy set within the negotiation set. Third, they may form a voluntary association, by deciding unanimously to adopt a set of rules for determining strategy sets. Thus the idea of a voluntary association can be derived either from the idea of a set of individuals with a common purpose but without a general will, or from the idea of a social group with a real general will but without a government.

This leads to our first decisive departure from the Weberian theory of organization. Among groups with an explicit governmental apparatus—that is, among organizations—we make no sharp theoretical distinction between "Gemeinschaft" and "Gesellschaft," "community" and "association." As a practical matter, the following influencing factors may be singled out, but purely on a relative basis, as a matter of degree.

1. The degree of technical rationalization. Technical rationalization of group decision making will bring out the associational side of the organization.

2. The degree to which the common interest is defined by a real general will. The higher this degree, the more the organization will lean toward the communal side. However, technical rationalization and the degree to which the common purpose is defined by a real general will do not inherently stand in inverse relationship to each other. High degree of technical rationalization and high degree of general will may go together; in fact this is precisely the defining characteristic of modern totalitarianism.

3. The origin of the governmental organization. On the one hand, a social group with a general will may exist for some time, even indefinitely, before an overt governmental apparatus is set up. For example, such seems to have been the case with the Catholic church as an organization, which grew out of the community of believers.[16] It is also argued that some modern states grew from the roots of nationhood, although an examination of these cases usually reveals that the picture is not as clear-cut as first appeared.[17] On the other hand, some organizations, such as political parties and many interest groups, appear to have come into being by a movement from alliance into voluntary

---

16. Harnack (1904), bk. 3, chap. 4; Klausner (ca. 1939), pp. 261–72.

17. In other words, the differences between the processes of the growth of nationality in European and non-European areas may not be as sharp as first might seem, and European nations, as well as non-European, can to a certain extent be regarded as the product, not the basis, of political action. See Emerson (1960), chap. 5, esp. pp. 93–94.

association.[18] Once again examination of specific instances reveals that the picture is often by no means clear-cut.[19]

4. The type of sanctions employed. In a voluntary association, a member may always leave the organization if he no longer consents to its actions. This defines the maximum sanction that can be brought to bear: expulsion from the group. It follows that voluntary associations cannot exercise physical coercion on their members, at least without their consent. A voluntary association which exercises physical coercion on its members is thereby no longer a voluntary association. The governmental organization of a social group with a real general will may exercise stronger sanctions, up to and including the death penalty. But the general will may prohibit certain forms of coercion and in fact limit sanctions to an extent equal to or less than those normally employed by a voluntary association.

5. Method of joining. In general, one attains membership in a voluntary association by an explicit act of joining (signing the compact), while one can be born into an organized social group with a real general will, for example, the members of a tribe governed by a tribal council. The point is that one cannot internalize the general will of a group by a single act; rather it is a process which takes time. Still, one can think of exceptions. A person can be adopted into a tribe, while if the organization of a voluntary association is relatively primitive, a person can join simply by participating in its activities, as with many political clubs.

For these reasons, we will not distinguish sharply between communities and associations as distinct types of organized groups and, instead, will adopt the following definitions: A *community* is a social group with a real general will, irrespec-

18. Duverger (1951), Introduction.

19. That is, voluntary associations often arise by deliberate initiative at the top, rather than as a gradual coalescence of like-minded persons, whose mode of cooperation becomes increasingly governed. Woll (1963), chap. 2; Wright (1964), chaps. 7, 8; Hoffman (1963), pp. 34–73; Ehrmann (1957).

tive of the organization of that group—that is, it may or may not be organized by a government. An *association* is the organization of a group whereby it is governed by a common purpose, regardless of whether the common purpose is in part or wholly a general will. Thus, for example, a nation is a community, a State is an association, and a nation-State is the organization which governs the nation according to a set of common purposes which include at least part of the general will of the nation. A *voluntary association* is an association which exhibits traits by and large on one side of the above list of distinguishing factors; an *integral association* exhibits traits by and large on the other side. It is assumed that a relatively large set of associations cannot be unequivocally identified either as voluntary or as integral.

An association is a type of governmental organization. It is to be distinguished from organizations whose members are ruled, but not by a common purpose, for example, an organization of slaves ruled by masters.

D. *Contractual Association*

In addition to voluntary and integral associations, there is a third type, which can be more sharply distinguished and defined, and which we shall term a *contractual association*. Like alliances and voluntary associations, contractual associations are based on a unanimous agreement; they differ from the former in that the agreement takes the form of a free and binding contract. It is thus necessary to inquire what makes a contract binding yet free.

The question what in fact makes a contract binding, and in what way, has long been a concern of political theory. The subject is so vast that I have no choice but to state my own view—that there are only two coherent ways to answer the question. The first was perhaps most clearly put by Hobbes—that contracts can be binding only in the sense that Bernouli's law is binding. They are obligatory only when it is to the actor's own interest to obey them.[20] We have already termed voluntary agreements of this kind "compacts" and have argued that such compacts form the bases of alliances and voluntary associations.

The second position, and the one adopted here, is that the validity of contracts, in common with the validity of all legal norms, rests directly or indirectly on the normative consensus of society: that contracts are binding if and only if they are backed by the authority of the general will. In effect, but in different ways, this point has been argued by Plato, Rousseau, Hegel, and even Hume.[21] The conclusion often drawn is that if the State is a contractual association, it must as a consequence be a community. I feel, however, that what logically follows is the more modest conclusion that if the State is a contractual association, it must at least *rest on* (i.e., be sanctioned by) a community, because the contents of a binding contract need not express the general will but need only be sanctioned by it.

As an ideal type (i.e., if we examine the meaning of the concept) a *free* contract is binding if and only if it is drawn in proper form, and by proper procedures. Its actual content may be anything at all to which the parties are willing to assent. In other words, the general will prescribes only the form of the contract; it is completely neutral about its content, which will hence be determined solely by the private wills of the parties.

The idea that it is the form, not the content, that makes a contract binding seems to have primitive origins, both anthropologically and psychologically. The oath that is indissolubly binding because of the manner in which it is made plays an important role in mythology, for example. Even a contract with the devil is binding, provided that it is signed in blood.

In contrast to communal obligations, the entry into a free contract and its terms are entirely voluntary matters, on which the general will is silent. What is authoritative is that, if it is

20. Goldsmith (1966), pp. 76–102, 115, 165.
21. Hume (1739).

drawn in proper form, the binding quality of the contract is independent of the particular wills of the parties and, instead, rests on the general will.

As a consequence, the actual wording of the contract and the precise meaning of its terms become of critical importance. The contract must be written, and its meaning clearly and unequivocally stated. Inconsistencies must be avoided. Hence, the idea of a free contract contains the germ of a full-scale legal rationalism.[22] This point, which leads to the philosophy of law, will not be pursued, except for one remark: A binding free contract requires an actor not party to the contract to determine the meaning of the contract in case of dispute between the parties. But to the extent that the meaning or force of a contract is determined by an authoritative judge, it is not determined by the voluntary assent of the parties. Hence legal authority, and behind it social authority, in a sense enters into the determination of the content as well as the form of any contract. That is, a given form or a given set of words in a contract has a meaning not determined by the parties to the contract. It is thus indispensable to the principle of free contract that the parties be able to determine in advance the legal meaning and force of any contract into which they enter. With this proviso, and perhaps others not developed here, the content of a free contract can be regarded as a result of the interaction of the particular wills of the parties. Since a binding contract presupposes a common authority, the parties to a contract must share a general will. By definition, however, the general will is neutral with respect to any possible content of a contract between the parties.

Perhaps the crucial difference that the opportunity to enter into a free contract makes will become clear from an additional matrix. Let A and B be the parties. A contract consists of a

---

22. The centrality of the free contract to the whole idea of legal rationality is emphasized by Flechtheim (1952), pp. 177–93, esp. p. 192. For a brilliant treatment of the idea of legal rationality and its relation to the free contract, see Neumann (1942), pp. 440–58.

promise of performance of a certain set of actions; hence a promise to perform a certain strategy. Let these possible strategies define a matrix such as that in figure 26.

	b_1	b_2	b_3	b_4
a_1	2,7	4,4	3,5	5,6
a_2	3,4	3,2	4,1	4,3
a_3	4,5	5,2	5,4	7,1
a_4	2,5	4,1	4,3	3,4

Fig. 26. Output matrix with nonoptimal solution

Assuming no common authority, this matrix has a solution at a_3b_1, with a utility of 4 for A and 5 for B, since a_3 and b_1 are the dominant strategies of the two actors in this matrix. It is true that both would be better off if the solution were a_1b_4, but if A has reason to believe that B will adopt b_4, he is best off adopting a_3 because B's outcome will be only one. But if B has reason to believe that A's strategy will be a_1, he is best off with b_1 because A's outcome will be only 2. An "agreement" or alliance by both to adopt a_1b_4 will have no effect, because of the "double-cross" possibilities treated earlier. Under the usual postulates of game theory, the outcome if both sides are rational will be a_3b_1, which represents the dominant strategy for each.

Since both A and B prefer a_1b_4 to a_3b_1, however, both would agree on this solution, provided that each had a guarantee that if he adopted the required strategy, the other would do likewise. The existence of a real general will which would validate a contract might enable this condition to be fulfilled in one or both of two ways:

1. First, suppose sanctions on nonperformance of the contract were both substantial (say, minus four utility units) and probable (say, 0.75 probability). Entering into the contract would, in this instance, alter the matrix in figure 26, producing the matrix in figure 27. As a result of the sanctions, a_1 is now

	b_1	b_2	b_3	b_4
a_1	2,4	4,1	3,2	5,6
a_2	0,1	0,-1	1,-2	1,3
a_3	1,2	2,-1	2,1	4,1
a_4	-1,2	1,-2	1,0	0,4

Fig. 27. Contract creates optimal solution through external sanctions of general will.

A's dominant strategy and b_4 is B's dominant strategy, and hence once the contract is signed both parties will adhere to it.

Notice how this solution differs from the one proposed by Hobbes. Hobbes assumes that both sides agree to submit themselves to a sovereign, who will enforce contracts with sanctions. But whence come the sanctions of the sovereign? As Hobbes himself points out, in the state of nature one person is not much stronger than another; and if so, it is hard to imagine a sovereign capable of applying heavy and certain sanctions. Of course, if A were not to perform, it might be reasonable for B to ally himself with the sovereign to apply sanctions on A, but—in the first place—why not enter into such an alliance at the outset, without bothering about the contract with A? (This is essentially Hume's point.)[23] In the second place, and more decisively, the configuration of the output matrix already precludes the possibility of an alliance.

In other words, against Hobbes we would argue that effective sanctions to a contract depend on the existence of authority, and this authority must exist prior to the institution of a binding contract.

2. A second condition enabling the above agreement to be binding occurs when the influence of the general will on the utilities of the actors is sufficient to ensure voluntary compliance. Assume that the general will commands that contracts drawn in proper form must be obeyed, and that the utility of

23. Hume (1742).

signing a contract and not obeying its terms is minus five, that the utility of obeying the contract is plus five units, and that the influence of the general will on the particular will is 0.4. Then, once the contract has been signed, the internal sanctions of the general will come into effect, producing the matrix in figure 28.

	b_1	b_2	b_3	b_4
a_1	4,5	6,2	5,3	7,8
a_2	1,2	1,0	2,−1	2,5
a_3	2,3	3,0	3,2	5,3
a_4	0,3	2,−1	2,1	1,6

Fig. 28. Contract creates optimal solution through internal sanctions of general will.

In this case, once the contract is signed, the general will itself, apart from sanctions, is sufficient to produce a solution at a_1b_4.

The existence of a general will supporting contractual relations in this way does not guarantee that contracts will always be honored. Provided, however, that the conflict of private interests is not too sharp, and provided that the combination of internal acceptance and external compulsion is sufficient, the general will can enable the creation of viable contractual relations where cooperative interaction could not otherwise exist.

From the above considerations it can be seen that the movement "from status to contract"[24] is essentially one of formalization of the general will; that is, the commands and prohibitions of the general will come to be applied to the formal as against the substantive properties of action.

From one point of view, the advantage of formalizing the general will lies in the fact that it may enable cooperative relations between subunits of a society which has developed different substantive normative standards. From another point of

24. Maine (1861).

view, however, the crucial aspect of the formalization of the general will may lie in the fact that it will alter the balance of social power among various groupings in society. Thus, the movement from status to contract of early modern society perhaps enabled the holding together of a social fabric increasingly torn by religious and class conflicts, while on the other hand giving a decisive edge to the rising bourgeoisie, who were the typical champions of the free contract and all that went with it.

Having defined a free contract, we now move to contractual association, which bears the same relation to contracts that voluntary associations do to alliances. In a contractual association, the contract does not specify a particular strategy by the signatory parties but, instead, defines a procedure by which group decisions are to be made. The contract may also rule out certain classes of substantive decisions, or specify that under certain circumstances decisions must fall within a specified range or both. A contractual association differs from a voluntary association only in that it is binding except by mutual assent of all parties.

The relationship between a voluntary and an integral association is mirrored by the relationship between a free contract and what we will call an integral contract. An integral contract represents the rationalization of mutual obligations contained in the general will. For example, it is widely held that when a man has cohabited with a woman for an undefined but lengthy period of time, he acquires obligations and rights vis-à-vis his partner different from those that would obtain for a shorter liaison. This social norm is rationalized by the common law of some States, which declares that a specific duration of cohabitation produces all the (fully specified by law) obligations and rights of a bona fide marriage contract. These contractual obligations hold regardless of any written agreements between the partners.[25] In many countries, the marriage contract itself is

---

25. Similarly, in many instances the contractual obligations between landlord and tenant are set by law, which supersedes the actual content of any agreement signed by the two.

integral. The legal feature of such a contract (as distinct from the social fact that it is the rationalization of substantive normative rights and obligations) is that often it may not be voidable even if both the partners assent.

Whether or not an integral contract is voidable by mutual assent depends on the substantive content of the social norm which has been rationalized, namely, whether or not the rights and obligations involved are absolute or contingent. Classical natural-law theories hold the basic contractual obligations of society to be integral and inalienable—that is, certain acts will be illegal whatever the actual parties involved agree on, and certain obligations are legally binding whatever the positive law happens to say.[26] This position stands at the opposite pole from the idea of a free contract, whose contents are entirely at the discretion of the contracting parties, and which is enforced by the sovereign solely because of its purely formal properties. The actual law of contracts stands between these two poles. In modern times it has moved toward the free-contract pole. So far in the twentieth century a reverse trend is clearly discernible.

Table 5 summarizes the classification of governmental organization developed in this chapter.

26. The most important statement of this doctrine is that of Aquinas.

TABLE 5

A Typology of Governmental Organizations
(Classification of Constitutions)

EXAMPLE	ALLIANCE Triple Entente	VOLUNTARY ASSOCIATION Elks Club	FREE CONTRACT Wage Agreement	FREE CONTRACTUAL ASSOCIATION I.B.M.	INTEGRAL CONTRACT Marriage (Roman Catholic)	INTEGRAL CONTRACTUAL ASSOCIATION Roman Catholic Church	INTEGRAL ASSOCIATION (COMMUNITY) Apache Tribe
ENTRY:							
Voluntary	X	X	X	X	X	X	
Involuntary							X
CHOOSE:							
Program	X		X		X		
Government		X		X		X	X
CHOOSE PROGRAM/ GOVT. BY:							
Assent	X	X	X	X	X	X	
Consent	X	X				X	
Neither							X

HOW CHOSEN:						
Unanimous Particular Wills		X	X	X	X	X
General Will	X					
VOIDABLE:						
Unilaterally		X			X	X
Unanimously			X	X	X	
Not at All	X	X	X			
NEW SANCTIONS CREATED BY ENTRY						
Enforcement by 'Third Party'		X	X	X	X	
Interaction Creates New Power Structures		X		X	X	X
New Moral Obligations from General Will		X	X		X	
No New Sanctions	X					

$13/$

POLITICAL AUTHORITY

AND POLITICAL POWER

$\mathbf{B}$Y IMPLICATION, THE concepts of political authority and political power have already been extensively used in the analysis in the previous chapters. Their explicit treatment can therefore be relatively brief.

It will be recalled that authority has been defined as legitimate power—the successful exercise of the right to command or the ability to do so. Political authority is here defined as the successful exercise of the right to make governmental actions. This is understood to cover the full range of govermental action —assessment, evaluation, choice, and execution. The discussion here, however, will center on governmental choice: the decision that the members of a group are to adopt a particular strategy set, or program.

Political authority may be personal or institutional. The distinction between personal and institutional authority has already been made, and we pointed out that institutional authority is regularly admixed with elements of personal authority. The constitution of a government is defined as the structure of its political authority. Some define a constitution (and law) as a system of right regardless of whether or not the right is observed in practice (for a command may be accepted as legitimate and yet be disobeyed), while others focus, as we have done here, on that which is both rightful and efficacious. Both positions present difficulties.[1] On the one hand, to define a constitution as a system of right is to include a set of deadletter laws (legally proper and rightful but not obeyed); hence the constitution will not describe the actual operation of the government. On the other hand, a certain portion of the authority of any governor is personal, and this personal authority will change as the office changes hands. Hence the constitution will be constantly changing. We will handle this problem by altering our definition slightly, and say that a constitution is the structure of institutional authority. Personal authority is hence extraconstitutional.

Public law is a system of rationalized and formalized institutional political (or public) authority. This distinguishes it from private law, which is a system of nonpolitical (private) authority. The general will, as written in the minds of the members of the group, is vague, unspecific, unstable, and variable from member to member, although we have assumed a substantial overlap which defines the real general will. These vague and shifting rules are made clear and specific by the law, which is written in such a way that its application to specific instances is unambiguous (although a certain doubtful borderline area is inevitable) and definite. This is not easy, and a thoroughly rationalized legal system is a very elaborate affair.

Here, however, a question enters. If the general will is vague in a specific instance, why should one interpretation rather than another be authoritative? By what right does this possible meaning of a commandment of the general will take precedence over that possible meaning? The answer, of course, is that there are persons who are assigned the authority to make this determination. Since the general will is not guiding in such instances (because its meaning is in doubt) it must be the particular will of

1. There is a third position, legal positivism, which defines laws simply as those rules which are obeyed.

the person charged with the determination which is decisive.[2] Hence, as law becomes rationalized, its content becomes more and more the product of the particular wills of certain individuals as against the general will. This is why law has been termed a system of political (as against governmental) authority.

This point underlies the often made statement that common law is made by judges. Common law jurists determine the meaning of the law (i.e., its content) according to their own particular wills. Although containing much truth, this statement is one-sided, for, as has also frequently been noted, common law tends to conform to the general will of society and to change content when the general will changes.[3] The matter may best be understood in terms of the general political situation. The general will defines a negotiation set of possible specific interpretations. In falling within this set, legal decisions will be in conformity with, and express the intent of, the common law. The exact interpretation within this set, however, is decided by the particular will (or particular wills) which happens to have the power to make the decision, and in that sense the decision bears no relation to the general will. In addition the possibility must not be overlooked that a particular individual (or group), through his control over the governmental process, will be able to turn the content of the positive law out of the negotiation set —that is, the law may no longer reflect the general will. Such an eventuality will always in principle undermine the authority of the law. Whether this undermining is decisive, and causes the law to fail as an effective or a legitimate command or both will depend on the total political configuration, but in principle a law which is not within the negotiation set defined by the general will does not possess authority and hence is not a law. In any event, the rationalization of the general will into a legal system is a dialectical process. On the one hand it promotes the precise, clear, and effective application of the general will; on

2. A good deal of the force of legal positivism derives from this point.

3. This point is associated with a philosophy of law known as sociological positivism. See Pound (1922).

the other hand it produces an ever widening gap between the content of the general will and the content of the law. The rationalization of the law is thus a profoundly political, not a purely legal, process.[4]

The formalization of the general will is the process of its development from commands concerning the concrete content of the strategies to be chosen by the actors to commands concerning the formal properties which strategies must possess. The idea of formalization is at once complex and subtle, and we cannot at this place enter into a full treatment. For present purposes, we wish to point out that the formalization increases the range of discretion of those who possess authority. We have already made this point in connection with our treatment of the free contract, which, being a formalized legal idea, allows far greater option to the contracting parties in the substantive content of their agreement. If legal rationalism is symbolized by the scales in the hand of Justice, surely the blindfold symbolizes legal formalism. It is not who or what are on the scale that counts, but the way the scale turns when they are placed on it. The highly abstract and formal property of the weight of legal evidence is all that counts.

A familiar aspect of legal formalism is the distinction between immorality and illegality. Two acts which in their substantive relationship to the normative standards of society appear to commit identical offenses may differ sharply in their legal standing because of purely formal differences. Furthermore, to commit an immoral act is not yet to act illegally. An act, the circumstances of which are known and acknowledged by all, has still to be judged as illegal. It must be ascertained whether or not in committing a given act the actor at the same time has violated a law.

The net effect of formalization is to open up a distance between the system of law and the general will. In particular, the options opened up for the particular will are often immensely

4. The position adopted here is thus an attempt to integrate legal and sociological positivism.

broadened. We are reminded of the dictum of Plunkett of Tammany Hall, that "a man who steals funds from the city treasury is worse than a crook; he's a fool." The point is that the robbery (in the moral sense) of public funds can readily be effected by a wide variety of legal means. In a less formalized system the options for legal robbery would be less.

The points which we have made with respect to the relationship between law and the general will also apply to the whole range of relations between government and the common purpose which government carries out. In principle, the common purpose of a group defines a negotiation set. Within this set, the result is determined by the relative power of the participants against each other. Government is inherently a combination of cooperation and conflict, a combination we have termed "politics." The net effect of formalization and rationalization is dialectical. On the one hand, the two processes serve better to enable the execution of the common purpose. On the other hand, the very same process broadens the negotiation set and places increasingly more powerful instruments of rule by one person over another in the hands of the governors. An analogy is to be found in the Marxist doctrine of immiserization. As capitalism developed, Marx claimed, the distribution of wealth in society would become increasingly unequal: the rich would get richer and the poor poorer.[5] The actual result of the (partial) technical rationalization of capitalism was more ambiguous. On the one hand virtually everyone was better off, rich and poor alike. On the other hand, and because of the very same process, the gap between rich and poor widened both in wealth and, it can be argued, in power. This is precisely the kind of situation produced by the formalization and rationalization of government. We have already cited a hypothetical illustration of this point in terms of the three farmers who moved from an alliance to an association. In that case, the decisive step was the formalization of the process of decision making. In an alliance, the substantive content of the strategy set is determined by unanimous

5. The relevant passages in Marx are collected in Freedman (1961), pp. 68–71.

vote. In an association, the form of the process whereby decisions are made, not the specific content of the decisions, is determined by unanimous agreement. This creates the possibility for a much wider range of strategy sets, since unanimous agreement on the specific set adopted is no longer necessary.

The status of political authority may be described formally as follows: Let A be an actor with political authority. Let $\mathbf{y}$ be the set of all possible governmental decisions. Let $\mathbf{y}'$ be the set of all decisions which A has the authority to make. Actor A then has power relative to $\mathbf{y}$ over the range of $\mathbf{y}'$. He will, of course, choose the value of $\mathbf{y}$ (within $\mathbf{y}'$) which will maximize his own utility. This situation is highly advantageous to A. Any choice of a governmental strategy set by him within the range $\mathbf{y}'$ will, since it is legitimate, be backed by the entire power of society. Thus the establishment of government, as purposive group action, greatly enhances the power of some individuals. This point, of course, is forcefully made by Rousseau. Economic authority (private property) and political authority (government) are the origins of inequality.[6] Notice, however, that the governor's power with respect to $\mathbf{y}'$ is not independent, for the members of society may choose not to support his decisions, even if they fall within $\mathbf{y}'$.

Political Power

Political power is often understood to be the ability to influence governmental action. This formulation has a difficulty, however. For example, it is possible to influence the result of an election by using economic power. It thus appears that in certain instances economic power is political power. Such confusions can be avoided by following the analysis already developed here, although the result will be somewhat at variance with common usage. Political power will be defined as power whose sanction is political authority. This may be worked out formally as follows:

6. Rousseau (1754), pp. 60–61, 70–79.

Let **y** be a set of governmental strategy sets. Let A have authority over this set, so that he has power relative to variable **y**. Let **x** be another variable of the field, over which A does not have authority. Let **x**′ be the set of values of **x** relative to which A has power. Now consider a field which is identical to the above field except in one respect, namely, that A does not have authority over **y**. Suppose **x**″ be the set of values of **x** relative to which A has power over the field. Returning to the original field, **x**′ minus **x**″ represents the political power of A relative to **x** which springs from his authority over **y**. Notice that **x** can be any variable at all and is not relegated to the political or any other area. Thus political power can be exercised over economic, religious, military, or any other processes. As with economic power, we have defined political power by its source, not its area of exercise.

The above definition of political power mirrors the definition of economic power. Perhaps, however, it is too narrow. Suppose, for example, in a given government an actor occupies a position which is not authoritative, but which nevertheless involves the exercise of governmental decision making. Such a position may be achieved by tacit consent or by default. This person has power relative to governmental policy. Since we have not specified the source of this power, we cannot tell whether it is economic, personal, material or technical, or what. If this power, however, is used as a sanction to influence something else, such influence may be said to constitute political power, at least in an extended sense.

For example suppose that, without any explicit decision to this effect, the secretary of a committee assumes the task of preparing the agenda of committee meetings, and that from time to time the order of topics on the agenda has a substantive impact on the decisions of the committee. If the rules of the committee, or its resolutions, stated that the secretary was to prepare the agenda, then authority would be involved, since we have pointed out that the rules and decisions of every association must directly or indirectly be authoritative. No such decision having been made, the secretary does not seem to have the authority to prepare the agenda, and hence strictly speaking the power which flows from his preparation of the agenda does not seem to be political. Perhaps one might argue that the secretarial office which he occupies makes him the natural (technically rational) person to prepare the agenda, and hence that his secretarial authority is the sanction from which springs the (political) power to prepare the agenda and thus to exercise further political influence. Alternatively, one might hold that the secretary has implicit authority to prepare the agenda, on analogy with the legal doctrine of implied powers.

These arguments, however, are not entirely compelling, and we will cover this possibility by expanding the idea of political power to include that springing from governmental "position," where this position involves the ability to make governmental decisions in cases where the authoritative basis is not clear. This point might seem of minor theoretical importance, but in practice political power can assume very complex, subtle, and indirect configurations; and we are inclined to think that a good deal of it springs from the strategic position which individuals occupy at intersections, gaps, or overlaps in the system of authority. In general, the operation of political power is often far less visible than either political authority or economic power.

Our theory does not prejudge which forms of influence will predominate in determining governmental decisions of groups. Political authority, political power, economic power, military power, and other forms may all play a role. We have suggested, however, that the formalization and rationalization of the governmental process will tend greatly to enhance the relative weight of political power. To cite a single example, the political authority of the United States presidency has expanded only moderately in the past two centuries, but its political power has become enormously enhanced. The underlying cause seems to have been the technical rationalization of the entire life of society, including especially the government of the State. It is of course no accident that our theory fits well with Weber's suggestion that the modern state has gone through three stages, in which first military, then economic, and finally political power have become the predominant forms of influence.

The classic work on the influence of the system of political authority on the system of political power is of course Michels's *Political Parties*. Michels argued, in effect, that one could predict the structure of power in an organization simply by examining its system of formal authority. Subsequent study has broadened this conception considerably, and Michels's formulation can now be restated by saying that the structure of power of a government is determined by the system of both formal and informal authority.[7]

Of course the influence is not merely one-way. Just as the rules for decision making determine the locus of political power within an organization (if external factors are ignored), so also those who possess the greater power may be able to effect a revision of these rules, including formal or informal changes in the process of decision, and thus alter the structure of power in such a way as to further enhance their own advantage. Michels thought the long-term shift in this respect was cyclical,[8] but an examination of this question must await a later volume. The point here is that at any one moment, the system of authoritative governmental action determines the distribution of political power, which thus rests directly or indirectly on authority rather than material power.

To help orient the reader, the view being presented here can be contrasted with that, for example, of Reinhold Niebuhr,[9] which sees the system of power as ultimately dependent on material power, especially ability to use violence. Instead, the present study sees a main, underlying, and indispensable source

7. Lipset et al. (1956); Blau and Scott (1962), chap. 9; Selznik (1949); Barnard (1938); Mills (1951); Whyte, Jr. (1956).

8. Michels (1915), p. 408.

9. Niebuhr (1932).

of influence as authority (legitimate power), and sees the other main (and partly derivative) source as position[10] within the social system. That is, the social system is not based on material power to any major degree but, instead, generates its own power in the form of authority and social power.

This idea is not as sharply anti-Marxist as might at first seem. While the psychological source of authority has been found in family relations, we have not yet examined how the concrete content of authority relations may be transformed by social, economic and material factors when we move from the family to larger groupings. To put it another way, authority arises out of interaction. We have treated its origin in family interaction but have not examined the impact of other institutional systems. In addition, technical (forces of production) and economic (relations of production) factors may influence the family, and hence the formation of authority relations.[11] Marx sees history as the product of two factors: an invariant set of human material needs, and the varying ways in which these needs are met. I agree with this (although not with a full Marxist determinism) but would define "material needs" in a far more psychological way.

From still another angle, the two components of a social system are activity and thought. Marx sees activity as strictly determining thought, at least on the level of sociological analysis.[12] In contrast, we regard both as partly independent variables at all levels of analysis, insofar as they are to be distinguished. Thus our position is closer to Weber than to Marx.

10. We have deliberately left this term somewhat vague, although subsequent discussion will introduce some clarification.

11. Cf. Engels (1884).

12. This qualification is important. See Engels to Conrad Schmidt, August, 1890, and Engels to Joseph Bloch, September, 1890, in Feuer (1959), pp. 395–400.

14/

THE POLITICAL SYSTEM

A. *The Emergence of Government*

IN DEVELOPING OUR idea of a political system we will use the time-honored device of a fictional history. This history may or may not correspond to the actual processes whereby political systems develop, but in any event its purpose is not descriptive, but instead to lay bare the meaning of the concepts and to describe and explain the basic nature of, and the intrinsic relations within, a political system.

Consider a community with a real general will, but without a government. A nation before the development of a national government, or clearly defined and highly self-conscious social classes, and certain tribes at the most primitive level of development approximate this situation. The group's mores—a code of strongly seated rules defining right and wrong behavior—are written not on paper but in the minds of the members and are enforced in an undifferentiated way by everyone. Of course, conformity to the general will is always a matter of more or less; but we assume that the informal control mechanisms are capable of keeping deviation within the range where it strengthens rather than weakens the group identity.

Probing deeper, we will also find that the exact concept of

the general will varies from individual to individual, both in the intensity of the identification and in the relative intensities of the various preferences that form the general will, perhaps even in their ranking. It is assumed that these variations are both *random* and *small,* terms which we will now define. If we take any aspect of the general will which can be measured in a linear way, and plot the position of each individual's concept of the general will along this line, the distribution will fall on a normal, or bell-shaped, curve. That is what is meant by random. Furthermore, the range of variation within which most (say, 98 percent) individuals fall will be small. This is of course a comparative idea. By "small" may be meant, "not much larger than most other communities," or, what is perhaps the same thing, "small compared with the range of variation beyond which the effectiveness of the general will in regulating behavior would be materially weakened."

Here, however, we must pause. While we have specified that the formulation and application of the general will is ungoverned, this does not mean that social action is completely unorganized. On the contrary, the general will consists of rules of behavior, and behavior according to the general will is of necessity organized by it. He who says "general will" must say "organization of behavior." It is hard to imagine a human society without at least *some* role differentiation—a certain amount occurs even in the most primitive societies. The very ability to meet minimal material needs seems to require the organization of behavior, including role differentiation. This means that different individuals will occupy different roles and hence different positions within the social organization. Their behavior will be different, and so will their modes of interaction with others, and different factors will be useful or harmful to the successful performance of their roles.

As thought affects behavior, so behavior affects thought. Those who occupy different positions within the social organization can be expected to have divergent particular wills, and divergent conceptions of the general will, while those who occupy similar positions can be expected to have congruent thoughts in this matter. If we examine the different attributes people have, these differences will not be random but will follow the main lines of the social organization and can be expected to reflect the different social positions people occupy. Furthermore, where an individual's particular will conflicts with his general will, we can expect the two wills to tend to drift toward each other.

In addition, we can expect certain groups to differ in the degree of authority with which they enunciate and enforce the general will. Perhaps prestige may vary with groups not differentiated by the social system, for example, the aged or the skillful. More likely, social position is at least an important contributing factor. The aged may perform special and esteemed tasks; what one is skillful at makes a difference according to the social system, etc. In short, some subgroups may be more influential than others in making their conception of the general will the operative one. This may in turn provide them with an important resource in the struggle to make their particular wills prevail over those of others, when conflict occurs. Already we can see the faint beginnings of a political system and political power.

What is lacking is government. The general will defines a range of strategies for each individual, who chooses in a unilateral way the strategy within this set which maximizes his utility. In making this choice the individual is influenced by the other actors: by his identifications with them and by the sanctions (rewards or punishments) they can bring to bear.

Looking at the whole field of interaction, the behavior of the group makes up a strategy set. The general will insures that this set falls within a range of strategy sets (the negotiation set). Within these limits, the actual strategy set is the unplanned product of individual interactions. The general will insures a certain amount of organization—perhaps a great deal of organization—in this strategy set, but no actor occupies himself with, or is charged with, determining what the strategy set as a coordinated whole, or the permissible boundaries of the strategy set, is to be. Group activity, as distinct from individual activity, is partly organized but wholly unplanned. The group exhibits activity but not action.

The next stage in our hypothetical development is the emergence of government. We may imagine government to arise to meet either a social or a technical need, or a combination of both. For example it might prove practical to have the crops sowed or harvested simultaneously and cooperatively by all of those engaged in agriculture, and to fix the date by custom might not be a practical arrangement. Better to have a designated member of the tribe set the day according to his judgment about the weather and other factors, possibly aided by various omens and portents. The norms would designate who should make the decision (e.g., the oldest male) but leave the choice of date to his discretion. We should imagine that questions of war or peace, and strategy during war, would best be governed by an individual or set of individuals, rather than left to the blind decree and broad limits of the general will. In this way, it is easy to imagine the allocation of governmental authority to specific individuals. The decisions of these individuals would be authoritative provided they fell within the broad range of permissible variation; they would, however, be the product of the particular wills of the governing individuals. The general will would influence these governmental decisions to the extent of determining a range within which these decisions must fall. This influence would be dual, first within the governors, as their particular wills are formed, and second on the governors in the form of sanctions or threatened sanctions by others.

To move to government as the product of a social need, suppose that difficulties were encountered in the informal administration of criminal justice. Perhaps a growing sharpness in the division of labor has produced somewhat different views of the rights and duties of various roles, and with it the need for a more reliable means of defining, discovering, and punishing transgressions. For example, suppose a tribal council is established. If anyone thinks an injustice has been committed, he takes his case before the council, which listens to testimony from those involved, deliberates, and then decides whether a violation has occurred, and if so what the punishment should be.

If we carry through this process of government formation over a period of time of indefinite duration we will arrive at a community with a full-scale government. The members of this government act consciously and purposively on behalf of the community in putting the general will into effect; that is, they assess the situation and examine possible alternative programs; they evaluate the possible results of these programs according to the scale of value that is the general will; they choose a strategy set (program) for the whole community; and they execute it. Some of these governmental actions will concern substantive commandments of the general will, for example, the conduct of criminal justice; for others a process of formalization may have occurred, and the process of decision (but not its content) will be in accordance with the general will. Still, the results of these discretionary powers will be judged in terms of the benefit to the community, as measured by the general will. In short, the government translates the general will into purposive group action—the actions of the community are rationally organized in the service of the general will. Just as rational individual actors maximize the utility of the result in their actions, so rational governmental action is supposed to maximize the utility of the result to the community—that is, it is charged with producing the result with the highest possible utility for the general will.

The above, of course, is nothing but the standard exposition of the nature, function, and rationale of government held by almost all political theorists from Plato through Aquinas. As a result of the theoretical development so far, however, we should be alerted to a difficulty. A government can act only by the particular will of its members. As we have seen, a certain amount of tension will always exist between the particular will of an individual and his general will. In the previous ungoverned community this tension was resolved by the informal tribal sanctions, which brought the particular will into relative harmony with the general will—that is, the system of sanctions insured that the particular will of a member more or less conformed to the general will. This system of informal controls, however, has now been superseded by the specialized and partly formalized activity of the government. The government, not the citizens at large, puts the general will into effect and, as the main sanctioning agent, possesses the preponderance of the means of coercive influence. In this circumstance, since the government itself is now in the main faced only with such sanctions as it chooses to apply to itself, it seems inevitable that this would produce a divergence between the particular will of the government and the general will. The governors, free of the threat of sanctions, will act to further their own particular wills as against the general will. Governmental policy will be nothing but the particular wills of the governors. When this coincides with the general will, so much the better; when it conflicts with the general will, so much the worse for the community.

The institutions of government have placed considerable power in the hands of the government. They have the mantle of authority; the instrumentalities of communication, of command, of coercion are at their disposal. The authority which was supposed to enable the fulfillment of the general will has instead created a repository of political power which is now used to serve the particular interests of the government. We are faced with the age-old question, Who is to guard the guardians? This, however, is not meant to be a rhetorical question. Our theory provides us with an approach to an answer.

B. *The Rise of Politics*

The formation of government has paradoxical consequences. On the one hand, the machinery for the purposive fulfillment of the general will is established; on the other hand, that very machinery sets up a tendency in opposition to the general will: the particular wills of the governors. This is what Rousseau had in mind when he said that the general will cannot be represented.[1] But the previous informal influence of the general will does not vanish; instead it continues to work in two ways, which combine to form a countertendency to the drift of the particular will of the governors away from the general will. First, the general will continues to operate within the minds of the governors. Within their psyches, their particular wills are formed by the interaction of the private and the general will. This always involves a certain amount of psychic conflict, and the conflict will be intensified as the particular will diverges more and more from the general. It is easy to be cynical about Bodin's answer to "Who shall guard the guardians?" (the conscience of the king), especially in view of the degree of rationalization to which most minds can go, but still it may not be a completely negligible force.

In addition, the authority of the government, on which its political power rests, depends on the governed's acceptance of their government as legitimate. If they become convinced that the government is not legitimate, then its authority will vanish, and with it its political power. It will then be thrown back on its material power, notably its command of the instrumentalities of violence. At that point it is no longer a government but a rule. Such a rule may be possible—indeed Machiavelli has written a book on how a ruler should conduct himself in these circumstances—but, as Machiavelli himself pointed out, such a regime is always a shaky affair, easily destroyed by ineptitude or mischance.[2]

"If thou hast not a virtue, assume it." The government is best off trying to convince everyone that it is actually serving the general will even if it is not. This corresponds to the process of rationalization whereby the governors convince themselves

1. Rousseau (1762), bk. 2, sec. 1.

2. Machiavelli (1532a), chaps. 1–3, 6–8, 25.

that their particular wills are really identical to the general will—in fact the two processes are complementary, for a government which deceives itself in this matter is far more likely to be able to deceive others.

We are adopting a "on the one hand but on the other" position at this point. On the one hand, in principle the general will exercises an influence on the government under our hypothetical circumstances. On the other hand, in practice this influence may be very small. In general, a tension always exists between the general will of the community and the particular wills of the governors, and in principle the resources of each will not be negligible.

It is common nowadays to regard the political process as an interplay of conflict and cooperation which is carried out within the bounds of a "political culture" or a set of agreed "rules of the game."[3] This assigns political culture an essentially negative or passive role. It constitutes, so to speak, the walls of the box within which politics occurs. We wish instead here to advance a more dynamic, or in a broad sense dialectical, view of the matter, assigning a more active role to the political culture, which is one of the reasons why the phrase "general will" has been chosen, for the term implies positive activity.

Although at this point in our hypothetical history it is only a glimmer, we wish to pick out the conflict between the general will of a community and the particular wills of its governors as the central or root dynamic of the political process. The political system is in a very primitive stage at this point but this conflict is nevertheless clearer than it will ever be later when it is heavily overlaid by a massive and more visible nexus of secondary elaborations and complications.

In this simplest State, in its role of making and executing decisions on behalf of the community, the governors are faced with a conflict between the general will and their particular wills. The course of this struggle will be called *the political pro-*

3. Almond and Powell, Jr. (1966); Truman (1953).

cess. The political process can be analyzed as an interplay of influence which predominately will take the form of political authority and its derivative political power. The institutional structure of this process will be called *the political system.*

The political process is not to be identified with the governmental process, for although the conflict between the general and particular wills tends to be pervasive, it is not ubiquitous. Thus it is not hard to find minor, routine, "administrative" decisions in which no one has a special stake and hence which can be decided on purely technical (as opposed to political) grounds. At the other extreme, governmental decisions of the greatest import can be made with the community and its government acting as one, without significant conflict. The process by which the government of the United States decided to declare war on Japan in 1941 cannot be described as political, for example. The whole complex apparatus which normally comes into play over major State decisions was as nothing; the decision was made as soon as the government could convene and the words be spoken, and the voice of the government was the voice of the nation. In addition there is often an element in the process of governmental decision, or the content of the decision, which is purely technical. Still, it is regularly difficult to separate out the political and the technical aspects of government, and appropriate to analyze them together. Political science may thus be defined as the study of government, with the understanding that the major focus is on politics.

C. *The Government as a Social Group*

To return to our fictional history, we left our community at the simplest stage of governmental organization. It has only one purposive organization, a government, which governs in the name of the general will. Rousseau has pointed out the dilemma this situation produces. On the one hand, if the government is weak, it will easily be kept subject to the general will by the informal and unorganized sanctions of the community, but it will have insufficient means to put the general will into effective, purposive group action. On the other hand, if it is strong it will have the capability of serving the general will but, having nothing to fear from the populace at large, will content itself with promoting its own particular interests, which, since the members of the government occupy a special position in the social system, will always be more or less at odds with the general will.[4] The community is thus left with the grim choice between anarchy and tyranny, or perhaps of deciding which combination of the two is the least onerous.

Rousseau felt that this dilemma could be escaped only if the community were very small, so that all could participate in legislation, and if in their execution of the laws the magistrates could be closely supervised and watched by the whole community.[5] It may be that he was right, and that government strictly according to the general will is impossible in all but small and very simply organized groups. However, it is not clear, as Rousseau supposed, that such a government would be altogether a desirable thing, at least to those who feel that their obligations to the social whole, while real, should not be allowed to supersede other obligations and interests of equal or greater importance. Furthermore, to stop our history at this point would be to throw scant light on modern political processes. Accordingly we will continue by assuming further developments in political organization.

Let us start by examining our simple government in some detail. This government will form a distinct subgroup in society, engaged in cooperative interaction. Its members will begin to identify with each other as fellow governors. As a consequence, the subgroup itself will become a distinct social group with its own general will. The general will of the government will be different from the general will of the community, because the

4. Rousseau (1762), bk. 3, chaps. 1–3.
5. Ibid.

social position and forms of interaction of a governor are different from those of a member of society at large. From the
point of view of the community, this general will is the particular will of a subgroup. This term must not be understood in a
metaphorical sense as a sum or aggregate or average of somewhat similar particular wills, but as a discrete utility scale, a
component of the psyche of each member of government, influencing the governors directly through superego control, and
indirectly through informal sanctions.

It is true that any subgroup in the community whose members interact with relatively high frequency and can perceive
similarities with each other, may form its own general will; indeed, social stratification with separate senses of identity and
separate normative systems among the subgroups appears to be
a universal phenomenon among communities. What is special
about government, however, and what gives its general will a
special strength and force, is that the government is organized
around the making and executing of decisions: it is more than
a social group; it is an organization. It is at once a community
and an association, and the general wills of the community and
the association are the same.

The way in which our government is organized will make a
difference. Supposing it to consist of, say, twelve individuals,
each with a separate sphere of jurisdiction, performing his
governmental functions individually, and without coordination
with the rest; then its general will might not form very strongly.
On the other hand, supposing that government ordinarily requires coordination, joint action, and that governmental decisions are made in the name of the government collectively, then
the general will of the government is more likely to form very
strongly.

For an entity to act purposefully, it must assess, evaluate,
choose, and execute. To do this, it must have a government. In
an individual, this government is called the ego. Our imaginary
community acts through its government. Subgroups within it

cannot act, because they have no government; hence the effect of any general wills of these subgroups will not be great. One subgroup, however, forms an exception: the government. The government acts *for* the community; it acts *in* itself. Its decisions will spring directly and unambiguously from its own general will, free of the paradoxes and internal contradicitions which characterize its relations to the general will of the community. The action of the government is purposive in a way altogether analogous to that of an individual; the government is an actor, and its actions carry out its general will in a straightforward and unambiguous way. Nothing else in the community can match its overwhelming coherence and power: not the particular wills of its members, not the general wills of the other subgroups, not the general will of the community itself, whose interests the government will serve only to the extent that its particular will is internally influenced. He who says purposive organization says power. With its monopoly of purposive organization, the position of the government is supreme and unchallengeable. We will call this kind of government *absolutism*.

It should be noted that while the power of an absolute government is supreme, it is not unlimited. As has already been pointed out, the government is drawn from the community and will share in the general will of the community. When we observe the government, we will see only its particular will in action. Beneath the surface, however, the general will of the community participates in the formation of the general will of the government and acts as its conscience—sometimes as its guide. In addition, as has also been pointed out, the government will be ill-advised to act in such a way as to undermine its legitimacy. Finally, there will be technical limitations on the power of the government: Its ability successfully to direct the activity of the community will be limited by the means at its disposal. The government may neither desire nor be able to regulate many areas of community activity. In fact, to depart momentarily from fiction, governments tend to be content with maintaining law and order, and not otherwise to meddle with the life of society except as is necessary to maintain their position, for example, in the raising of taxes or the conduct of war. The enormous expansion of the role of government in modern times is essentially a response to a challenge to its existence, as was, to take another example, the transformation of the government of the Roman Empire in the third century.[6]

Since the conflict between the general will of the community and the general will of the government is overwhelmed by the preponderance of the latter, there is little of a political system in absolute government. Politics is mainly the struggle among the governors and others who exercise power over governmental decisions, to determine which strategy set among the negotiation set of the general will of the government will be chosen. The main systemic aspect is the internal psychological struggle in the minds of the governors, whereby their private wills, the general will of the community, and the general will of the government strive for supremacy. The informal sanctions within the government, however, ensure that by and large the actions of the governors will be in conformity to the general will of the government, and from there on it is only a question of which program in this range will be chosen. The individual members of the government will of course use the power conferred by their authority to their own individual benefit (i.e., to the advantage of their particular wills). That goes without saying for any form of government. Here, however, they will do so in a way which will not conflict with the general will of the government; for example, they will squeeze private profits out of the general public rather than each other, usually in such a way as not to endanger the governmental stability.

D. *The Primary Organization of the Government*

So far, the organization of our government has been simple and straightforward. It has been assigned, or has assumed, the task of translating the general will of the community into effective

6. Walbank (1946).

group action. The accomplishment of this task will require a division of labor among the governors. We have not, however, assumed that the governors are so numerous, nor their tasks so complex, that they must be organized into subgroups. Of course, some person or persons must figure out what the most effective division of labor is within the government, recruit members for these posts, see that the tasks are effectively carried out and coordinated with each other, etc. In other words, the activity through which the government regulates the activity of the community must itself be regulated. It would be a mistake, however, to say that there must be two governments, a government of the community and a government of the government. The matter must be stated more carefully.

Given the common purpose of the community, the task of creating the necessary organization to translate this task into effective group action is purely technical. Now the governors are members of the community; they govern themselves along with everyone else. As long as government is understood as a purely technical problem, there is no need to assign special status to those governors who govern members of the government as against those who govern members of the community, for example, a tax collector as against a person who oversees and coordinates the activity of tax collectors. The government of the government is simply a part of the government of the community—one aspect among others of the division of governmental labor.

We may call the level of government we are now considering its *primary organization*, which is the organization technically rational to the accomplishment of the general will. This is the nonpolitical, "purely administrative" level of governmental organization.

On the level of primary organization, the basic situation does not change if, as a result of the increasing size and complexity of the government, it becomes necessary to divide the government into subgroups, each with its own special task. One of these subgroups may be the government of the government, or, more generally, in the organizational chart of primary organization, we may be able to distinguish between the line organization and the staff organization.

While the suborganizations of the primary organization create no new problems as long as we focus only on the problem of carrying out the general will, as we shall see, it has results of the greatest importance for the political organization of the government.

E. *The Secondary Organization of the Government*

Our government has by now developed considerably beyond a simple primary organization. The system of political authority created by the primary organization has given rise to a system of political power. The general will defines a negotiation set of governmental strategies, relative to which the members of the government have conflicting purposes. A struggle will ensue, in which each member of the government will use the authority and power at his disposal in an attempt to produce the governmental strategy with the highest utility to his own particular will. But the decisions which emerge will not only define certain behavior by the members of the community; it will also define a system of governmental action and interaction. Thrown into this system of interaction, the governors will begin to identify with each other. The government, as a social group, will generate its own general will, which will influence governmental activity through both its psychological force and the exercise of sanctions.

Our government now faces much the same situation as did our unorganized community formerly. It has a general will, but no government. This statement does not contradict our previous discussion of the "government of the government." In the primary organization the government of the government has the task of putting the general will of the community into effect.

There does not, however, exist any organization whose task it is to put the general will of the government into effect. If, therefore, the members of the community felt impelled to establish a government in order to promote their general will, so now, by the same token, the government will feel impelled to create its own government. Hence, our primary governmental organization will give rise to a secondary governmental organization.

At first, we can assume, this secondary government will take the form of alliances and systems of alliance among the governors, and perhaps even the most advanced governmental systems will be heavily infused with such alliances. In the end, as the size and complexity of the governmental organization grows, the technical superiority of association over alliance will loom ever larger, and the government will form an association, or series of associations, for the purpose of promoting its own general will.

There is one critical respect in which the government's position here differs from that of the community prior to the formation of government. We assumed our original community to have no associational organization whatsoever; the government started with a blank state. Now, however, our government not only needs an association; it *is* an association. Hence it may be possible for it to utilize the existing organization, or parts of the existing organization, to serve its own general will in addition to the general will of the community. Thus, the secondary organization may politicize the primary organization by growing into it, or infusing it in a parasitic or symbiotic way. Indeed, this can be expected to happen, to a greater or lesser degree, to the entire primary organization of the government. In these circumstances, when we say that the government has a government, we mean something far different from our previous statement. We are now stating that the governmental system has become a political system.

Perhaps an example will make this point clear. The main elements of the primary organization of the United States

Congress are defined by the Constitution. The function of this organization is to pass laws in furtherance of the general welfare of the nation, as defined formally in the Preamble to the Constitution and substantively by the general will of the nation.

Preliminary research and deliberation with a view to eventual legislation seems technically impossible for as large a body as a house of Congress, and the system of committees, each with a specialized area, and with a chairman, staff, etc., is clearly a logical development from the primary organization. In the same way, the authority of the committee chairmen to set the time and place of meetings and otherwise oversee the committee activity appears technically rational to the primary organization. The committee system, however, and in particular the committee chairmen play a key role in the secondary (political) organization of Congress, whereby the two houses govern themselves according to their own general wills. The very great authority of the committee chairmen derives from the role which they play in both organizational systems, but perhaps predominantly from the latter.[7]

Despite their close interlocking, however, the two systems have an uneasy relationship to each other at various points. To take a single instance, the rule is that the committee chairman shall be the member of the majority party with the longest continuous service on the committee (the seniority rule). From the point of view of the secondary organization, this rule has a good deal to be said for it. It elevates to posts of formal leadership those who are likely to possess personal authority. Members of Congress with long service are the most likely to have firmly internalized the group norms, to have experience and hence skill at internal congressional government, and to command the respect of their colleagues. Above all, it provides a ready way to avoid the central problem faced by the political organizations of any group of peers, fraternal dissension and squabbling.

7. Berman (1964), pp. 117–36.

On the other hand, the seniority rule has been widely attacked as technically irrational to the primary organization. Being aged, it is argued, the chairmen lack vigor. They are oriented to the ideals and purposes of past decades and neither understand nor support recent changes in national sentiment. They come from safe rural districts or States and are unsympathetic to the problems of urban civilization. Above all, their main focus is inward toward their colleagues in Congress, rather than outward toward their constituents and the nation.[8]

Irrespective of the merits of these arguments, the general point is valid, that when a given organization or post in an organization plays an authoritative role in both the primary and the secondary organizations, it is unlikely to perform both tasks with equal effectiveness.

Alternatively to growing up within the primary organization, political organization can emerge as largely separate. For example, the party system in the United States and Great Britain grew up largely in separation from the primary governmental organization. This principle is carried to its extreme in communist states, with their complete organizational separation of the primary and secondary levels, that is, between the regular governmental apparatus and the communist party.

The group which governs the government according to the general will of the government may emerge as a distinct subgroup within the government. It, too, will constitute a social group, with, in time, its own general will. In turn this group itself may develop a government, leading to a tertiary level of organization, and so on.

F. *The Emergence of the Political System*

We have pointed out that as it develops, our primary government organization will become divided into subgroups. From a purely technical point of view, assigning an individual to a

8. Ibid., p. 129–36.

task does not differ in principle from assigning that task to a group of individuals. From a psychological point of view, however, there is a most significant difference. When an individual is assigned a post in a formal or informal organization, there will, of course, be an impact on his preferences: indeed, his whole self-concept may be altered. As far as its impact on the organization is concerned, what happens is that the individual's particular will undergoes more or less of a transformation. An organizational theorist must examine the psychological question How do organizational roles affect the individuals who occupy them, and how, in turn, does their behavior affect the organization?

If a group, as against an individual, is assigned a role, something radically new occurs. The group becomes, not just a functionally or technically rational entity, but a psychological entity; it becomes a social group with a real general will, and just as we assumed that our original group formed an organization to further its general will, so we must assume that the newly formed group will, informally or formally, itself organize to further *its* general will. So organization begets organization in an apparently endless chain, spreading horizontally with the division of labor and vertically with the increasingly elaborate chain of command and the development of secondary, tetiary, quarternary, etc., levels of government. Given the two principles, first, rational organization to pursue a common purpose, and second, the psychological consequences of this organization, the proliferation of organization and the multiplication of general wills will spread to the boundaries fixed by the limits of technical feasibility and the law of diminishing psychological force as group identifications multiply in the minds of the members (i.e., presumably there will come a point where the intensity of the identifications among the members is too weak to support a viable organization). As an illustration, one need only glance at the almost incredible organizational complexity of the modern state or the modern corporate giant.

The distinction between primary and secondary organizations is purely one of point of view. In our previous example, we distinguished the secondary organization of a house of Congress, but from the point of view of the body of legislators, that is its own primary organization—the organization which promotes the general will of the legislators—while the original primary organization, serving the general will of the nation, is something external. Hence our distinction resembles Homans's distinction between the "external system" and the "internal system." There are, however, two important differences. First, from the point of view of the organization of a given general will there will be an external environment (the larger organization and the larger general will of which it is a part) and the internal environment (the suborganizations, with their general wills which are a part of *it*). Second, neither the larger nor the smaller organizations are psychologically external. Both are internalized in the minds of the members. The organizational nexus is linked together by three factors: the technical requirements of organizational interdependence, the power of sanctions, and the psychological forces of interlinking group identifications.

The whole apparatus governs the actions of its members, on many levels and in many sections, with the levels and sections linked together by the above three forces into a system of conflicting and cooperating wills, which we will call the political system.

G. *The Operation of the Political System*

Our hypothetical government now exhibits an indefinite proliferation of suborganization on both a vertical and a horizontal level. This creates an entirely different situation than the former one, where the government is simply a set of individuals, with their own particular wills, who also share the general will of the government and of the community. In the former case, we could expect the general will of the government to gain sway in nearly all circumstances, so that one could discern a clear-cut set of interests of government, or "reasons of State," which governmental policy could be exhibited as representing. The operation of government could not in normal circumstances be seriously jeopardized either by the general will of the community or by the diversity of private wills within the government. The general will of the community would be influential only insofar as it harmonized with the governmental interests. The interplay of the private wills of the members of the government would be more visible and, as it were, noisy. Each member of the government would have his own interests, and his own resources of power, based on his authority within the government. The process of governmental action would then, from one perspective, be nothing but the struggle among the governors to turn the governmental policy to their own particular interests. Nevertheless, this struggle would in no way impede the orderly flow of the general will of the government into purposive action. The struggle within the government will be, so to speak, a fight within the family, and where the interests of the family itself are concerned, all would unite.

In this case, the political process will interweave three things, with the following results:

1. The general will of the community contends with the general will of the government. Result: Insofar as they conflict, the general will of the government will prevail.

2. The private wills of the governors conflict with the general will of the government. Result: Insofar as they conflict, the general will of the government will prevail.

3. The private wills of the governors conflict with each other. Result: The outcome will be heavily influenced, but not uniquely determined by, the relative power of the members of the government, compounded of the power conferred by position and the skill with which it is used. In fact, the politics of this section of the system will be much the same as the politics of the contractual organization outlined above.

On the other hand, where government is viewed as a set of organizations, the political process assumes an altogether different course. The underlying reason was developed earlier: When it comes to a conflict between the particular will of an individual and the general will of his group, the general will almost always prevails because of the twin pressures on the individual: inward from his superego, and outward from the readiness of others to sanction departures from the general will, even (or especially) in cases where the sanctioner himself might wish to violate the general will. On the other hand, when it comes to a subgroup which develops its own general will, a conflict between the general will of the subgroup and the general will of the overall group is far less unequal. In the first place, the internal forces will be far more unclear: the superegos of the individuals involved will be caught in a conflict of loyalties toward the two groups. In the same way, the sanctions of the group may be far less overwhelming in the face of the united strength of the subgroup. In short, a suborganization is in a much stronger position vis-à-vis the overall organization than an individual is vis-à-vis the organization. The result will be to create a complex political system wherein the governmental policy will be much less an unequivocal expression of its general will. The relative weakening of the general will of the government creates the possibility that the governmental programs will express the general will of the community and the wills of the subgroups at the expense of the general will of the government.

At this highest level of generalization, it is hard to get a clear idea of what our political system will look like; nevertheless a few very broad conclusions seem to emerge. Taking the system layer by layer:

1. *The individual.* Every member of the government will at all times act to maximize his expected utility. His utility scale constitutes his particular will. This will is compounded of several elements: his private will and the general wills of the com-

munity, the government, his branch of the government, and the subgroup within this branch that he occupies. He may be aware that in part these wills conflict with each other, or he may have rationalized the conflicts away. In any event, by hypothesis he has worked these into a coherent preference scale. In actual practice, conflicts between subscales will regularly produce results other than an integrated particular will. The effects of conflicts of loyalty have received a good deal of study.[9]

Apart from outside resources and personal skill, the power which an individual possesses will spring from the position which he occupies. The main source of this power is the authority of his office, both formal and informal. He will act according to the rules defining his authority, and on the whole his actions will have the effect of putting the general will of his subgroup into action, although perhaps with varying degrees of vigor and effectiveness. He will, however, always have a certain amount of discretion in the way he fulfills his duties, and in addition, his authority and the position he occupies will create a wide range of options beyond, but not in contradiction to, his official duties. The political power thus generated will be used to influence group decisions toward the outcome which has the highest utility for his own particular will—for example, in enhancing the power or prestige of his office, acquiring promotion, increasing his monetary rewards, as well as advancing the interests of the subgroup, the government, or the community as a whole. Private gain and public weal do not stand in contradiction in his mind. His objectives will be a blend of the two, and in those areas where the two stand in opposition, his own evaluations will consist of that accommodation most congenial to him. This point has been insisted on because a conclusion of great theoretical importance flows from it, as follows:

On the concrete empirical level, politics consists of actions by individuals, which in turn are an amalgam of mental and

9. Some of the literature is discussed in Blau and Scott (1962), pp. 82–83, 155, 199.

physical activity. If we examine this action, we will not see any private or general wills, but only particular wills, that is, the actual utility scales of the actors. (The word "see" is perhaps too strong, for we infer these scales from individual preferences and infer the preferences from the words and deeds of the actors.) It is the particular wills of the actors which are, so to speak, on the stage, and from which (in conjunction with assessment and choice) action proceeds. On the empirical level, private wills and general wills may not be at all visible. They may be pure fictions, or, to put a better face on it, purely theoretical ideas used to explain the specific content of particular wills. By analogy, for example, we may say that a particular shade of green contains two parts yellow to one part blue. This is a purely analytical statement; it does not imply that one can see yellow or blue, given a powerful enough microscope (thought this might be), nor that the color was actually produced by adding yellow and blue. Similarly, we are not arguing that in fact an individual forms two utility scales, a private and a general, and then combines them in some way. The actual process of preference formation is demonstrably very different. The idea of the particular will, though somewhat artificial, is closer to what is observable. We can observe activity, draw inferences about the thought processes involved, and from this draw conclusions about sets and patterns of preferences held by the individual. The theoretical idea of a particular will can be translated into this observed and inferred preference pattern fairly readily.

There may be instances where the ideas of private will and general will can be given a straightforward empirical reference. For example suppose that when faced with a choice an individual is aware of a conflict between his private interests and his duty to his country. In that case it might not be stretching things too much to say that, as an empirical fact, his private and general wills are in conflict.

2. *The general will*. It is relatively easy to locate the general will of a small, informally organized group. When asked,

the participants will usually respond with a list of the normatively sanctioned rules of behavior characteristic of the group, and these lists will usually be quite similar. It is then easy to iron our minor discrepancies and come up with a general will of the group. Strictly speaking this is a purely theoretical idea: the utility scale of an ideal group member with which each has identified; but the close correspondence between the theoretical idea of the general will and the empirical data of the list of rules as perceived by the participants makes the procedure of identifying the two at least plausible.

When we move to larger groups, especially with complex formal organizations, the problem becomes far more difficult. Many political scientists insist that on the national level there is no such thing as a general will, a national interest, or a national welfare and in effect assert that all that they can observe is the interaction of particular wills—which of course is perfectly true.[10] For example, Gabriel Almond started with a concept close to the idea being developed here, but he has abandoned it.[11] The same can be said for David Truman's concept of "the rules of the game."[12] W. W. Rostow distinguishes a "national style," and a "national purpose" in foreign policy, but it seems to have little impact on his actual analyses and prescriptions.[13] The theory developed here, while asserting the existence and pervasive influence of a real general will on the

10. Bentley (1908); Gross (1953), p. 10; Latham (1952), p. 37; Beard (1934); Schilling (1962), pp. 5–27. For recent discussions of this theme see Friederich (1958) and Leys and Perry (1959).

11. Almond (1950), pp. 158–91; Almond and Powell, Jr. (1966), pp. 50–72.

12. Truman (1953).

13. Rostow (1960), pp. 12–28, 476–84, 543–50. We feel that, in common with many such treatments, Rostow's fails to show any real connection between his essentially moral (or moralistic?) conception of the national purpose, and his geopolitical conception of the national interest. That is, his "national interest" would remain unaltered if, for example, the United States were a communist state. Hence the idea of a "national purpose" has no operational meaning when it comes to foreign policy and the definition of the "national interest."

national level altogether commensurate in importance with the normative system of a small informal group, also serves to explain how something so important can be so invisible.

The central reason concerns the paradoxical nature of the results when attempts are made to supply purposive organization and action to the general will. Purposive organization requires a government. Following Rousseau's argument, unless government includes every citizen of the group, and unless there is absolutely no role differentiation among the governors (that is, unless there is a radical democracy with complete equality and no officers) then the government will constitute a distinct group or subgroup within the community which will develop and act according to its own general will, not that of the community. The purposes of the government will be at odds with those of the community. This in turn means that there is no effective way in which the general will of a community can carry out the processes of assessment, choice, and execution required for its translation into action.

The general will itself cannot act. It only manifests itself as it influences the attitudes of, and hence the actions of, the individual actors within the community. This influence in turn will be enormously difficult to ascertain, first, because the general will is the precipitate of only one of the many identifications which contribute to the formation of an individual's values, and normally it will be of less importance than many of these; second, because each individual's perception of the general will differs somewhat from the others' perceptions; and third, because the conflicts between the various wills which make up a person's particular will are mostly heavily blurred and overlaid by a blanket of rationalization. As a consequence, it appears to be a problem of the utmost difficulty to ascertain the general will of a large organized community by direct observation.

Even if these difficulties are waived, and assuming that the general will is known, it may be a highly uncertain task to try to relate this will to specific policy problems faced by the government of the community, especially since the general will only determines a range of possible policies. When one examines the literature which attempts to relate governmental policy to a "national purpose," one sees that the relation of this national purpose to concrete policy problems is often very unclear. In addition, the suspicion keeps arising in the reader's mind that the author has mistaken his own particular will for the general will.[14]

Nevertheless, there are times when the operation of the general will can be discerned even if an exact specification is elusive. The ready mobilization of national energies in times of crisis, especially when a danger from without threatens; the widespread feelings surrounding great public occasions; the general indignation when a public official is caught doing something which would be only mildly disapproved as a private act; the intense emotion associated with national symbols, such as the flag—all attest the existence of something akin to what is here called a general will. I was first led to take this view seriously by my reflections on the impact that the assassination of President Kennedy seemed to have on most United States citizens, and by my readings on the French Revolution. Both seem totally inexplicable unless one posits something like a national will at work. The roles of the committee of public safety and especially of Rousseau's disciple Robespierre seem especially notable in this respect. The phenomenon of nationalism—that most powerful and least understood[15] ideological force in modern history, next to which liberalism and communism appear but pale shadows—bespeaks a national consciousness and a national will.

We should expect the general will to be the most visible

14. See notes 11–13 above.

15. Although there is an enormous literature on the subject. For a survey of the literature through 1950, see Snyder (1954). For more recent treatments dealing with non-European aspects, see Kedourie (1960) and Emerson (1960), among others.

when the organizational structures of society whose general wills compete with the overall general will are weak, either disintegrating or not yet built up. In this connection the clearest emergence of all appears to occur around the phenomenon of charismatic leadership. The charismatic leader typically stands for the destruction of existing organizational forms, and a return or advance to the direct expression of the national will through the personal authority of the charismatic leader. Here the underlying tension between the general will and the organizational apparatus which is supposed to serve it, but in fact does not, emerges for once out in the open. The personal leadership of the charismatic leader stands in antithesis to organizational or institutional authority and the legalistic formal codes they spawn: "It is written but *I* say unto you . . ., etc." In its modern form it almost uniformly expresses the sentiments of nationalism. In fact we may use these characteristics to define charismatic leadership: Charismatic leadership is personal authority which expresses the general will of a community in opposition to the values of existing organizations and institutions within the community. Charismatic leadership must as a consequence be more or less ephemeral, because to achieve success, or even to pursue it, a charismatic-led movement must develop an organization, and the pursuit of the general will of the organization will gradually supplant the expression of the original goal. Weber has termed this process "the routinization of charisma."[16]

Thus the general will may "break through" the institutional structure and assume a dramatic, indeed dominant, role in setting governmental policy, but only temporarily. It will soon return underground, its operation remaining pervasive, but indirect and largely unseen.

Returning to our fictional government: If it is a stable affair

16. Weber (1925*a*), pp. 124–25. But contrast this passage with pp. 262–64. Weber's use of the idea of charismatic leadership is not always consistent.

and has endured for awhile, we can generally describe the operation of its political system in terms of the interaction of the
particular wills involved (i.e., the general wills of the government and its suborganizations and the particular wills of the
individuals), with the understanding that the overall general
will makes itself felt mostly in the process of the formation of
these wills. The term is of not much use in describing the ordi-
nary workaday operation of politics.

3. *Intermediate wills.* It is otherwise with the general will
of the government and its suborganizations, for there is a critical difference. In our hypothetical history, the governmental
organization is a product of the general will, while in all other
cases the general wills of the suborganizations are products of
their organization. The central proposition here is that the general will springs from the organization of action. In the community, it springs from the informal, nonpurposive organization
of the community. The community does not act, and hence its
general will does not. In contrast, governmental organization
is purposive; hence the general wills of the government and its
subunits will be expressed in their actions. This is not to say
that a tension may not exist from time to time between the organization of action and the general will of a governmental organ.
Homans has vividly described how informal organization grows
up within formal organization, only to become crystallized into
new formal organization. Official organizational goals can stand
in conflict with the actual goals, and interactions between the
two produce a new and unplanned set of objectives. These tensions and conflicts produce the dynamics of much organizational change and development and will be examined at length
in the following volume. In lieu of that treatment, we may here
support Homans's conclusion that normally the general trend
is toward congruence: that usually we find an equilibrium process between the organizational structure and its normative
system, with equilibrium, disequilibrium, and new equilibrium
succeeding each other in an endless chain which he has called

a "moving equilibrium."[17] If we take a cross-section of this process at any moment of time we will find a fair consonance between the two. Hence, in contrast with the general will of a community, the general will of an organization readily finds its purposive expression in organizational activity.

When we come to the impact of suborganization on the government, however, this statement must be modified. As has been pointed out, compared with the general will, and the particular wills of the individual members, the influence of the general wills of the subgroups will be large. Hence, the governmental policy will not simply be a product of the general will of the government but instead will be a complex amalgam, influenced by the wills of the various subunits, the specific content of which will depend on the strength of the general will of the government in the minds of the members and on the relative power of the subunits. In other words, the general will of the government stands in much the same relation to the suborganization as the general will of the community stands to the government, and it is in danger of vanishing as the direct determinant of policy and retreating to one of the factors forming the general wills of the subunits.

On the other hand, there are critical differences which will tend to give the general will of the government an advantage. First, the government has been assumed to be divided into a set of subunits, possibly a very large set. This will, so to speak, divide the opposition and give the general will of the government a great weight. It should be noted that the community itself is also presumably divided into subgroups, for example, social classes, with their own general wills. In contrast with the relation of the suborganization to the government, these divisions within the overall community have an unmitigatedly weakening effect on the general will, because the community is not itself a decision-making apparatus and hence is unable to play a role of "divide and conquer."

17. Homans (1950), pp. 421–23.

In addition, we have assumed that the governmental subunits are in turn subdivided. This means that a unit on the intermediate level will be caught between the government as a whole and its own subunits; that is, it faces a war on both fronts, thus weakening its position vis-à-vis the former and correspondingly strengthening the latter. It will be noted that the only suborganization not caught between the two millstones is the lowest level, whose subunits are individuals only. For reasons already indicated, in this case the general will of the organizational unit can be expected to prevail in a relatively unimpeded way. Hence there will be two relatively advantaged levels of organization: the highest and the lowest.

4. *The convergence of wills.* Finally, there is a more decisive advantage which will accrue to the overall government, which can be exhibited by continuing our fictional history another step. Our government is now organized in a complex set of suborganizations, arranged in levels and sections. Without regard, for the time being, to the relative influence of these subunits, we assume that the political process results in decisions which are executed; that is, there is neither deadlock nor failure of authority and the government succeeds in governing. Now the decisions of the government are authoritative; that is, they are accepted by the community, and the members of the government will be obeyed as they exercise their authority. Suppose that we focus on three actors, A from suborganization Alpha, B from Beta, and D from Delta. Suppose that there are four policy alternatives, w, x, y, and z. Actor A reflects the prevailing view in department Alpha and prefers w to the other three, B prefers x in common with his fellows, and D is indifferent to all four. In other words, w is the general will of Alpha, x of Beta, and Delta has no general will on the subject. We are in some doubt about what the general will of the government is, since all we perceive is the varying wills of the particular departments. Let us suppose, however, that by delving into the psyches of the participants we discover that the general will of

the government is z, although this corresponds to the general will of none of the departments. Actors A, B, and D have handled the problem of the conflict between the general wills of their departments and the general will of the government by rationalizing away the conflict; that is, by means of incorrect assessments of reality they have reconciled their preferred departmental policies with the general will. This is very easy, since the likely consequences of a governmental policy, and hence its utility, are often very difficult to determine—if this can be done at all. By this means the general will of the government has been shunted out of the political process and exercises no influence.

Now let us suppose that the policy that eventually emerges is y. By hypothesis, y now possesses authority, and A and B will obey it because it is legitimate. The situation is now rather complex. The actual general will is z, actor A thinks that the general will is w, actor B thinks it is x, and D thinks there is no general will on the question; yet all agree that y is the legitimate policy. The legitimacy involved is formal legitimacy—all agree that y has been arrived at through the prescribed channels—and is hence binding, not because of its content, but because of the way in which it has been formulated.

Policies which are accepted as formally legitimate, however, tend in time to become accepted as substantively legitimate (within unspecified boundary conditions). At first A will say to himself, "y is a mistaken policy. It does not reflect the real general will, which is w, but I will obey it because it is legal, and it is wrong to break the law." But this is psychologically a difficult attitude to sustain: there will be a pull in two directions, first toward a denial of legitimacy and overt disobedience, and second toward revision of evaluation and acceptance of y as a substantively legitimate dictate of the general will. By hypothesis, the general will of the government, in conjunction with the general will of the community, is sufficiently strong to maintain the authority of the governmental acts.

Therefore the movement will be toward the psychologically more stable alternative of accepting y as substantively legitimate.

We are here asserting that any viable political system will show a strong pull toward general acceptance of the actual governmental policy as substantively legitimate. Hence y will tend to become the general will of the government and of the community. Rousseau put this point very succinctly.

> The citizen consents to all the laws, even to those which have been passed in spite of him, even to those which will visit punishment upon him should he dare to violate any of them. . . . When, therefore, a view which is at odds with my own wins the day, it proves only that I was deceived, and that what I took to be the general will was no such thing.[18]

It is this consideration which has led some political philosophers to assert that might makes right, for when by the application of superior power a set of rules is imposed on a population, either the populace will successfully resist these rules and overthrow them, or else eventually it will come to regard them as legitimate. In the latter case, therefore, justice is nothing else but the interests of the stronger.

This point throws another factor into the balance: first, there will always be a pull of governmental decisions away from the general will of the community. This is a consequence of the process of organization. On the other hand, the general will exerts a pull on governmental decisions through its operation on the consciences of the government, while the governmental decisions will exert a pull on the general will because of their formal legitimacy. When a system is stable, it is a sign that these forces are in balance. When changes are occurring, it is a sign of imbalance.

5. *Recapitulation.* We will summarize this section on the operation of the political system before proceeding to the final steps of our fictional history.

18. Rousseau (1762), bk. 4, chap. 2.

Government has traditionally been justified as an instrument for translating the general will of the community into purposive action; but government cannot be a neutral means to this end. Its organization sets in motion a complex of conflicting forces. Each governmental unit and subunit will develop its own general will. Insofar as all these wills are convergent, government is a technical matter of assessment, choice, and execution. Insofar as these wills are conflicting, government will involve politics, that is, the struggle to influence governmental choice and execution in which the resources of the contending parties consist of the political authority and political power conferred by their positions within the governmental structure. Organization thus creates conflict, and in this conflict the greatest advantage will be to the most comprehensive governmental unit on the one hand, and the smallest units on the other. In normal times, the general will of the community will be relatively weak and indirect in its influence, although occasionally it may break through in the most striking fashion.

While organization creates a plurality of divergent wills, the process of conflict among these wills tends to lessen the divergence and to bring the conflicting wills closer together, providing the system is able to achieve authoritative policy. A stable political system will thus be an equilibrium of opposing forces.

H. *The Expansion of the Political System*

To resume the development of our government, little has so far been said about the relations between the community and the government. It has only been pointed out that the requirement that the policies of the government be accepted as legitimate imposes certain restraints on its actions. In this relationship much depends on the tasks which the government performs or attempts to perform. Near one extreme, the government may confine its activities to the definition and enforcement of criminal law, defense of the territory of the community (where "territory" may be taken literally or figuratively), and such functions as the establishment of currency, weights and measures, etc. At the other extreme the government may attempt to regulate the entire life of the community, down to the smallest detail, including the very thoughts of the members. It might appear that the larger the area of authority of government, the greater will be its power relative to the community, and hence the more absolute it will be (i.e., independent of the general will). In fact, such an assumption underlies much of modern political theory. On the contrary, I will argue that area of control and extent of governmental autonomy do not necessarily go together, because extension of the area of control may set in motion processes which will create countervailing centers of power.

Suppose for example that our government has a law which declares murder a criminal offense. The execution of this law will not require either an extensive governmental apparatus or any significant organization of the community. Murder is in most communities a relatively rare event. It is easy to tell when a person is dead, and persons discovering a body will almost uniformly notify the authorities immediately and voluntarily. The authorities will usually be able to tell fairly easily whether the death was by homicide simply by observing the body and its surroundings. If homicide has occurred, it is then necessary to determine the exact circumstances by observing the details of the crime and asking appropriate questions of those who might have knowledge of the event.

The whole process of executing justice in such instances will not usually be a technically difficult job, providing only that the public is willing to report dead bodies and to answer questions for the most part truthfully. This is not asking a great deal. Little public cooperation is needed, although this small amount is still indispensable, for if people do not report dead bodies voluntarily, or are reluctant or evasive under questioning, the execution of justice becomes an entirely different task.

At the other extreme, suppose that the government is faced with a major war. Here a great deal of cooperative activity by the citizens may be required. Substantial resources must be raised, economic activity will have to be regulated, and a large army must be recruited, presumably from the citizenry.

Let us assume that our government initially was of a minimal kind, that is, its functions mainly those of justice and defense, but that over a period of time it extends its regulatory functions into the economic sphere. This spread can occur in various ways. The government can enlist the cooperation of social organizations already existing, for example, business concerns or associations; it can encourage the development of such organization; it can create semigovernmental organizations; or it can create official governmental organizations to enlist the necessary societal cooperation.

We have not so far spoken of the relation of our government to the other forms of organization in society, an omission that it is now necessary to repair. Suppose, first, that outside of the government the organization of society is mainly informal, and focused on families and social classes.[19] The social organization even of relatively modern societies can be mainly informal; for example, if one examines formal organization in France prior to the twentieth century (even to a considerable extent prior to World War II), one finds the State, the church, the family, and very little else.[20] Business firms were mainly extensions of family organization.[21]

Suppose, as has often been the case, that the members of the government are predominantly drawn from a single social class. We can therefore expect the members of the government to reflect the values of that class in the way they conduct their

19. For a definition of a social class as an informal organization of action, see Homans (1950), chaps. 1, 2.

20. Rose (1954); Hoffman et al. (1963).

21. Hoffman et al. (1963), pp. 129–31, 249–54 et passim.

business; the general will of that class will greatly influence governmental policy. Should this be carried to the extreme, in that the policy of the government is not influenced by the overall general will at all, then the government *rules* society but *governs* its own social class, of which it is, in Marx's phrase, the executive committee. We should, however, expect a divergence between the general will of this class and the general will of the government for the same reasons which produced the split between the general will of the government and the general will of the whole community. We will not here go into the conditions which will aggravate or mitigate this split, except to say that we can expect it to be entirely absent only if the social class and the government are coextensive, that is, if a member of the social class normally finds his career in governmental service or in a closely allied field. This was largely the case, for example, with the Mandarin system in China and perhaps explains its extraordinary tenacity.[22]

If the social class from which the government is drawn is also the base for another organization, then the two organizations may be thrown into conflict in areas where their values differ but be drawn into cooperation by virtue of sharing the same general will (of the social class). So, for example, with a separation of church and government, both drawn mainly from the landed aristocracy, as in the Middle Ages.

The existence of purposive social organization outside the government, and drawn from a different social class from that of the governors, seems always to pose a threat to it, and an acute struggle is likely to break out if the government attempts to regulate or in any way extend its authority over the operation of such organizations. In general, the greater the purposive organization outside the government, the harder it is to govern; and the greater the area of governmental regulation, the more acute this problem becomes.

The source of such a conflict is double. In the first place,

22. Weber (1922).

the general will of the two organizations will be to a certain extent at odds, especially if there is an overlap of claimed jurisdiction. In the second place, the nongovernmental organization will feel that the government has to a certain extent neglected the general will in favor of its own interests (and will often be correct in this). While this organization will be myopic with respect to differences between its own general will and the general will of the community, and tend to rationalize these differences away, its vision will be keen with respect to any mote in its neighbor's eye. As a consequence, its opposition to the government will always be carried out in the name of the general will, and with considerable justification in many cases. As a result, the organization may be able to recruit support for its opposition from those who are not its members. In short, to the extent that the general will fails to find expression in purposive governmental action, it may for that very reason find a champion elsewhere. Hence the organization of society into a multiplicity of organized particular wills engaged in purposive action is not necessarily, as Rousseau supposed, at the expense of the general will.[23]

We are not here advancing the argument that pluralistic forms of social organization are best because they promote purposive expression of the general will of the community. In the first place, the general will of some communities may best be left unexpressed; perhaps indeed the full and unhampered expression of *any* general will is bad. Second, we are pointing out that the entry of additional organized partial wills into a political system does not necessarily weaken the influence of the general will and may even increase it. A multiplicity of organized interests may or may not promote the purposive expression of the general will; what will always happen is that the government will become less absolute.

While an increase in the area of governmental function will

23. Rousseau (1762), bk. 2, chap. 3.

tend to bring the interests of governmental and nongovernmental organizations more strongly into conflict, at the same time it will bring the two more in need of each other. The expanded role of the government places it increasingly in need of active cooperation from those not in the government, while at the same time making the ability of nongovernmental elements to influence governmental policy an increasingly attractive goal. The area of conflict grows, while at the same time each increasingly needs the assistance of the other. The ground has now been prepared for an associational relationship between the two. If this relationship is formed, it may go no further than that of an alliance. This, for example, is still more or less the case in the United States. If it does go further—that is, if the cooperation reaches the stage of voluntary association or contractual association—then a new suborganization and new partial wills have been added to the political system. Such a process, for example, is very far advanced in France.

The process may take on still different directions. Nongovernmental organizations may gradually move into governmental roles. Political parties are often the vehicles for such developments. Parties are governmental organizations (e.g., they regulate recruitment into governmental office), but in performing their tasks they may enter into alliances with groups such as labor unions or business associations and eventually incorporate them into the party. Alternatively, interest groups may grow into parties or quasi-parties.[24]

Finally the government itself may reach into society and create organization that in other systems would be nongovernmental.[25] Earlier, we noted centripetal tendencies in the relations of government to nongovernmental units, and so now we must note a centrifugal tendency as the government extends its organization deeper and deeper into society.

24. Duverger (1951), Introduction.

25. As in Nazi Germany and the Soviet Union.

I. *Summary*

The reader will perhaps have lost patience with being led at breakneck pace through a highly abstract analysis filled with expressions such as "tends to," "might," "to some extent," "more or less," "on the one hand and on the other hand," etc. Despite the unsatisfactory nature of this discussion, it has been included for two reasons. First, I felt it desirable, toward the close of the volume, to give the reader a glimpse of the main architectonic ideas of the theoretical system in the process of construction, prior to plunging into the highly microscopic considerations which will occupy much of the following volume (and which will undoubtedly end up by modifying considerably the larger ideas here very briefly outlined). Second, it was felt that some context was needed for our definition of the concept of a political system, which otherwise might have been largely unintelligible because of the very general nature of the propositions it contains. We will now summarize the argument and present an explicit definition of a political system.

A political system is a set of actors organized into stable forms of political interaction. It is first necessary to inquire who these actors are. In part, the actors are individuals; indeed individuals at times can play an important role and have an important impact on the system. Mainly, however, the actors are groups. This raises the question how a group can be an actor—that is, behave purposively in more than a figurative sense.

Action involves assessment, evaluation, choice, and execution. Group action requires regulation from within according to a common purpose, that is, government. While individuals choose strategies, governments choose strategy sets.

A typology of governmental organization has been developed. The governmental organization of an alliance is rudimentary because the group strategy set must be chosen unanimously. An association differs from an alliance in that the form, rather than the content, of group decisions is unanimously chosen. This enables the development of a specialized governmental appartus.

The effective operation of an association requires that its decisions be authoritative, that is, that the common purpose of the association include a real general will, either that of a larger social group or of one specific to the association (normally both).

Associations may be voluntary, contractual, or integral, depending on whether the agreement on the form of governmental is voidable unilaterally or by mutual consent, or not voidable at all, except under special circumstances.

A community is a social group (with a real general will) whose organization performs a function or functions. To be governed, a community must form an association.

Governmental action has a technical and a political aspect. Action is technical when there is no conflict of evaluation among the subactors (individuals or subgroups). Action is political when there is such a conflict. Although any form of influence may occur in politics, the characteristic forms are political authority and political power. Political authority is authority to govern. Political power is power whose sanction is political authority, or, more broadly, governmental position. Any aspect of governmental action may be political, although the political process tends to center in governmental choice (decision making). In practice, however, choice and execution are not sharply separable.

The actors of a political system are thus a government, its subunits, and its individual members, plus nongovernmental associations, their subunits, and individual members who engage in politics. Some of these actors may be the product of the system; for example, system activity may bring an individual into politics or create a group which engages in politics.

Each actor occupies a position in the system. A position is the set of all strategies (programs) available to the actor which will influence governmental action. The influence of a position stems mainly from its authority, and the political power that springs from this authority, but may include other factors.

The activity of a political system is the sum of the actions of each of its actors as they relate to governmental action. If the position of each actor and the outcome matrix are known, then, on the assumption of rationality, the activity of the system can be predicted. (The significance of this point is theoretical rather than practical.) Position and value (utility scale) are not independent variables; each influences the other, but neither uniquely determines the other. To these two a third basic variable must be added, the technical opportunities and limitations for action by the actor, that is, the material base. This technical system both influences and is influenced by the other two basic variables. The content of a political system is the sum of the positions of the actors in the governmental process. The structure of a political system is the stable relations among these positions. The process of a political system is its activity in relation to the function of governing.

The content of this chapter up to the summary is a set of generalizations about the interrelations between position (P), value (V), and technical or material base (T) in a political system. For example:

1. The translation of the general will of a group into purposive action requires a government $(V, T \rightarrow P)$.

2. In groups above a very small size, the government must be a subgroup $(T \rightarrow P)$.

3. Individuals in stable cooperative interaction will form a real general will $(P \rightarrow V)$.

This discussion may be summarized as follows: A political system may be looked at as a network of opposing forces generated by the values (evaluations) of its actors (both groups and individuals, but especially the former), the positions they occupy, and the technical necessities of action. If these forces are in balance, the system will be in a state of equilibrium. If they are not in balance, the system will undergo change which will lead either to a new equilibrium or to the destruction of the system. (In the latter case, government will either vanish or turn into rule.)

The possibilities of equilibrium are created by the fact that the generation of forces is highly dialectical: the process of generating a force tends to create an opposing force. This point was worked out in connection with the relations of the general will to the will of the government, the will of the government to the wills of the governmental subunits, the will of the government to the wills of nongovernmental groups, and finally the system of partial wills to the general will.

J. *The State*

The theory developed so far has been intended to apply to any group whatsoever, even though most of the illustrative examples have concerned the political system of a State. We move now to a definition of a State, and a consideration of the ways in which the political system of a State differs from the political system of other organized communities.

A State is an association organized for the purpose of putting the general will of a community into action; that is, it is the governmental organization of a community. It differs from other governed communities in the nature of the community, in the nature of the authority of the government, and in the authorized sanctions at the government's disposal.

The State is a territorial idea. The jurisdiction of the government of the community covers a given geographical area which, unless the State has an empire, is roughly coterminal with the area inhabited by the community. The community is the most inclusive one within the area. Exception may be made for the situation where the government rules another group within the territory (for example, slaves, selots, metics), which is not in the community. The critical factor, however, is that the general will of the community takes precedence over any other will in the territory, and hence the authority of its government is the highest in the land. Sometimes two associations share the highest authority, for example, church and State. Here the two associations, taken together, form the State. Each government is the supreme authority within its own sphere and each draws its authority from the same community. Such a separation, for example according to the Gelasian doctrine,[26] means that the government has no government, and does not differ in principle from the separation of authority in the United States Constitution. Finally, the government of a State seems always to have a monopoly on the right to use the sanction of violence (but not a monopoly on the right to use force; for example, when a person locks his door at night this is force but not violence). There appear to be theoretical reasons why this should be so, but we will not examine them here.

This definition can be contrasted with Weber's, which is the most often used.[27] The only significant substantive difference, but a fundamental one, is that Weber defines the State without reference to any purpose it might have, but only with respect to the means that it employs. This enables him to avoid a whole set of knotty theoretical problems. Leaving aside whether there is any purpose that every State has had (criminal justice and defense of territory appear to be quite general ends), the fact that the State has a purpose is of the utmost theoretical importance, quite apart from any inquiry into what this purpose may be. The central question, with which we have tried to deal, is whose purpose it is, and how this purpose is translated into action.

It is possible, of course, to argue that the State has no purpose—only its subunits. While this position has been rejected here, there is a good deal to be said for it, mainly because the

26. R. W. Carlyle and A. J. Carlyle (1939), vol. 1, pp. 184–93.
27. Weber (1925a), p. 78.

impact of the general will is usually so indirect and uncertain. The point is, however, that one must choose one or the other of the two positions before one can begin to grapple with the main problems of political theory in a coherent way. In failing to make this choice Weber has defined himself as a sociologist rather than as a political theorist.

Our answer to the question is that the community from which the State springs has common purposes, but that if the community is beyond a minimum size, these can be translated into action only by a government which, though drawn from the community, is separate from it. The general will can have purposes and can act only through the purposive action of an agent. Hence, all government is representative. Paradoxically, however, the actual purposes of all governments stand more or less in contradiction to the purposes of the general will of the community, and to that extent the regulation by government of the community is rule from the outside rather than government from the inside. Representation and rule, the two forms of purposive regulation of a community, stand in a dialectical relationship to each other.

Bibliography

Where two dates are given, the first refers to the date of original public issuance, and the second to the publication date of the edition cited.

Adorno, T. W.; Frenkel-Brunswik, Else; Levinson, Daniel J.; and Sanford, R. Levitt. 1950. *The Authoritarian Personality*. New York: Harper & Bros.

Almond, Gabriel A. 1950. *The American People and Foreign Policy*. New York: Harcourt, Brace & Co.

Almond, Gabriel A., and Powell, G. Bingham, Jr. 1966. *Comparative Politics: A Developmental Approach*. Boston: Little, Brown & Co.

Aristotle. 1941. *Metaphysics*. In *The Basic Works of Aristotle*, ed. Richard Mckeon. New York: Random House.

————. 1948. *The Politics of Aristotle*, trans. Ernest Barker. London: Oxford University Press.

Arrow, K. 1951. *Social Choice and Individual Values*. New York: John Wiley & Sons.

Bailey, Stephen K. 1950, *Congress Makes a Law*. New York: Columbia University Press.

Balint, Alice. (1943), 1954. "Identification." In Balint, *The Early Years of Life*. New York: Basic Books.

Barnard, Chester I. (1938), 1962. *The Functions of the Executive*. Cambridge, Mass.: Harvard University Press.

Beard, Charles A. 1934. *The Idea of the National Interest*. New York: Macmillan Co.

Bendix, Reinhard. 1960. *Max Weber: An Intellectual Portrait*. Garden City, N.Y.: Doubleday & Co.

Bentley, Arthur. (1908), 1967. *The Process of Government*, ed.

Peter H. Odegard. Cambridge, Mass.: Harvard University Press.

Berman, Daniel. 1964. *In Congress Assembled*. New York: Macmillan Co.

Bierstedt, Robert. 1950. "An Analysis of Social Power." *American Sociological Review* 15:730–38.

Blau, Peter M., and Scott, W. Richard. 1962. *Formal Organizations*. San Francisco: Chandler Publishing Co.

Braithwaite, Richard Bevan. (1953), 1960. *Scientific Explanation*. New York: Harper & Bros.

Bréhier, Émile. 1965. *The Hellenistic and Roman Age*, trans. Wade Baskin. Vol. 2 of *The History of Philosophy*. Chicago: University of Chicago Press.

Brenner, Charles. 1955. *An Elementary Textbook of Psychoanalysis*. Garden City, N.Y.: Doubleday & Co.

Bridgeman, P. W. (1927), 1948. *The Logic of Modern Physics*. New York: Macmillan Co.

Calhoun, John C. (1853), 1953. *A Disquisition on Government*. In Calhoun, *A Disquisition on Government, and Selections from the Discourse*, ed. C. G. Post. New York: Liberal Arts Press.

Carlyle, R. W., and Carlyle, A. J. 1939. *A History of Medieval Political Theory in the West*. Vol. 1. London: William Blackwood & Sons.

Carnap, Rudolf. 1966. *Philosophical Foundations of Physics*. New York: Basic Books.

Coser, Lewis A. 1956. *The Functions of Social Conflict*. Glencoe, Ill.: Free Press.

Dahl, Robert A. 1957. "The Concept of Power." *Behavioral Science* 2:201–15.

————. 1963. *Modern Political Analysis*. Englewood Cliffs, N.J.: Prentice-Hall.

Davis, Kingsley. (1948), 1949. *Human Society*. New York: Macmillan Co.

Dean, Herbert A. 1963. *The Political and Social Ideas of St. Augustine*. New York: Columbia University Press.

Dentler, Robert A. and Erikson, Kai T. 1959. "The Functions of Deviance in Groups." *Social Problems* 7 (Fall):98–107.

Dodds, Eric R. 1951. *The Greeks and the Irrational*. Berkeley and Los Angeles: University of California Press.

Dostoevsky, Fyodor. (1880), 1950. *The Brothers Karamazov*, trans. Constance Garnett. New York: Modern Library.

Duverger, M. (1951), 1954. *Political Parties*. 2d ed. New York: John Wiley & Sons.

Ehrmann, Henry W. 1957. *Organized Business in France*. Princeton: Princeton University Press.

Emerson, Rupert. (1960), 1962. *From Empire to Nation*. Cambridge, Mass.: Harvard University Press.

Emmet, Dorothy. 1954. "The Concept of Power." *Proceedings of the Aristotlian Society*, vol. 54. London: Harrison & Sons, Ltd.

Engels, Frederick. (1884), 1942. *Origin of the Family, Private Property and the State*, New York: International Publishers.

————. (1880), 1959. *Socialism: Utopian and Scientific*. In *Marx and Engels: Basic Writings on Politics and Philosophy*, ed. Lewis S. Feurer. Garden City, N.Y.: Doubleday & Co.

Erikson, Erik H. 1950. *Childhood and Society*. New York: Norton & Co.

————. 1968. *Identity, Youth, and Crisis*. New York: Norton & Co.

Fenichel, Otto. 1945. *The Psychoanalytic Theory of Neurosis*. New York: Norton & Co.

Feuer, Lewis S., ed. 1959. *Marx and Engels: Basic Writings on Politics and Philosophy*. Garden City, N.W.: Doubleday & Co.

Flechtheim, Ossip K. 1952. *Fundamentals of Political Science*. New York: Ronald Press Co.

Freedman, Robert, ed. 1961. *Marx on Economics*. New York: Harcourt, Brace & Co.

French, John R. D. 1956. "A Formal Theory of Social Power." *Psychological Review* 63:181–94.

Freud, Anna. 1946. *The Ego and the Mechanisms of Defense*. New York: International Universities Press.

Freud, Sigmund. (1905), 1953. *Three Contribution to the Theory of Sex*. In *The Complete Psychological Works of Sigmund Freud*, ed. James Strachey. Vol. 7. London: Hogarth Press.

————. (1915), 1953. "Instincts and Their Vicissitudes." In *Collected Papers*. Vol. 4, ed. Ernest Jones. London: Hogarth Press.

————. (1920), 1955. *Beyond the Pleasure Principle*. In *Complete Psychological Works*. Vol. 18. London: Hogarth Press.

————. (1921), 1955. *Group Psychology and the Analysis of the*

Ego. In *Complete Psychological Works.* Vol. 18. London: Hogarth Press.

———. (1923), 1961. *The Ego and the Id.* In *Complete Psychological Works.* Vol. 19. London: Hogarth Press.

———. (1926), 1961. *Inhibitions, Symptoms and Anxiety.* In *Complete Psychological Works.* Vol. 20. London: Hogarth Press.

———. (1927), 1961. *The Future of an Illusion.* In *Complete Psychological Works.* Vol. 21. London: Hogarth Press.

———. (1930), 1961. *Civilization and its Discontents.* In *Complete Psychological Works.* Vol. 21. London: Hogarth Press.

———. (1938), 1964. *An Outline of Psychoanalysis.* In *Complete Psychological Works.* Vol. 23. London: Hogarth Press.

Friedrich, Carl J., ed. 1958. *Authority* (Nomos I). Cambridge, Mass.: Harvard University Press.

———, ed. 1966. *The Public Interest* (Nomos V). New York: Atherton Press.

Fromm, Erich. 1942. *The Fear of Freedom* (American title: *Escape From Freedom*). London: Routledge & Kegan Paul.

Fruchter, Benjamin. 1954. *Introduction to Factor Analysis.* New York: Van Nostrand.

Goldhammer, Herbert, and Shils, Edward A. 1939. "Types of Power and Status." *American Journal of Sociology* 45:171–82.

Goldsmith, M. M. 1966. *Hobbes's Science of Politics.* New York: Columbia University Press.

Green, Thomas Hill. (1895), 1941. *Lectures on the Principles of Political Obligation.* London: Longmans Green & Co.

Gross, Bertram. 1953. *The Legislative Struggle: A Study in Social Combat.* New York: McGraw-Hill.

Hampshire, Stuart. 1951. *Spinoza.* London: Penguin Books.

Harnack, Adolf. (1904), 1962. *The Mission and Expansion of Christianity in the First Three Centuries,* trans. and ed. James Mofatt. New York: Harper & Bros.

Harsanyi, John. (1962), 1964. "The Measurement of Social Power." In *Game Theory and Related Approaches to Social Behavior,* ed. Martin Shubik. New York: John Wiley & Sons.

Hartmann, Heinz. (1939), 1958. *Ego Psychology and the Problems of Adaption,* trans. David Rapoport. New York: International Universities Press.

————. (1947), 1964. "On Rational and Irrational Action." In Hartmann, *Essays on Ego Psychology: Selected Problems in Psychoanalytic Theory*. New York: International Universities Press.

————. (1948), 1964. "Comments on the Psychoanalytic Theory of Instinctual Drives." In Hartmann, *Essays*. New York: International Universities Press.

————. (1950), 1964. "Comments on the Psychoanalytic Theory of the Ego. In Hartmann, *Essays*. New York: International Universities Press.

Hartmann, Heinz; Kris, Ernest; and Lowenstein, Rudolph M. 1942. "Comments on the Formation of Psychic Structure." In *The Psychoanalytic Study of the Child*. Vol. 2. New York: International Universities Press.

Hartmann, Heinz, and Lowenstein, Rudolph M. 1962. "Notes on the Superego." In *The Psychoanalytic Study of the Child*. Vol. 17. New York: International Universities Press.

Hegel, Georg Wilhelm Friedrich. (1831), 1944. *The Philosophy of History*. Rev. ed., trans. J. Sibree. New York: Wiley Book Co.

Hicks, R. D. (1910), 1911. *Stoic and Epicurean*. London: Longmans Green & Co.

Hobbes, Thomas. (1651), 1958. *Leviathan,* ed. Herbert W. Schneider. Pts. 1, 2. New York: Liberal Arts Press.

Hoffmann, Stanley. 1963. "The Paradoxes of the French Political Community." In Hoffmann et al., *In Search of France*. Cambridge, Mass.: Harvard University Press.

Homans, George. 1950. *The Human Group*. New York: Harcourt, Brace & Co.

Hook, Sidney, ed. (1959), 1960. *Psychoanalysis, Scientific Method, and Philosophy*. New York: Grove Press.

Hume, David. (1739), 1896. *A Treatise of Human Nature*. 3 vols. Oxford: Clarendon Press.

————. (1742), 1948. "Of the Original Contract." In *Hume's Moral and Political Philosophy*, ed. Henry D. Aiken. New York: Haffner Publishing Co.

Kant, Immanuel. (1785), 1959. *Foundations of the Metaphysics of Morals, and What Is Enlightenment*, trans. Lewis W. Beck. New York: Bobbs-Merrill (Library of Liberal Arts).

Kaplan, Abraham. 1964. *The Conduct of Inquiry*. San Francisco: Chandler Publishing Co.

Kedourie, Elie. 1960. *Nationalism*. London: Hutchinson & Co.

Kelsen, Hans. 1945. *A General Theory of Law and the State*. Cambridge, Mass.: Harvard University Press.

Kennan, George. 1967. *Memoirs, 1925–1950*. Boston: Little, Brown & Co.

Klausner, Joseph. (ca. 1939), 1943. *From Jesus to Paul*. Boston: Beacon Press.

Kris, Ernest. 1950. "On the Preconscious Mental Processes." *Psychoanalytic Quarterly* 19:540–60.

Lasswell, Harold D. 1930. *Psychopathology and Politics*. Chicago: University of Chicago Press.

———. (1934), 1950. *World Politics and Personal Insecurity*. Glencoe, Ill.: Free Press.

Lasswell, Harold, and Kaplan, Abraham. 1950. *Power and Society*. New Haven: Yale University Press.

Latham, Earl. 1952. *The Group Basis of Politics*. New York: Octagon Books.

Lenzen, Victor. 1954. *Causality in Natural Science*. Springfield, Ill.: Charles C Thomas.

Leys, Wayne A. R., and Perry, Charner Marques. 1959. *Philosophy and the Public Interest*. American Philosophical Association, Western Division.

Lipset, Seymore; Trow, Martin A.; and Coleman, James S. 1956. *Union Democracy: The Internal Politics of the International Typographical Union*. Glencoe, Ill.: Free Press.

Locke, John (1690), 1947. *Two Treatises of Government*, ed. Thomas I. Cook. New York: Harper & Bros.

Luce, Robert D, and Raiffa, Howard. 1957. *Games and Decisions*. New York: John Wiley & Sons.

McIntosh, Donald. 1959. "Psychoanalysis and the Theory of Liberal Democracy." Ph.D. Dissertation. Columbia University.

———. 1963. "Power and Social Control." *American Political Science Review* 57, no. 1:619–31.

Machiavelli, Niccolo. (1532*a*), 1950. *The Prince*, trans. Luigi Ricci. In *The Prince and the Discourses*. New York: Modern Library.

———. (1532*b*), 1950. *The Discourses on the First Ten Books of*

Titus Livius, trans. Christian E. Detmold. In *The Prince and the Discourses*. New York: Modern Library.

Maine, Henry S. (1861), 1887. *Ancient Law*. 11th London ed. London: John Murray.

Mannheim, Karl. (1929), 1949. *Ideology and Utopia*. New York: Harcourt, Brace & Co.

Mao Tse-tung. 1965. *Selected Works*. 4 vols. Peking: Foreign Languages Press.

March, James G., 1955. "An Introduction to the Theory of Measurement of Influence." *The American Political Science Review* 49:431–51.

March, James G., and Simon, Herbert A. 1958. *Organizations*. New York: John Wiley & Sons.

Maritain, Jacques. 1951. *Man and the State*. Chicago: University of Chicago Press.

Mead, George Herbert. 1934. *Mind, Self, and Society: From the Standpoint of a Social Behaviorist*. Chicago: University of Chicago Press.

Meehan, Eugene J. 1965. *The Theory and Method of Political Analysis*. Homewood, Ill.: Dorsey Press.

————. 1968. *Explanation in Social Science: A System Paradigm*. Homewood, Ill.: Dorsey Press.

Menninger, Karl. 1968. *The Crime of Punishment*. New York: Viking Press.

Merton, Robert K. 1949. "Social Structure and Anomie." In Merton, *Social Theory and Social Structure*. Glencoe, Ill.: Free Press.

Michels, Robert. (1915), 1949. *Political Parties: A Sociological Study of the Oligarchical Tendencies of Modern Democracy*, trans. Eden Paul and Cedar Paul. Glencoe, Ill.: Free Press.

Mills, C. Wright. 1951. *White Collar*. New York: Oxford University Press.

Moore, Barrington. 1958. *Political Power and Social Theory*. Cambridge, Mass.: Harvard University Press.

Nagel, Ernest. 1961. *The Structure of Science: Problems in the Logic of Scientific Explanation*. New York: Harcourt, Brace & World.

Nash, J. J. 1950. "The Bargaining Problem." *Econometrica* 19: 155–62.

Neumann, Franz C. (1942), 1944. *Behemoth.* New York: Oxford University Press.

Neustadt, Richard. 1960. *Presidential Power.* New York: John Wiley & Sons.

Niebuhr, Reinhold. (1932), 1955. *Moral Man and Immoral Society.* New York: Charles Scribner's Sons.

Nigel, Howard. 1966. "The Theory of Meta-Games," and "The Mathematics of Meta-Games." *General Systems* 61:167–200.

Oppenheim, Felix E. 1961. *Dimensions of Freedom: An Analysis.* New York: St. Martin's Press.

Parsons, Talcott. (1937), 1949. *The Structure of Social Action.* 2d ed. Glencoe, Ill.: Free Press.

———. 1964. "The Superego and the Theory of Social Systems," in Parsons, *Social Structure and Personality.* Glencoe, Ill.: Free Press.

Piaget, Jean. (1947), 1950. *The Psychology of Intelligence*, trans. Malcolm Piercy and D. E. Berlyne. London: Routledge & Kegan Paul.

———. 1953. *The Origin of Intelligence in the Child*, trans. Margaret Cook. London: Routledge & Kegan Paul.

Plato. 1954. *The Republic* (Cornford Trans.). New York: Oxford University Press.

Popper, Karl R. (1934), 1959. *The Logic of Scientific Discovery.* New York: Basic Books.

Pound, Roscoe. (1922), 1954. *An Introduction to the Philosophy of Law.* Rev. ed. New Haven: Yale University Press.

Rapaport, David, ed. 1951. *The Organization and Pathology of Thought: Selected Sources.* ("Toward a Theory of Thinking," by D. Rapaport.) New York: Columbia University Press.

Rapoport, Anatol. 1960. *Fights, Games, and Debates.* Ann Arbor: University of Michigan Press.

———. 1966. *Two-Person Game Theory: The Essential Ideas.* Ann Arbor. University of Michigan Press.

Rapoport, Anatol, and Chammah, Albert M. 1965. *Prisoner's Dilemma*, Ann Arbor, University of Michigan Press.

Redl, F. 1942. "Group Emotion and Leadership." *Psychiatry* 5: 573–96.

Riker, W. H. 1962. *The Theory of Political Coalitions.* New Haven: Yale University Press.

Rose, Arnold. 1954. "Voluntary Associations in France." In Rose, *Theory and Method in the Social Sciences.* Minneapolis: University of Minnesota Press.

Rostow, W. W. 1960. *The United States in the World Arena.* New York: Harper & Bros.

Rousseau, Jean-Jacques. (1754), 1949. *On the Origin of Inequality.* Chicago: Henry Regnery Co.

————. (1755), 1949. *A Discourse on Political Economy.* Chicago: Henry Regnery Co.

————. (1762), 1960. *The Social Contract.* In *Social Contract*, ed. Barker, Ernest. New York: Oxford University Press.

Russell, Bertram. 1912. "Truth and Falsehood." in Russell, *Problems of Philosophy.* New York: Oxford University Press.

Sabine, George H. (1937), 1961. *A History of Political Theory.* 3rd ed. New York: Holt, Rinehart & Winston.

Santillana, Giorgio de. 1961. *The Origins of Scientific Thought: From Anaximander to Proclus, 600 B.C. to A.D. 500.* New York: Mentor Books.

Scheidlinger, Saul. 1952. *Psychoanalysis and Group Behavior: A Study of Freudian Group Psychology.* New York: W. W. Norton & Co.

————. 1955. "The Concept of Identification in Group Psychotherapy." *American Journal of Psychotherapy* 9:661–72.

————. 1964. "Identification, the Sense of Belonging, and of Identity in Small Groups." *International Journal of Group Psychotherapy* 14, no. 3:291–306.

Schelling, Thomas C. 1960. *The Strategy of Conflict.* Cambridge, Mass.: Harvard University Press.

Schilling, Warner R. 1962. "The Politics of National Defense. 1950." In Schilling, Hammond, and Snyder, *Strategy, Politics, and Defense Budgets.* New York: Columbia University Press.

Selznick, Philip. 1949. *TVA and the Grass Roots: A Study in the Sociology of Formal Organization.* Berkeley and Los Angeles: University of California Press.

————. 1957. *Leadership in Administration: A Sociological Interpretation.* Evanston, Ill.: Row, Peterson.

Shapley, L. S., and Shubik, Martin. 1954. "A Method for Evaluating the Distribution of Power in a Committee System." *American Political Science Review* 47:787–92.

Shubik, Martin, ed. 1964. *Game Theory and Related Approaches to Social Behavior*. New York: John Wiley & Sons.

Silberstein, Ludwik. 1933. *Causality: A Law of Nature or a Maxim of the Naturalist*. London: Macmillan & Co.

Simon, Herbert A. 1953. "Notes on the Observation and Measurement of Political Power." *Journal of Politics* 15:500–516.

Smith, Adam. (1776), 1937. *The Wealth of Nations*. New York: Modern Library.

Snyder, Louis L. 1954. *The Meaning of Nationalism*. New Brunswick, N.J.: Rutgers University Press.

Spinoza, Benedict de. (1677), 1951. *Ethics*. In *The Chief Works of Benedict de Spinoza*. 3d ed. Translated by R. H. M. Elwes. Vol. 2. New York: Dover Publications.

Tillich, Paul. 1951. *Systematic Theology*. Vol. 1. Chicago: University of Chicago Press.

Tocqueville, Alexis de. (1835), (1840), 1954. *Democracy in America*, trans. Henry Reeve. 2 vols. New York: Random House.

Tönnies, Ferdinand. (1926), 1963. *Community and Society*, ed. and trans. C. P. Loomis. New York: Harper & Row.

Truman, David B. 1951. *The Governmental Process*. New York: Alfred A. Knopf.

Von Neumann, John, and Morgenstern, Oskar. (1944), 1964. *Theory of Games and Economic Behavior*. 3d ed. New York: John Wiley & Sons.

Walbank, Frank W. 1946. *The Decline of the Roman Empire in the West*. London: Cobbett Press.

Weber, Max. (1903–17), 1949. *Max Weber on the Methodology of the Social Sciences*, trans. and ed. Edward A. Shils and Henry A. Finch. Glencoe, Ill.: Free Press.

———. (1919), 1946. "Politics as a Vocation." In *From Max Weber: Essays in Sociology*, ed. H. H. Gerth and C. Wright Mills. New York: Oxford University Press.

———. (1922), 1951. *The Religion of China: Confucianism and Taoism,* trans. H. H. Gerth. Glencoe, Ill.: Free Press.

———. (1925a), 1946. *From Max Weber: Essays in Sociology*, ed.

H. H. Gerth and C. Wright Mills. New York: Oxford University Press.

————. (1925*b*), 1947. *Max Weber: The Theory of Social and Economic Organization*, ed. Talcott Parsons and trans. A. M. Henderson and T. Parsons. New York: Oxford University Press.

Whyte, William H., Jr. 1956. *The Organization Man*, New York: Simon & Schuster.

Wiener, Norbert. 1948. *Cybernetics*. New York: John Wiley & Sons.

Woll, Peter. 1963. *American Bureaucracy*. New York: W. W. Norton.

Wright, Gordon. 1964. *Rural Revolution in France*. Stanford, Calif.: Stanford University Press.

Index

Absolutism, 283–85
Action (voluntary or purposeful behavior), 7–8, 16, 32, 43.(*See also* Drive; Irrational action; Rational action
  definition, 7–8, 16
  development of, 117–23
  economic, 205–6
    definition, 205
  governmental, 313 (*see also* Government)
  group *v.* individual, 216, 283–84, 312 (*see also* Actors; Political system, actors in)
  political, 313 (*see also* Politics)
Actor, 31. *See also* Action, group, *v.* individual; Person; Political system, actors in; State, as actor
Actual will. *See* Particular will
Adaption (Adaptation), 18–19, 118, 122
Adorno, T.W., 9 n, 74 n, 201 n, 203 n
Aim. *See* Drive, aim of
Aim inhibition, 147–49. *See also* Drive, aim of; Drive, object of
Alienation, 55
Alliance, 225, 227, 228, 231–33, 234–37, 239, 260–61, 267, 312
  v. coalition, 234
  definition, 227, 231
  and general will, 225
  and identification, 235
  and nation-state, 235
  pure, (defined), 237

and voluntary asociation, 238–40, 245, 248
Almond, Gabriel A., 280 n, 297
Aquinas, Thomas, 259 n, 277
Aristotle, 3, 18, 24, 87–88, 96, 97 n, 109 n, 117, 198, 223, 225
Arrow, Kenneth, 27
Assent (defined), 232
Assessment, 31–34, 40, 119–22, 128
  probabilistic, 53–54
  strategic, 53–54
Association, 238, 267, 313. *See also* Alliance; Contractual association; Free contractual association; Integral association; Integral contractual association; Voluntary association
  defined, 252
Augustine, 24
Authoritarianism, 203
Authority, 146, 158–59, 163–64, 168, 175–76, 195, 226
  charismatic, 160, 161–63 (*see also* Leadership, charismatic)
  defined, 159
  economic, 213
    defined, 208
    and economic power, 205–13
  institutional, 159, 163–64; 175, 263
    defined, 163
    v. personal, 163
  personal, 159, 160, 175, 263
    defined, 160
    v. institutional, 163
    v. personal influence, 159–60

primary organization of, 285–87,
288
defined, 286
and secondary organization,
288–90
representative, 145, 226 (*see also*
Representation)
defined, 233
secondary organization of, 287–90
defined, 288
as social group, 281–85
Green, Thomas Hill, 206 n
Gross, Bertram, 297 n
Group norms. *See* Social norms

Hampshire, Stuart, 90 n
Harnack, Adolf, 250 n
Harsanyi, John, 102 n, 104 n
Hartmann, Heinz, 10, 18, 111 n,
117 n, 125 n, 127 n, 137 n
Hate, 196–97. *See also* Identification,
negative
Hawthorne study, 147
Hegel, Georg W.F., 152, 238, 253
Herodotus, 116 n
Hicks, R.D., 17 n
Hitler, Adolf, 110, 162
Hobbes, Thomas, 25, 65, 116, 157,
168, 183 n, 200, 224, 238,
252, 256
Hoffmann, Stanley, 246 n, 251 n,
308 n
Homans, George, 147 n, 154–55,
159 n, 228 n, 246, 292, 301–2,
308 n
Hook, Sidney, 12 n
Hume, David, 17, 69, 94, 238, 253,
256

Id, 124
Ideal group member, 147, 149, 158,
179, 248
Idealization, 137, 140, 173–74
Identification, 15–16, 24–28, 71–75,
76, 140, 172–73, 196–97, 224.
See also Love; Social groups,
emotional relations within
among allies, 235
in army and church, 142–43

defined, 91
degree of, 73
and idealization, 140, 173–74
mutual, 82–85, 182
negative, 74–75, 85, 92, 186–87
partial, 78–82
personal *v.* institutional, 175–76
positive, 74 (*see also* Identification,
simple)
primary, 173–74 (*see also* Superego identification)
defined, 173
and projections, 73–74
and rationality, 26
secondary, 174–77
simple, 71–86, 92, 135–36, 172–
73, 182, (*see also* Ego identification)
defined, 74
in social groups, 139–46 (*see also*
Identification, primary; Identification, secondary)
total, 77–78
"Impersonality," 90–92, 181, 197
defined, 68
of power relations, 90
Imputation sets, 26, 224, 225
Indifference. *See* Impersonality
Individual. *See also* Actor; Person
political system and, 294–96
Influence, 133–36. *See also* Authority; Power
causal, 98–100
personal, 135, 159–60
defined, 135
distinguished from authority,
159–60
typology of, 157–169
Innovation, 165
Instincts, 118
Integral association (integral government), 249, 258, 260–61,
313. *See also* Community, organized; Integral contractual
association
defined, 249, 252
and voluntary association, 258
Integral contract. *See* Contract, integral

What is it to be human? What is a social group? What holds it together? What does living in a social order mean to its members? What is government? How does it work? What forms does it take? What is a political system?

These questions provide a framework for this theoretical analysis of the basic forms of interaction which make up and support human society. The answers are worked out in terms of a general theory of human action, constructed in stages: individual action, interaction among individuals, social interaction, and, finally, the outlines of a theory of group action and interaction. The author has developed a typology of the ways in which individuals and groups influence each other's actions, and he examines the patterns of influence which characterize and hold together human groups, organizations, and political systems.

Reminiscent of the comprehensive political and philosophical analyses written before the age of specialization, this work is strongly influenced by traditional political theory, particularly as found in the works of Plato, Aristotle, and Rousseau. While the approach is traditional, the materials

(Continued on back flap)